Vadim Khramov, PhD & John Ridings Lee, Jr.

I0392395

THE 5-MINUTE ECONOMIST

YOU DON'T NEED A PHD
TO UNDERSTAND THE ECONOMY

ISBN: 1536825743
ISBN-13: 978-1536825749

In loving memory of John Ridings Lee, Jr.
who envisioned empowered people creating a better world.

YOU DON'T NEED A PHD TO UNDERSTAND THE ECONOMY

Every news report and newspaper article will tell you something different about what is going on in the economy. One economist says things are great, but another says things look bleak. Regardless of the deluge of statistics and the amount of time that the media devotes to discussing the economy, most people remain bewildered by it all. Rather than informing them, it only serves to confuse them at best and mislead them at worst. How is the average person supposed to know what's really going on in the economy?

Wouldn't it be great if there were an easy way anyone could see how the economy was *really* doing?

That's why the authors created the Economic Performance Index, or EPI, currently the *only* patented index of economic activity, that was published at the International Monetary Fund, the largest global economic policy institution in the world. It uses four macro-indicators (easily found online) that capture the broad health of nearly any economy—from individual US states to regional country blocs—at any point in modern history!

Five years of research along with the publication at the IMF gives you certainty that it will provide you with a clear, unbiased and competent understanding of the economy.

Not only does *The 5-Minute Economist* show you how to use the index for yourself, where you can apply it to the US economy and individual states as well as other countries, but it answers major questions that everyone wants to know:

- Who's better: Democrats or Republicans?
- Is war good for the economy?
- Is the media biased?
- Has the US lost to China?
- Do high taxes help or hurt?
- Should we model Texas or California?
- Who was the best president in managing the economy?
- And many more!

In short, this book provides the reader with a clear but powerful method of evaluating the performance of any economic entity, in a way that will profoundly change your understanding of the economy, as well as that of millions of other people forever.

Don't wait for the "experts" to tell you how the economy is doing—find out for yourself!

"The 5-Minute Economist provides an innovative way to get a quick idea of what's going on in the economy of any country. Anyone can quickly "score" the economic performance of any country with just a few economic variables."

Aleksei Mozhin
Executive Director, International Monetary Fund

"I always believed there was no simple way to see the full picture of the correct economy. But this books proved me wrong. This is exactly what this country has needed for decades—a solid frame work that allows anyone to get an independent evaluation to see how we are doing. No bias, no spin, only numbers and grades."

Ray Wallace
Chairman, Trinity Industries

"The 5-Minute Economist is an innovative and clear, powerful and approachable way to understand what's going on in the world economy. It's a must read if you want your own view on the economy."

Rodney T. Madden
CEO, Madden Asset Management

CONTENTS

INTRODUCTION

I n the past, the public relied on economists, politicians, business leaders, and other such experts to tell them how the economy was doing. Accurately measuring the economy's health is exceedingly complex and difficult, to say the least. People have devoted a lifetime to understanding it.

In the wake of the Great Recession in 2008, though, the public learned that it could not depend on those experts. After all, few of them saw the crash coming and the global economic recession that ensued. From the boom years of the 1990s, the acceleration of the global economy, and the breathtaking expansion of emerging markets, most people believed such economic success would continue unabated. Like the eve of WWI, few leaders could imagine such devastation (in this case, economic) on such a global scale.

Unfortunately, their optimism was soon dispelled.

While the aftermath of the Great Recession is abating, it is clear we cannot depend on Wall Street, Washington, and world leaders to keep us informed on the economy. Fluctuations in the global economy affect the average citizen more strongly than ever. Whether it is in managing the allocation of their 401(k), doing business with overseas suppliers, or traveling for leisure, individuals feel the impact of the nation's economic health in their everyday lives.

We cannot wait for the next economic report to come out or for analysts in ivory towers to declare whether things are better or worse than last quarter.

We need a tool that is easy, yet accurate,—a tool that anyone should be able to use, from blue-collar workers worried about their retirement to CEOs planning international expansion, a tool that captures the overall health of an economy.

The late John Ridings Lee, Jr. envisioned such a tool more than two decades ago but was unable to complete the formula. He partnered with economist Vadim Khramov, PhD to finish it. After subjecting the method to rigorous academic scrutiny and comparing the results against historical data, they were satisfied that they had finally created an elegant solution to this decades-old problem:

The Economic Performance Index.

In Part I of *The 5-Minute Economist*, the authors demonstrate how the four macro indicators used in the Index accurately capture the broad health of an economy and demonstrate how effectively it works in the real-world.

In Part II the authors demonstrate the *real* power of the Economic Performance Index: its ability to be used in any situation, in any period in modern history.

The authors address the questions everyone asks but can never seem to get a straight answer to. Is the US doing better or worse against the rest of the world? How do we compare the US economic performance against individual countries, such as China? Does the average person grasp how the economy is doing?

Moreover, they answer some politically divisive questions, like whether Democrats or Republicans are better at managing the nation and if war actually boosts the economy. Which presidents were best for the economy… and which were worst?

The beauty of the Economic Performance Index is that anyone can use it to answer any economic question. It works for measuring state economies all the way to regional economic blocs such as the European Union.

No more does the average person have to wait for economists and analysts to tell them whether to be excited or dismayed about the economy. No more do people have to be confused when one report is positive while another remains negative. No more do they have to trust pundits to help them sift through economic data to figure out if they should be cheering or jeering one political policy over another.

They can now find out for themselves.

PART 1

CREATING THE ECONOMIC PERFORMANCE INDEX

CHAPTER 1

WHAT'S GOING ON WITH THE ECONOMY?

"The index of leading [economic] indicators does not lead and it does not indicate!"

Economists Diebold and Rosebush

Despite impressive strides in measuring economic activity, few people truly understand what is going on in the economy. Politicians tout one number or another to support their legislation. TV pundits seize a statistic released that day and both the left and the right say why it is a good thing or not. Newspapers publish editorials about what one economic indicator means for the future.

Regardless of the deluge of statistics and amount of time the media devotes to discussing it, most people remain bewildered by it all. Rather than inform them, it only serves to confuse them at best and mislead them at worst. The average person and even the well-educated cannot determine how well or poorly the economy is doing, and are forced to rely on politicians, pundits, and the newspapers to tell them whether it is getting better or worse.

Moreover, when the statistics are released, they are often compared to the same numbers from last month or last quarter. Only a few economic indicators are put into historical context. Without any sort of reference point, the reported numbers are meaningless. Can 3% growth be considered high? Does unemployment of 6% mean recovery? Is 3% inflation too high? Worse yet, where can the average person go to find a trustworthy interpretation of it all? The media? Most people would agree it cannot be trusted to be fair and unbiased all the time. Government and government agencies? By mandate, they can offer little interpretation and analysis as to whether an indicator is good or bad; their purpose is to collect and report data. Private businesses, investment bankers, or individuals? Few have completely altruistic motivations.

This lack of knowledge affects everyone's everyday lives. Is it a good time for them to invest in real estate, or should they rent? Is the stock market too volatile, or is it a smart time to buy? Is the recession over, or are we about to sink further? Is it a good time to get a job, or should they stay in school? Business owners face the same uncertainty with corporate decisions as well. Should they prepare their factories to get ready for an economic boom and invest now to produce more in the future, or should they get ready for a fall in orders? Is the domestic market the best place to grow, or should they expand elsewhere? Is it a smart time to borrow, or should they deleverage and quickly get rid of debt?

"Real GDP rose by 2.6% in 2015…" "Unemployment fell to 5.3% …" "New housing starts were up by 1.5% this month compared to the past year…" "Consumer spending reached an all-time high this quarter…" "The Federal Reserve announced its decision to keep interest rates at record lows…"

It seems everywhere the public eye turns, someone is using an economic measure to support their position, such as why everyone should buy gold (or not), invest in the stock market (or not), refinance their mortgage (or not), or be worried about the future of America (or not).

What does it all mean? Does it make sense? What is really going on with the economy? Even expert policy advisors—the people who influence the president, members of Congress, private investors, and others who affect large parts of the economy—lack the tools to properly assess and compare economic performance across time and against other economies. How is the US doing vis-à-vis China, the UK, and the euro area countries? Is current legislation helping or hurting the economy? Should decisions be based on any one indicator or index?

Everyone wants to know what is going on with the economy but no one seems to know.

Well, almost no one.

We wrote this book because we believe that everyone should be able to answer the question "What's going on with the economy?" This book offers a clear but powerful method of evaluating the performance of any economic entity, be it a nation, a US state, or an economic bloc like the EU. It took us five years of research, including many consultations with economists, businesspeople, representatives of Congress, and others to create our own economic index. It is currently the only patented index of economic activity.

We call it the Economic Performance Index, or EPI for short.

Of course, the Index is not perfect, as some can say that it might be too simple. Others may argue that it does not take every economic data release into account. We are aware of that, but it accomplishes its original goal: to allow anyone to get an independent evaluation of the performance of the economy. Our Index empowers anyone to evaluate what is happening in any major economy, letting them draw their own conclusions about what they need to decide when it comes to their investments, their personal finances, their education choices, and, ultimately, their own economic future.

In just three simple steps, we can teach anyone how to construct the EPI and apply it to virtually any economic entity – a country, a state, or an economic bloc. As part of demonstrating how to use and interpret the Index, we have evaluated all major periods of US history. In addition, we demonstrate the ability of this simple index to catch economic recessions and evaluate stock market fundamentals. But after showing you the EPI's capabilities, we proceed in the second part of the book to answer the real secrets of the economy, i.e. "everything you always wanted to know but were too afraid or embarrassed to ask."

CURRENT INDICATORS AND INDEXES

But before we delve into our Index, let's examine the current tools economists, statisticians, financial experts, and others use to answer these pressing questions. Over the past few decades, experts created dozens upon dozens of economic measures. To list just a few covering various segments:

▼ **VARIOUS CURRENT ECONOMIC INDICATORS AND INDEXES**

Macroeconomic aggregates
- Gross Domestic Product
- Gross National Product
- Consumer Spending
- Total personal income
- Disposable income
- Corporate Profits After Tax

Money and Interest Rates
- Federal Funds Rate
- 30-year treasury constant maturity rate
- 10- year treasury constant maturity rate
- 1- year treasury constant maturity rate
- M1 money stock
- M2 money stock

Business
- Manufacturer's new orders of durable goods
- Lightweight vehicle sales
- Industrial production
- Capacity utilization
- Manufacturing: Purchasing Managers Index
- Industrial production: durable manufacturing

Fiscal stance
- Budget deficit as a share of GDP
- Gross federal debt
- Nominal debt
- Federal surplus/deficit
- Debt-to-GDP ratio

Credit
- Consumer credit outstanding
- Revolving credit outstanding

Employment
- Civilian unemployment rate
- Number of unemployed
- Median duration of unemployment
- Total non-farm payrolls
- Initial claims of unemployment insurance

Housing
- Housing starts of new, privately-owned, single-family housing units
- New single-family houses sold

Trade
- Exports of goods and services
- Imports of goods and services
- Exchange rate

Inflation
- Consumer price index for all urban consumers
- Consumer price index for all urban consumers, less food and energy

...and those are just a sample of the most commonly used indicators, much less the more obscure measures.

Each indicator describes only a part of the economy or its respective sector. For example:

1. The Federal Funds Rate can tell us whether the Federal Reserve wants to stimulate or to cool down the economy.

2. The number of new single-family houses sold is important in evaluating the health of the housing market.

3. The debt-to-GDP ratio of the government might help us expect higher or lower taxes in the future.

Unfortunately, all these indicators are made available at different times: GDP is reported quarterly, the unemployment and inflation rates are reported monthly but at different dates, interest rates are observed daily, etc.

In short, there is no simple way to see the full picture of the current economy.

It reminds us of the Indian fable about the blind men who came upon an elephant. They could hear the animal but had to rely on their other senses to figure out what it was. One man touched the ears and declared the animal was like a hand fan, thin and supple. Another man touched the elephant's tusk and decided the first man was mistaken: the animal was like a spear, hard with a pointed tip. The third man touched the trunk and said the animal was like a snake, thick and coiling. Likewise, other men in turn touched the elephant's feet, side, and tail, all disagreeing with the others as to the true nature of the animal.

It is impossible to see the whole truth from only one perspective.

But since one number by itself cannot tell the full story, economists have combined certain indicators to create indexes, hoping that for each one, the whole would be greater than the sum of its parts. Today's widely used indicators attempt to measure a country's economic performance but their ability to convey useful information and trends is less than optimal. Normally these indicators incorporate a number of economic variables and are based on complicated econometric procedures that render them too complex to be of much value to the general public or even to policymakers.

The Chicago Fed National Activity Index (CFNAI) is one such index. It uses eighty-five different economic indicators to measure the growth of the national economy. A zero value for the index means that the economy grew at its historical growth rate; a positive value, that it grew above that rate; a negative value, that it grew below that rate. A typical report of the Chicago Fed states, "The CFNAI was +0.02 in December, down from +0.27 in November." So the economy grew above its usual growth rate, but was it by a little or a lot? How much of a difference is there between 0.02 and 0.27?

Another index of economic activity reported by the media, and perhaps the most well known, is the Conference Board Coincident Economic Index (CEI). The board typically releases such announcements as, "The CEI for the US increased 0.4% in January to 106.5 (2004=100), following a 1.0% increase in December, and a 0.9% increase in November."

These figures by themselves may not be absolutely clear even for economists trained in understanding them. There are no definitive meanings behind these values. Changes in these indexes are not the same as changes in common economic variables, such as GDP or inflation, but are instead relative to the indexes themselves.

These indexes attempt to get the complete picture of economic activity, from interest rates to monetary aggregates, from industrial production to consumer spending, from the stock market to government debt. The problem with these indexes is that they go to the other extreme, involving complicated econometrics and filtering procedures, including principal components analysis, regression analysis, normalization procedures, and other calculations beyond the skills of everyday people. Furthermore, the structure of these types of indexes is so complex that it does not give room for a reasonable interpretation of their changes or levels.

TO TRUST OR TO KNOW?

Currently, we can either attempt to understand the economy from a single, limited perspective or use scientific methods that are so complicated that they are realistically unusable for the vast majority of people (and even trained specialists).

From here, we have two options. We can either remain in the dark, having to trust other experts—often just as clueless as the rest of us—to interpret the data for us, or, more obviously, we should look for a better solution. We need to find a way that provides the complete picture of the economy and yet is easy enough that the average adult could use it. We need ease and convenience (not to mention accuracy) that reveals the performance of the economy right now. And it would be far more powerful if, in addition to all that, we could also compare economies to each other (say, US economic performance vs. the EU's) as well to it-self across time (say, US economic performance during the Great Recession vs. the Great Depression).

But where do we begin?

We asked ourselves the same question. As we said earlier, over a period of five years and countless hours, our efforts yielded the Economic Performance Index. Easy, intuitive, accurate, and versatile, the EPI can be explained in just three simple steps. In the next three chapters, we explain what those steps are and how anyone can quickly "score" the economy's performance. In doing so, we will demonstrate both the convenience and the effective-ness of the Index, as well as its ability to reflect all major events in US history, to capture economic recessions, and even to eval-uate the stock market.

CHAPTER 2

STEP 1: THE "BIG FOUR"—THE PILLARS OF THE ECONOMIC PERFORMANCE INDEX

"If all the economists were laid end to end, they'd never reach a conclusion."

George Bernard Shaw

Economists tend to agree that a good indicator of economic activity should reflect the performance of the key components of the economy—households, firms, and government. These three sectors reflect virtually all of an economy's domestic activity. In order to assess the health of each sector, we should think what each sector cares mostly about:

1. For households: **the monetary stance**—what are the economy's inflation level and effective interest rates?

2. For firms: **the production stance**—how productive is the economy and whether firms are in good shape?

3. For government: **the fiscal stance**—how well is the government managing its budget?

Each of these stances reflects what happens in the real world. If any one of them deteriorates, they exert a negative influence simultaneously on households, firms, and the government.

While GDP growth is an easy way to measure these three sectors, it is not enough to see the big picture, as we will explain later in the book. In addition to GDP, we need three proxy variables to more accurately capture what happens with households, firms, and government. Our approach does not use complicated procedures and, in our view and in the view of many economists, is a clear and coherent way to measure the performance of the economy in a straightforward manner.

The right choice of variables was the most complicated part in creating the EPI. As we said, it took us five years of research, many consultations with economists, policymakers, businessmen, and people from academia, as well as multiple trials of different variables and different filtering procedures, to conclude that the following four simple variables can comprehensively explain economic performance. Together with real GDP growth, these variables are:

- The **inflation rate**, as a measure of the economy's monetary stance
- The **unemployment rate**, as a measure of the economy's production stance
- The **budget deficit as a percentage of GDP**, as a measure of the economy's fiscal stance
- The **change in real GDP**, as a measure of the aggregate performance of the entire economy.

The combination of these four variables (The "Big Four") allows for a birds-eye view of the economy and also neutralizes specific fluctuations of its components. Later in the book, we will show that the EPI, based on the appropriate weighting of these variables enables us to track almost all major events in US history since 1790, to capture the occurrence and severity of all US economic recessions, and to demonstrate how the economy's fundamentals are important for the stock market.

Earlier, we talked about the Indian fable of the blind men and the elephant. Just like the blind men, each of the Big Four represents a piece of the total, but it is impossible to see it in its entirety from just one perspective. In the end, all four must work together. But let's examine each of these in turn to see why all four are critical pillars in building an overarching economic indicator.

In the rest of this chapter, we will discuss in detail the four components of the EPI: GDP growth, inflation, unemployment rate, and the budget deficit (as a share of GDP).

GDP

As we said, real gross domestic product (GDP) is the typical measure economists use to describe the overall performance of an economy. GDP is a good rule of thumb since it attempts to capture the market value of all final goods and services bought and sold in the country by individuals, businesses, the government, and other nations. In other words, a way to measure GDP is to total up all spending of all agents in the economy. This would reflect how much households, government, and firms spend but will not show whether they are currently in good or bad shape, right? As an example, the government usually spends more money during recessions to support the economy.

As such, GDP is a proxy measure for how much activity takes place throughout the entire economy over the course of a year, which we can then compare to the previous year to see how much the economy grew or shrank. In this section, we explain why GDP growth is important and yet why it still fails to accurately reflect the big picture of the economy.

The importance of GDP growth is usually underestimated by the media and the public in general. Does an extra percentage point of GDP growth a year really matter? Absolutely! Even one percentage point change in GDP can affect a nation's entire future. Why?

If GDP were an individual savings account, the growth rate would act like an interest rate: the higher the interest rate, the more money the account would earn in compound interest. Unlike one person's saving account, though, GDP represents the income of an entire nation. The GDP growth, therefore, represents the growth of this income.

Let's say someone wanted to buy a $10,000 certificate of deposit (CD) they wanted to leave to their children for their inheritance. As they shopped around for the best deal, they came across a few different interest rates: 1%, 3%, 5%, and 7%. Obviously, they would want to leave the most money possible for their children. But what if the banker offering the slightly lower rate of 5% was nice, the bank was familiar to them, and they did not have to drive so far to do all the paperwork? Would one or two percent really be worth all the extra hassle?

Let's do the math and calculate the amount of money that would be on the couple's CD in different years at different interest rates:

▼ **EXAMPLE OF A $10 000 CERTIFICATE GROWTH AND THE LEVEL OF THE INTEREST RATE**

			Interest rate		
Year	0%	1%	3%	5%	7%
0	$10,000	$10,000	$10,000	$10,000	$10,000
1	$10,000	$10,100	$10,300	$10,500	$10,700
2	$10,000	$10,201	$10,609	$11,025	$11,449
3	$10,000	$10,303	$10,927	$11,576	$12,250
4	$10,000	$10,406	$11,255	$12,155	$13,108
5	$10,000	$10,510	$11,593	$12,763	$14,026
10	$10,000	$11,046	$13,439	$16,289	$19,672
15	$10,000	$11,610	$15,580	$20,789	$27,590
20	$10,000	$12,202	$18,061	$26,533	$38,697
25	$10,000	$12,824	$20,938	$33,864	$54,274
30	$10,000	$13,478	$24,273	$43,219	$76,123
40	**$10,000**	**$14,889**	**$32,620**	**$70,400**	**$149,745**

If the interest rate is zero, the deposited $10,000 will be the same $10,000 in forty years. If the interest rate is at least 1%, the couple will have almost $15,000 to pass on. If the interest rate is 5%, the sum jumps to more than $70,000, and so on. Looking at all the possible options, we find that, of course, the bank with the highest interest rate returns the most money. But compare the difference in compound growth between 5% and 7%. When their children inherit the CD in forty years, do they want them to receive $70,000 from "the nice bank" with a 5% rate or nearly $150,000 from the bank with the 7% rate?

GDP growth works in the same way for the entire nation and the whole economy. If the US could consistently grow at about 3%, by the time those parents' children were just twenty-five years old, there would be twice as much wealth in the US as when they started their family. This means that, as long as the overall population was about the same, their children would be twice as wealthy as their parents. In other words, a 3% GDP growth rate would result in each generation living twice as well as their forefathers. The growth of 5% a year on average would make their children three times wealthier than their forefathers.

Historically, GDP has grown over time with different growth rates. It went from about $1 trillion (in 2009 dollars) in the 1930s to almost $16.5 trillion in 2015. At the same time, the average person cannot really interpret much from these dynamics. Therefore, economists usually look at real GDP growth. That is, instead of seeing how many dollars there are in the pool, they look at how much the pool has grown over time.

But while GDP is a convenient measure to evaluate the general performance of the economy, it is not enough to see the whole picture. GDP does not accurately capture other important structural elements of the economy. Take unemployment, for example. Most people think whether they have a job or not is pretty important, but GDP does not capture how many households are out of work. In theory, a higher GDP should alleviate unemployment, but that does not always work out to be the case.

Furthermore, as government spending is a part of GDP, it can grow if the government simply spends more money. Of course, this would mean that the government ran budget deficits and accumulated more debt. Does the national debt (and its consequences) affect the economy? Of course it does. However, the GDP rate does not quantify those legislative decisions in the present. It takes a period of time—sometimes years—before the results of those actions show up in the economy (in, for example, higher taxes, defaults, and less money put toward other government programs). It is the economic equivalent of "eat, drink, and be merry, for tomorrow we die."

Finally, economists usually talk about real GDP growth, or growth excluding inflation. In this case, negative inflation effects are already taken out from the real productions. That is fine. But think about two economies with 1% and 10% inflation rates with the same GDP growth. Which one would you prefer to be in? Of course in the one with lower inflation. However, that is not captured by real GDP growth.

Thus, it is clear that, although GDP is an important pillar in any major economic index, we cannot see the full health of the overall economy from just this one number.

INFLATION

Inflation is the second component of the EPI and reflects one of the most critical areas of the economy—its monetary stance. The actual goods and services produced by all three sectors are one thing; assigning them a dollar value is something quite different. We experience inflation when average prices of goods and services increase; and deflation, when prices fall.

The classic layman's definition of inflation is "more dollars chasing fewer goods." As more money goes into circulation, people and businesses have more cash to buy the same amount of goods and services. Most people know inflation is bad for the economy, especially when their income does not rise in lockstep with inflation. Their nominal income stays the same but everything they need to buy costs more. In effect, their so-called real income falls and they are effectively making less money than they did a year ago.

But few people realize that the opposite of inflation—a.k.a. deflation—is also bad. On the surface, it looks like a good thing. Everything people need to buy becomes cheaper, so their dollar stretches further. However, at the same time, their incomes decrease with deflation in nominal terms, while financial loans remain the same. This means that their car loan, mortgage, and credit card debt do not decrease. As their income eventually goes down, their debt payments (negotiated and agreed on years earlier) eat up a bigger piece of the household income. This affects not only individuals but businesses (paying leases on their offices and factories) and the government (paying back government debt).

Basically, inflation *and* deflation are bad for the economy; ergo, a good economic indicator would negatively reflect a change either way.

UNEMPLOYMENT

The third component of the EPI is the unemployment rate, which reflects the health of the production stance or firms' ability to hire people. Officially, the unemployment rate is the percentage rate of the total labor force that is unemployed and actively seeking employment and willing to work. Firms hire labor to produce goods and services. Therefore, unemployment is a good proxy for measuring firms' health but also their expectations about the future, as firms hire if they have a positive perspective about the future.

Moreover, unemployed people represent underutilized production opportunities. It is comparable to an eight-cylinder racing car engine running on six cylinders; while it may continue to move forward, it is not going as fast as it could. While an economy may grow despite a relatively high unemployment rate, it could grow faster if more people were contributing to the growth. As more people are put to work, the more output they generate. That, in turn, increases the country's overall GDP both by firms having more output and by households earning more income. Therefore, a good economic indicator should reflect how efficiently the economy makes use of its human capital.

At the same time, unemployment alone cannot tell the entire story. Other parts of the economy can grow even without adding additional people to the labor force, as evidenced by the Great Recession's jobless recovery, when GDP growth was positive but unemployment stayed high. As such, while the unemployment rate may provide a perspective on the relative health of the production stance of the economy, it is still insufficient to serve as an accurate gauge of the economy on its own.

THE BUDGET DEFICIT (AS A PERCENTAGE OF GDP)

The last component of the EPI is the budget deficit, which primarily reflects the fiscal health of the government sector in a certain year. As a quick refresher course: the government deficit is the difference between how much the government spends and how much it collects (primarily through taxes) in one budget year. Usually, the government has to borrow money if it runs a deficit, resulting in debt accumulation. The national debt is the total amount of how much the government owes because it had to borrow money to cover the previous years' deficits.

It makes sense to use the deficit as an indicator because it primarily reflects the fiscal health of the government sector. If the economy is bad, the government collects fewer revenues and has to spend more, running budget deficits that it eventually has to repay. Therefore, the government would either have to raise taxes or decrease spending in the future. Economists sometimes compare the government's finances with a household's: if a family spends more today, they will have to save more tomorrow to pay it back. Similar to the share in income from the household's perspective, economists usually measure budget deficit as a share of GDP.

Although the budget deficit as a percentage of GDP largely reflects the fiscal health of the government sector, it also affects the other two sectors (households and firms). A fiscally irresponsible government will eventually have to raise taxes, devalue its currency, and/or default on its debts, thereby putting the burden of high debt on households or firms. As such, the budget deficit as a percentage of GDP is a good proxy indicator of the true health of the government sector.

If a family buys furniture on "no money down and no payments for twenty months," they would technically be immediately wealthier from one perspective. Their income has remained the same and their total assets have increased by several thousand dollars. However, if their total finances were considered, then they would actually be poorer: their income has remained the same, their increase in assets would have been offset by the principal amount they borrowed, and on top of that, they now owe the financed interest.

Similarly, when the government borrows money to inject into the economy—by investing in the country's defense systems, building new infrastructure projects, covering government programs, etc.—the overall economy gets a boost and GDP goes up. But GDP does not reflect the big picture: the government is not getting richer. Instead, it has had to borrow the money and it will, at some point, have to repay it with interest.

BRINGING THE BIG FOUR TOGETHER

Now that we have examined the three major stances of the economy, let's recap the proxy indicators we use to measure them:

- **Inflation**, as a measure of the economy's monetary stance
- **Unemployment**, as a measure of the economy's production stance
- **Deficit-to-GDP**, as a measure of the economy's fiscal stance
- **GDP growth**, as a measure of the aggregate performance of all three sectors

In isolation, they each reveal a different piece of the puzzle. Unfortunately, there is no readily discernible way to see the whole picture by looking at each individual component. All four together should reveal the whole picture. However, if we take them at face value, they reveal little more than the other indicators we looked at.

As all four are released at different dates throughout the year—absent any historical context—it is difficult to see how any of them is affecting or being affected by the other three. Even the graphs of their historical trends do not reveal the position and direction of the overall economy. They convey a smattering of information without conveying the performance of the economy as a whole:

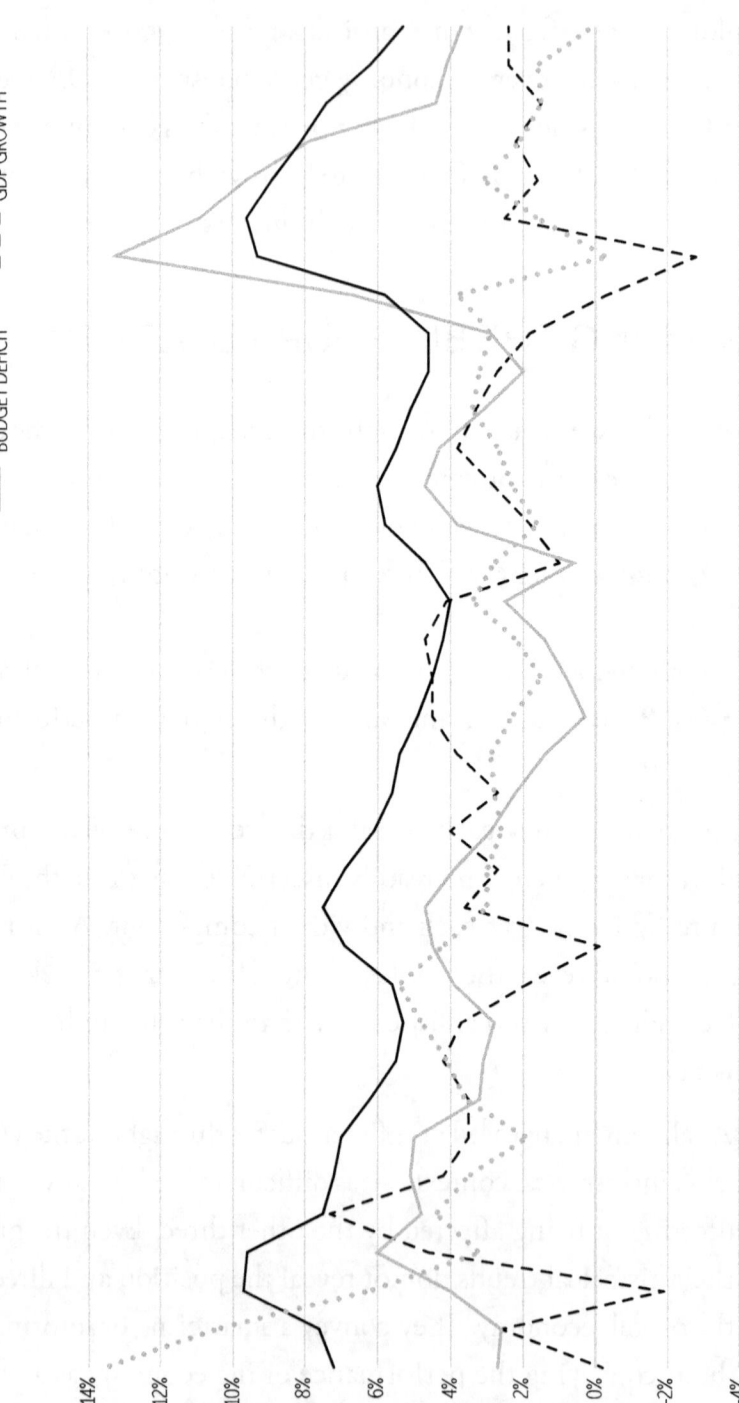

▸ **DYNAMICS OF INFLATION, UNEMPLOYMENT, BUDGET DEFICIT, AND GDP GROWTH**

INFLATION   UNEMPLOYMENT

BUDGET DEFICIT   GDP GROWTH

Is it any wonder that people are confused? Does it come as a surprise that economists create complex indexes with eighty-five different indicators in an attempt to unravel the mysteries of the economy? The economy is such an intricate web of so many different people, actions, decisions, and activities,—can we ever realistically hope to find a sound way to truly understand exactly what is going on?

Fortunately, there is a solution: the Economic Performance Index, or EPI for short!

CHAPTER 3

STEP 2: THE ECONOMIC PERFORMANCE INDEX—PUTTING THE PIECES TOGETHER

"We've taken the world apart but we have no idea what to do with the pieces."

Chuck Palahniuk, Asfixia

When GDP rises, we usually consider it a good sign. But did that growth come from higher government spending? If so, then the economy "robbed Peter to pay Paul," as the old saying goes. If unemployment is high but the economy seems to be recovering, how do we interpret these two conflicting indicators? If unemployment goes down but inflation goes up, have we made any progress?

How can we make heads or tails of any of this?

We can argue about why some numbers rise even as others fall. We can discuss why one number may be more or less important in one specific instance. We can debate the merits of data collection. But to date, there has not been a single method to easily and effectively use these major economic indicators together.

Therefore, we saw the need for an economic indicator that is:

1. comprehensive, so that it captures the whole picture of the economy

2. accurate, so that it can be relied on to provide a credible measure of the economy's health

3. easy to construct and understand, so that anyone can use it with no special skills or education required

To date, people have had only two options. One was using indexes that were comprehensive and accurate, but that required a dedicated specialist to use and understand—so complicated as to require a PhD to calculate. The other was to rely on an easy proxy, such as GDP growth or President Carter's "Misery Index." Having all three—scope, precision, and convenience—was unheard of, and even considered impossible by many.

Until now.

The EPI[1] is the only patented macroeconomic indicator that examines the overall performance of a country's economy and reports any deviation from the desired level of economic performance. It incorporates the variables we have already presented that simultaneously influence all sectors of the economy:

- The **inflation rate** measures the economy's monetary stance.
- The **unemployment rate** measures the economy's production stance.
- The **budget deficit as a percentage of GDP** measures the economy's fiscal stance.

---

[1] The official name on the patent is the "Country Economic Performance and Prudence Indicator." We had originally planned on referring to it as the CEPPI for short, but a quick consumer survey revealed that "the Economic Performance Index" would be far easier to remember.

• The **change in real GDP** measures the aggregate performance of the entire economy.

But what we have yet to discuss is how we took the Big Four and made them work together in such a way as to be useful to the average person. There is a straightforward calculation that allows us to quickly construct the EPI, resulting in an easy to understand number that automatically "scores" the performance of the economy. How does it work?

THE MATH BEHIND THE INDEX

We constructed the EPI such that it:
• falls when there is inflation or deflation
• falls when the unemployment rate rises
• falls when the government deficit rises
• rises with positive GDP growth

We begin with a total score of 100% (i.e. the economy at "perfect performance") and then subtract the inflation rate, then the unemployment rate, then the budget deficit as a percentage of GDP and, finally, add back the percentage change in real GDP, all weighted and calculated as deviations from their desired values. A letter grade is then assigned to these scores to further communicate economic performance in a methodology easily understood by everyone.

The above calculation is what we refer to as "the Weighted Economic Performance Index." But since it is a bit involved to assign desired values and calculate standard deviations, we also created what we call "the Raw Economic Performance Index," or just the Economic Performance Index, which uses equal weights for its components. In Appendix III *"Raw and Weighted EPI"*, we show that the Weighted Economic Performance Index and the Raw Economic Performance Index are almost identical for the US. With equal weights, the complicated formula boils down to a straightforward calculation that is virtually as accurate as the weighted version.

In other words, **the EPI is just the following: 100% minus the absolute value of the inflation rate[2], minus the unemployment rate, minus the budget deficit as a percentage of GDP, plus the percentage change in GDP.**

Or, quantitatively:

100%

– Inflation (%)

– Unemployment (%)

– Budget deficit (% of GDP)

+ GDP growth (%)

= The Economic Performance Index

It is really as easy as that!

Changes in the economy affect the EPI in a very straightforward manner. For example, if the inflation rate increases from 2% to 3%, the Index score falls by one percentage point; if an equal change occurs in the opposite direction, the score rises by the same amount. Similarly, a one-percentage-point increase in the unemployment rate would lead to a one-percentage-point decrease

---

[2] We consider any deviation from a stable price level (i.e. positive or negative rates of inflation) as leading to welfare losses, so the absolute value of inflation is taken in the formula.

in the score. On the other hand, a fall in the unemployment rate (i.e. an improvement) improves the score respectively. The same inverse relationship holds for the budget deficit: if the deficit increases, the score falls; if the budget deficit shrinks, the score rises. Finally, if the percentage growth rate of GDP rises, so, too, does the score; when the percentage growth rate drops, the Index falls proportionately.

Imagine a perfect world, in which inflation is zero, the unemployment rate is 4.75%, the government budget is balanced (zero deficit), and GDP growth is 4.75%. In this case, the EPI score would be:

100%

– 0% inflation

– 4.75% unemployment

– 0% budget deficit

+ 4.75% GDP growth

= 100%

This is just one example of a "perfect" score. It is clear that 100% can be achieved in many different ways. For example, an economy with 1% inflation, 5% unemployment, 2% budget surplus, and 4% growth rate would also score 100%. Note that the score can be more than 100% if the economy is experiencing high economic growth. For example, if the GDP growth in the previous example were 5% instead of 4%, the economy would score 101%. While a "perfect" score of 100% may not seem realistic, our research shows that the US economy has achieved this score and even higher in one year out of every ten, on average, throughout US history since 1790.

The provided EPI formula might seem to be too simple. Many economists would say that the volatility of its components is different and averages are different, too. They would also say that, when our Index is applied to different countries, the weights of components should not be the same. We had similar reservations about this simple formula when we started analyzing it.

To overcome problems of consistency during periods of high economic volatility and to make scores comparable across countries, we initially created the Weighted Index that normalizes the data by introducing weights and desired values to each sub-component (see Appendix III). Weights are determined by calculating the inverse standard deviation of each economic variable multiplied by the average standard deviation of all variables such that the sum of weights is equal to one[3]. The results of our research show that there is very little difference between the raw score and weighted score for many developed economies. For the US, the simple and weighted Index formulas give almost identical dynamics of the Index throughout US history. At the same time, the weighted formula has better applications in emerging market economies.

As such, we will use the raw formula throughout our book as the best means for gauging the true performance of an economy, with the caveat that it works best in developed countries.

---

[3] More detailed discussion of the Weighted Economic Performance Index is presented in Appendix III *"Raw and Weighted EPI".*

THE ECONOMIC PERFORMANCE INDEX FOR 2014 AND 2015

So let's see what the Index looks like when we actually do the math. The official government statistics for the US in 2014 and 2015 are as follows:

▼ **THE US INFLATION, UNEMPLOYMENT, BUDGET DEFICIT, AND GDP GROWTH DATA**

Year	Inflation (%)	Unemploy-ment (%)	Budget Deficit (%)	GDP growth (%)
2014	1.6	6.2	4.1	2.4
2015	0.1	5.3	3.7	2.4

To determine the Index score for 2014, we would begin with 100%, then subtract the inflation rate of 1.6%, subtract the unemployment rate of 6.2%, subtract the budget deficit of 4.1%, and then add the GDP growth of 2.4%:

100%

– 1.6% inflation

– 6.2% unemployment

– 4.1% budget deficit

+ 2.4% GDP

= 90.5% EPI Score.

The value of 90.5% has an important meaning. It indicates that economy was about ten percentage points away from perfect condition. According to our Index, in 2014 the principal factors that depressed a better economic performance were the unemployment rate and the budget deficit.

If we do the same for 2015, we have:

100%

– 0.1% inflation

– 5.3% unemployment

– 3.7% budget deficit

+ 2.4% GDP

= 93.3% EPI Score.

From 2014 to 2015, inflation fell almost to zero, the unemployment rate got marginally better, the budget deficit slightly diminished, and the GDP growth rate improved. Subsequently, the EPI rose. So we can see that, according to our Index, 2015 was a better year than 2014. Instinctively, most people would agree with this. In 2015, the US economy was still recovering from the recession, but it had made gains from the year before.

But let's look back a few years from before the Great Recession to see what our Index can reveal. We calculate the EPI scores for 2007-2015 and graph them on the chart below.

Most people would agree with the general interpretation: the economy plunged into the Great Recession in 2008, as the EPI dipped to 74.5%, the lowest score since the Great Depression. George W. Bush and Barak Obama both took stances of pro-intervention, including a tax stimulus package and industry bail-out plans. Despite heavy

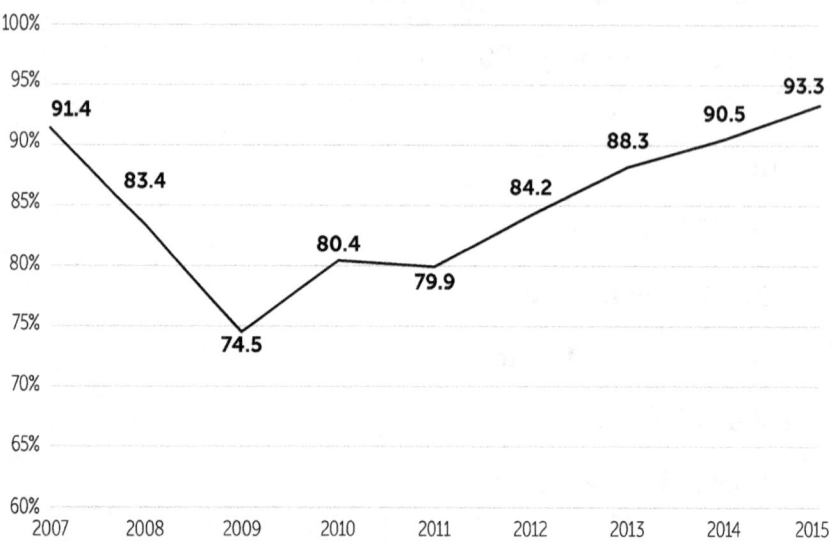

▼ **THE ECONOMIC PERFORMANCE INDEX FOR THE US, 2007–2015**

government involvement, the recession continued for a few years but eventually the recovery in the housing market and production sector started providing support to the rest of the economy. The economy returned to its pre-recession performance in 2015.

While it might seem that all the graph does is tell us what we already know, what it really allows us to do is compare the performance of the economy during these years to other years so that we can understand how much better things are and how today compares to pre-recession performance.

GRADING THE US ECONOMY

The EPI's true benefit lies in its ability to use four simple numbers to accurately compare the performance of the economy at any two points in time.

That is, we can *quantify* just how good or how bad the economy was in two completely different economic times, stretching all the way back to 1790, just fourteen years after the US declared independence. We can compare "the Roaring Twenties" to see how they stack up against the boom years of the 1990s, or to see how the economy fared during times of war.

For instance, let's see if the Great Recession came anywhere near the Great Depression. According to the numbers, the lowest point of the Great Recession was 2009. According to historians, the lowest point of the Great Depression was 1932. These are the official statistics for those years:

▼ **THE GREAT DEPRESSION (1932) AND THE GREAT RECESSION (2009)**

Year	Inflation (%)	Unemployment (%)	Budget Deficit (%)	GDP growth (%)	EPI (%)
1932	-9.9	23.6	4.0	-13.0	49.5
2009	-0.3	9.3	13.2	-2.8	74.5

A score of 49.5% in 1932 is a far cry from 74.5% in 2009. While the Great Recession was the worst recession in recent history, 2009's score was about on par with the years around 1980. In fact, despite its reputation as "the worst period in economic history since the Great Depression," the recent recession was not even as bad as the economy in World War II, as we will discuss later.

When we score the US's economic performance since 1790, we find the historical scores can be grouped together, as follows:

▼ **THE DISTRIBUTION OF THE US EPI SCORES SINCE 1790**

Performance	Number of years	Percent Occurring
Above 100	26	12%
(95–100)	60	27%
(90–95)	63	28%
(80–90)	54	24%
(60–80)	22	10%
(below 60)	1.0	0%
Total	**226**	**100%**

The average historical score is about 92%, which is not far from a perfect score. When we graph this table, we see that it is distributed in a bell-shaped curve:

▼ **DISTRIBUTION OF U.S. INDEX SCORES SINCE 1790**

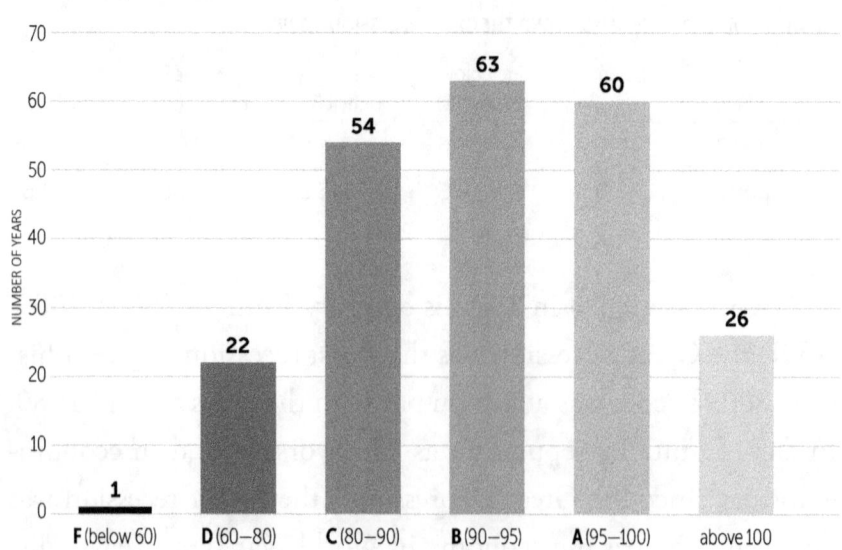

After much deliberation, we decided to assign letter grades to these value ranges, like a teacher might in school or college. Our reasons were: firstly, we are grading the performance of the economy with 100 being a perfect score; and secondly, we set out to create an intuitive, convenient tool to understand how well the economy is doing, and people readily relate to the grades they received in school. If someone says, "Well, this economist gives the US economy an A+," no one needs any more explanation to understand that the economist says the economy is doing extremely well. On the other hand, if the economist gives the economy a C, then people quickly understand that the economy is not doing well, but it is not in the tank, either.

As a result, we assigned the following score intervals to the following grades:

▼ THE EPI GRADES

EPI Score	Grade	Economic Performance
95+	A	Excellent
90–95	B	Good
80–90	C	Fair
60–80	D	Poor
< 60	F	Failure

This way, we can easily refer to an economy's performance with a designated letter grade, making it easy for everyone to quickly grasp how well or how poorly the economy did in a given period. Within each grade interval, we further distinguish between higher and lower performance with a "plus" or "minus": i.e. a 94.5% would be a B+ but 90.1% would be a B–. Thus, the top third of an interval is designated by a "+" sign, the middle third is without a sign (i.e. a letter by itself), and the bottom third is designated by a "–" sign.

With this grading scale in hand, we can begin discussing how the EPI reflects the reality of the US's entire history and scoring how the economy fared during every period—just as soon as we talk about how and where to find the Big Four in the first place.

FINDING THE DATA TO CALCULATE THE ECONOMIC PERFORMANCE INDEX

The US has kept reliable data records on inflation, unemployment, economic growth, and budget deficits or surpluses almost since its inception. Today, individual agencies are responsible for calculating modern statistics. Inflation and unemployment are handled by the US Bureau of Labor Statistics (BLS); budget deficits and surpluses, the Congressional Budget Office (CBO); and GDP growth by the Bureau of Economic Analysis (BEA).

Unfortunately, these agencies do not always publish all the data in a ready-to-use format. For instance, while the BLS collects inflation figures, the number it makes available on its website is the Consumer Price Index (CPI). While the CPI is indicative of the price level, inflation is a change in the CPI. We could download the official numbers in order to calculate the inflation rate… but doing all that math would defeat the goal of having an easy-to-use EPI.

The good news is that many organizations do it already. One of them is the International Monetary Fund (IMF), which makes official data on the Big Four readily available on its website for not only the US but for every country. In its online World Economic Outlook (WEO) database, the EPI components can be found as follows:

- The inflation rate is labeled as "Inflation, average consumer prices (Percent change)"
- The GDP growth rate is labeled as "Gross domestic product, constant prices (Percent change)"
- The unemployment rate is labeled as "Unemployment rate (Percent of total labor force)"
- The budget deficit is labeled as "General government net lending/borrowing (Percent of GDP)."

With just those four numbers, any person who can do basic math can see exactly how the economy is doing and how it has fared over the entire history of the country.

CHAPTER 4

STEP 3: TESTING THE ECONOMIC PERFORMANCE INDEX ON US HISTORY

"Those who cannot remember the past are condemned to repeat it."

George Santayana, The Life of Reason

A fter putting together the formula for the Economic Performance Index (EPI), one of the very first things we did was to score every year in US history, stretching as far back as 1790, and then graph the result. It was important to be sure that the Index is able to trace major historical events and recessions.

The results of our research show that:

1. **The EPI tracks the major events in US history,** from wars and stagflation to booms and periods of prosperity. Out of all economic indexes, only the EPI can accurately compare the performance of the US economy across time.

2. **The EPI catches almost all official US recessions**, from the Great Depression to the dot-com bubble, falling substantially during these periods. Furthermore, the EPI is the only index that allows comparing the severity of recessions in a transparent way.

3. **The EPI reflects the same economic behavior as the stock markets.** Since the EPI reflects the fundamentals of the econo-

my just like the financial markets do, it follows that the dynamics of the EPI should rise and fall in tandem with the market.

Later in this Chapter we assign the letter scores (as discussed in Chapter 3) to easily compare the performance of the economy across time periods. For convenience's sake, we also highlighted the dramatic rises or falls to underscore how accurately the EPI reflects even outlier events.

As an example, history remembers the Roaring Twenties as a time of great prosperity and optimism. It is no surprise then that the EPI reflects a superior economy during these times. History also records the Great Depression as the worst economic period in the US, beginning at the end of 1929. Right on cue, the EPI drops dramatically. Then, too, the 1950s and 60s are remembered as the golden era of American capitalism. When we look at the Index for those two decades, we see consistently high economic scores.

Below we provide a Table with the US fourteen economic periods and their average EPI scores. We also chart the EPI for the US since 1790 to 2015 and divide it into fourteen period as well as mark all major recession and panics.

Our research shows that this simple Index is extremely powerful in reflecting the performance of the economy throughout US history. The EPI is able to catch all major historic events, like the War of 1812, the Civil War, World War I, the Great Depression, World War II, as well as almost all economic panics and conflicts.

▼ **RANKING THE US FOURTEEN ECONOMIC PERIODS BY AVERAGE EPI SCORES**

1	The Gilded Age	1866–1889	Deflation, moderate unemployment, budget surpluses and rapid GDP growth	Reconstruction, the "Wild West," Industrial Revolution, beginning of Labor Movement, rapid expansion of the Railroads, Sherman Antitrust Act	97.5	A
2	Post War Prosperity	1948–1967	Very low rates of inflation, unemployment and deficits combined with relatively high GDP growth	The beginning of the Cold War; the Korean Conflict, the beginning of the Vietnam War, peak of Labor Movement	96.9	A
3	The Roaring 20s	1921–1929	Low inflation, unemployment and budget deficits, high rate of GDP growth	Mellon Tax Cuts, rapid growth of automobiles and telephones	96.8	A
4	The Progressive Era (excluding WWI)	1890–1913	Low inflation and budget deficits, moderate unemployment and GDP growth until WWI	Federal Reserve Act of 1913, introduction of the Income Tax, Mass Production	96.4	A
5	The Mid Industrial Revolution	1816–1860	Deflation, moderate (estimated) unemployment, budget surpluses, rapid GDP growth	Panic of 1837, beginning of the Industrial Revolution, Manifest Destiny	94.1	B+
6	The Founding Years	1790–1811	Low inflation, average unemployment, budget surpluses, moderate growth in GDP	Establishment of basic government institutions, Federalist vs. Jeffersonian debates, large agricultural economy, small industry	92.7	B
7	Reagan Revolution and the New Economy	1982–2000	Low inflation, falling unemployment, moderate to high budget deficits and higher rates of growth in GDP	Reagan Revolution, escalation and end of the Cold War, Gulf War, NAFTA, rise of the Internet, Tech Bubble	90.4	B-

8	The Post Millennium Period: 2000- the present	2001– present	Relatively low inflation and unemployment, moderate budget deficits and slowing growth in GDP	9/11 Terrorist Attacks, Iraqi and Afghan Wars, Housing Bubble, Banking Crisis, The Great Recession	87.7	C
9	1st Modern Stagnation	1968– 1981	Worsening economic performance marked by high rates of inflation, increasing unemployment, moderate budget deficits and slower growth inGDP	The continuation of the Cold War, Vietnam War, the Great Society, Medicare, Medicaid, Watergate Scandal, Stagflation	87.8	C
10	The War of 1812	1812– 1815	A doubling of the inflation rate, (assumed) higher unemployment, significant budget deficits, lower growth in GDP	Agricultural blockade, Burning of Washington, Capture of Detroit, Battle of New Orleans	83.4	C
11	World War II and War Decommission	1941– 1947	Moderate inflation, rapidly falling and low unemployment, unprecedented budget deficits, rapid GDP growth	World War II, Nuclear Fission and the "atom bomb"	81.8	C-
12	World War I and its aftermath	1914– 1920	High budget deficits and increasing inflation	Mass Production, World War I	81.2	C-
13	The Great Depression	1930– 1940	Deflation and low inflation, very high unemployment, moderate budget deficits, two contractions in GDP followed by growth	The New Deal, introduction of Social Security, broad based rise in business regulation	77.4	D+
14	The American Civil War	1861– 1865	High inflation, low estimated unemployment, large budget deficits and moderate GDP-growth	Civil War, Emancipation Proclamation	75.3	D+

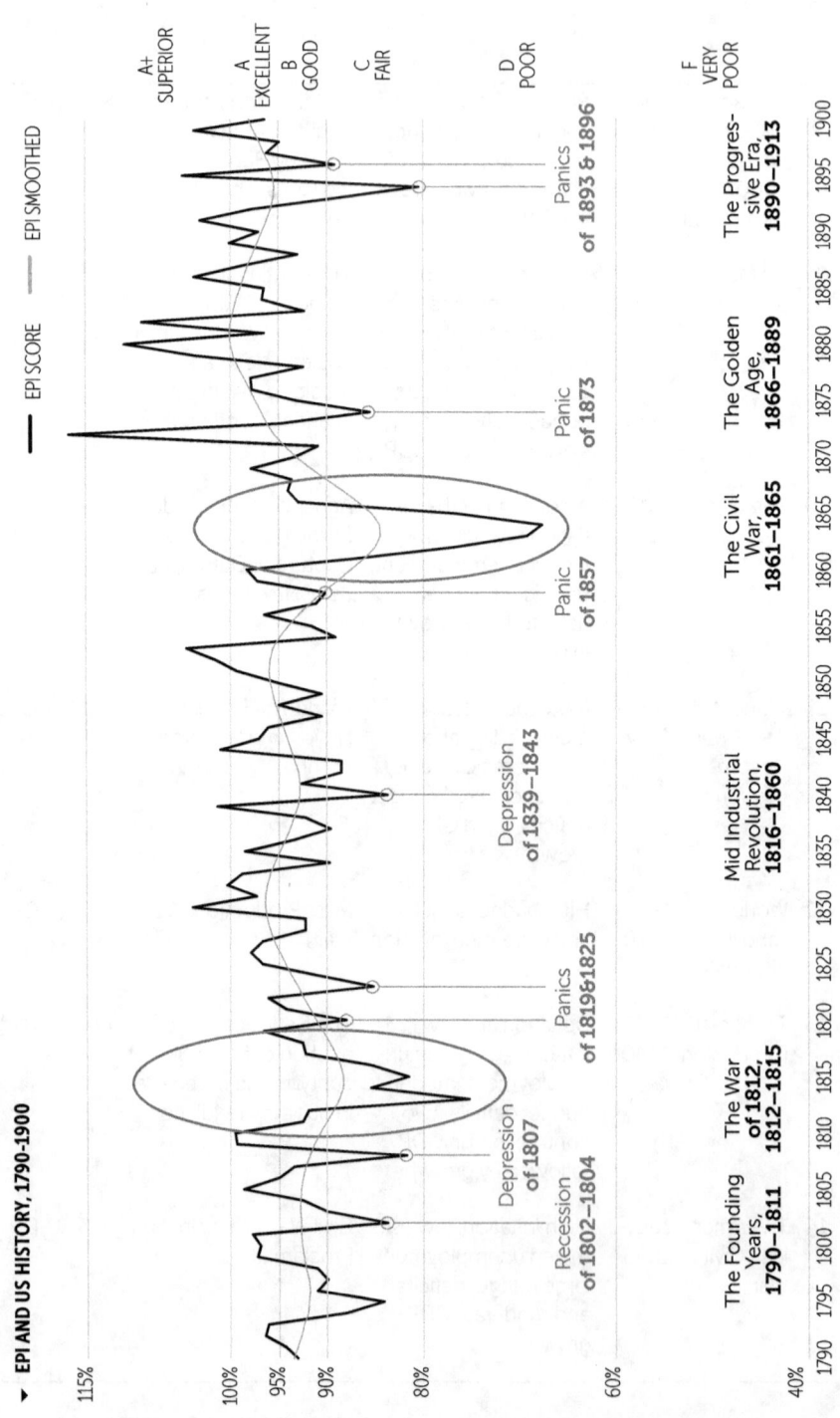

▶ EPI AND US HISTORY, 1790-1900

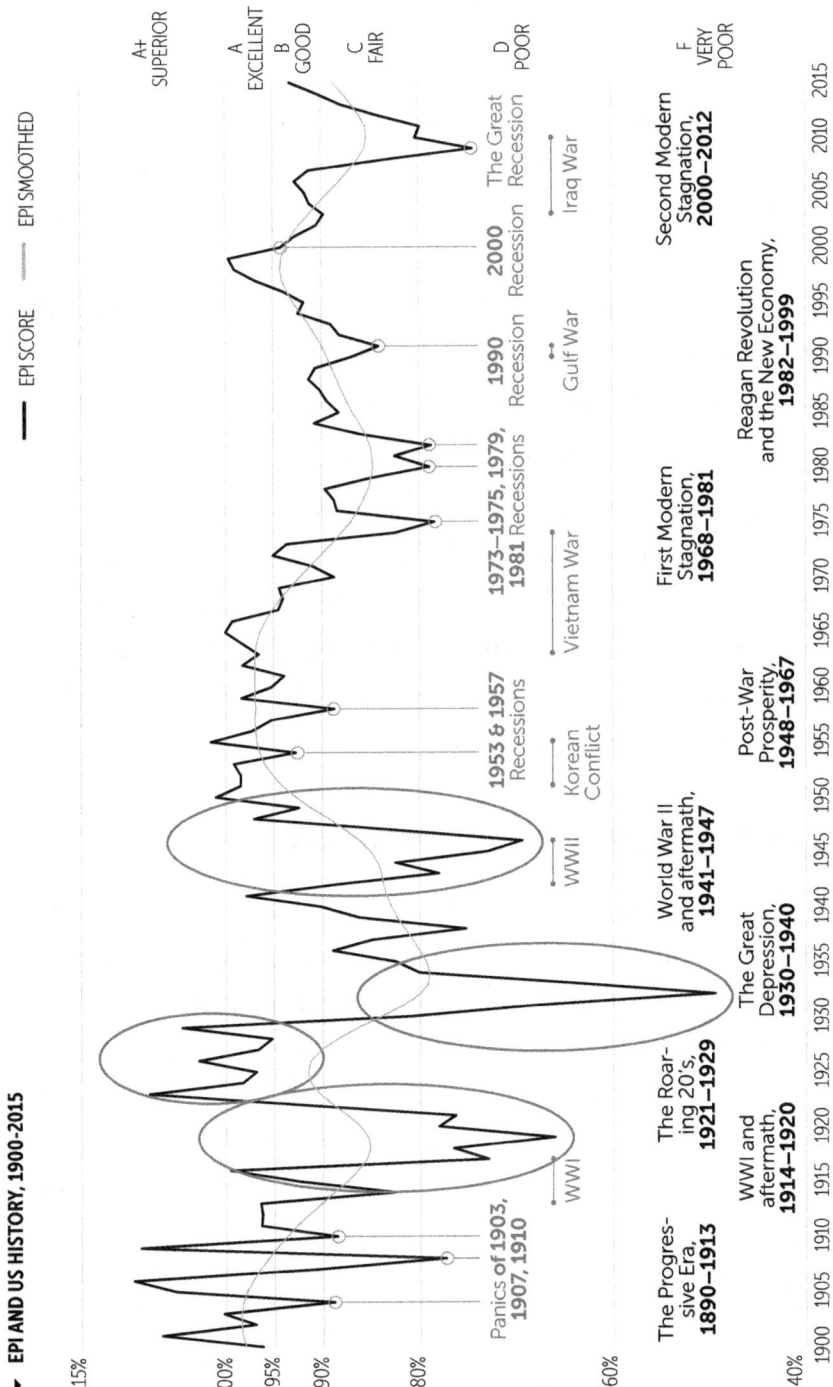

▶ **EPI AND US HISTORY, 1900-2015**

EPI SCORE ——   EPI SMOOTHED - - -

THE ECONOMIC PERFORMANCE INDEX AND THE US ECONOMY

In this section, we examine US economic history using the EPI as a tool to help explain overall economic performance. Economists and historians generally agree that the US has experienced a number of historical periods that include both favorable and unfavorable economic conditions. Each period is characterized by a variety of sociological changes, domestic political upheaval, technological innovation, and exogenous shocks such as wars.

Beginning with 1790, we have divided the graph of the EPI into fourteen general economic periods (in close agreement with most historians' division of US history) so that we can take a better look at how closely EPI reflects the events during each period that would influence the economy's health. Following a quick explanation of those events, we provide a brief analysis and rank each period's performance[1].

THE FOUNDING YEARS: 1790-1811

In 1787, the US had just adopted the Constitution, establishing a unified nation with a common market and no internal tariffs or taxes on interstate commerce. The national culture was dominated by three primary trends: the development of government institutions, western expansion, and early industrialization marked by the growth of small cities. The major national events included in the western expansion were the Louisiana Pur-

---

[1] Statistics from 1790 are generally available, with the exception of unemployment data, which is available starting at 1869, and the average unemployment of 6.7% was used for years before 1869. Most historical statistical data for inflation, unemployment, budget deficits, and change in GDP were taken from *Historical Statistics of the United States: Millennial Edition* (2006), edited by Richard Sutch, Susan B. Carter, etc. Cambridge University Press. A complete discussion of data sources can be found in Appendix IV *Data Sources*.

chase in 1803; the expansion of plantations' output (including slave labor); the growth of industrialization in small cities; and the development of government institutions. Great Britain was the fledgling country's main trading partner, receiving 50% of all exports, and even 80% of all cotton. Towards the end of this period however, Britain began to institute trade restrictions to impede the US's ability to trade with other nations with whom Britain was at war with.

The Founding Years were a time of growth and optimism. Even though there were substantial drops in the EPI values during the recessionary period of 1802-1804 and the depression of 1807, the period's score averaged 92.7%, a solid B grade. Despite relatively high inflation in 1794-95 and then considerable deflation in 1802, prices rose only 2% annually, on average. The national budget was basically balanced or ran a surplus seventeen years out of the twenty-one. GDP growth averaged an admirable 3.9%.

THE WAR OF 1812: 1812-1815

As the Napoleonic Wars engulfed Europe, Britain sought to keep US goods from reaching its enemies, including a blockade of American ports. Exports fell from $130 million in 1807 to just $7 million in 1814. By 1812, the US had declared war on Great Britain. By 1814, British troops had razed Washington, D.C.

To pay for the war, the government borrowed heavily. Consequently, the national deficit rose from $45 million at the beginning of the war to $127 million by its end. Exports were almost nonexistent and trade came to a virtual standstill by the end of the war. In 1814, both sides recognized a stalemate and sought to end the conflict, signing a treaty in 1815.

The EPI clearly measures a fall in economic conditions during the war. In 1812, the economy enjoyed a score of about 91.8%, or a B grade; by 1815, it had fallen to 81.4%, or a C- grade. The EPI reflects that the war and blockade strangled the economy. Inflation surged in 1813-14 with prices rising by almost 30%. Though dwarfed by today's standards, the budget deficit rose above 2% of GDP as the national debt tripled. The only thing saving the score from being worse was a respectable 3% GDP growth (perhaps because of continued expansion and industrialization), resulting in an average score of 83.4%, or a C grade.

MID-INDUSTRIAL REVOLUTION: 1816-1860

The forty-four-year period of the Industrial Revolution was a time of economic growth and expansion for not only the US but for much of the Western world. The US government took a stronger, more centralized role in the economy by instituting high tariffs to protect industry and generate revenue, continuing with the Bank of the United States to stabilize the currency, and providing investments in infrastructure such as roads and canals to knit the vast territory together. Despite political struggles among politicians, banks, and investors, the US economy boomed as steamboats, railroads, capital investments, factories, and immigrant settlers, among other factors, all contributed to a surge in economic activity.

Even though 1816-1860 saw three panics and an outright depression (all captured by the EPI), the period averaged a score of 94.1% and for six years even saw a score of over 100%. Despite those panics and a few years of higher inflation, inflation averaged a negative 1.3% and the average GDP growth was 4.1%.

THE CIVIL WAR: 1861-1865

Much of the industrialization of the US occurred in the North and the West as the South remained largely rural with the economy dependent upon slave labor. With the election of the pro-abolition Republicans to Congress, seven states seceded, eventually resulting in the Civil War. The war was costly, both financially and casualty-wise. Over 620,000 soldiers and an undetermined number of civilians died on both sides.

To pay for the war effort, the North imposed higher tariffs than ever before, in addition to borrowing heavily. The South collected comparatively little in tariff funding, resorting to inflating the Southern currency to cover its own costs. Trade and economic activity fell severely as the entire nation was swept up in its own internal battles.

Overall, the era's score averaged 75.3%, one of the worst economic scores, on average, of any period measured by the Index. The economic effects of the war were immediately evident: the economy fell from an excellent economic performance with a score of 98.2% (an A grade) the year before the war began to a poor performance with a score of 76.4% (a D+ grade) by the time it ended. Inflation averaged about 15%, although both 1863 and 1864 saw prices surge to around 25%. The government deficit increased to 10.2% of GDP by the end of the war. The only thing that kept the score from being any lower was strong GDP growth (including a high growth of 8.8% in 1863), though even that dropped to -2.9% in 1865.

THE GILDED AGE: 1866-1889

The Gilded Age is named as such because it is seen as a period of prosperity and the golden years in many regards. With the Civil War behind it, the US turned its full attention toward recovery and growth. The US quickly surpassed other developed nations in economic output and rose second only to Britain in economic power. The corporation became the major form of business and well financed capital markets sprang up, especially on Wall Street. The laissez-faire model dominated business thought.

Along with the rapid expansion came sharp declines, including the notable panics of 1873 and 1884 and the prolonged economic contraction known as the Long Depression (1873-1879). However, the Long Depression was more of a perception than a reality, as GDP actually grew in every year except 1874, including a 10.2% rate in the last year of the "depression." Its moniker is largely a reflection of economic events in Europe as well as the high rates of deflation in the US.

Overall, the Gilded Age enjoyed an average EPI score of 97.5%—near perfect. This includes a high score of an astonishing 116.8% in 1872, the best economic performance in US history. Inflation and the deficit as a percent of GDP averaged -2.3% and -0.7%, respectively. Unemployment averaged a manageable 5.1% level. Consequently, the EPI reflects that, yes, the period deserves being remembered as "gilded." The performance of the economy was excellent, with an average score of 97.5%, an A grade. The period ranks first out of the fourteen total periods examined.

THE PROGRESSIVE ERA: 1890-1913

At the end of the nineteenth century, the government still held a general attitude of laissez-faire towards the economy. However, around that time, a number of interest groups began lobbying Washington to intervene in certain markets. Their stated goal was to temper rapid economic expansion after becoming skeptical of the consequences of commercial empires of the likes of John D. Rockefeller and Andrew Carnegie. With these influences and following a series of financial panics, the government instituted the Federal Reserve in 1913.

Despite the financial crises, economic conditions during the Progressive Era were generally excellent with low inflation; mild unemployment; budget surpluses or, at least, mild deficits; and growth of 3.7%. The EPI reflects all major economic events and records an average score of 96.4%—a solid A—including a high of almost 110% in 1906. The lowest score of 77.4% (a D+) reflects the aftermath of the Panic of 1907.

WORLD WAR I AND ITS AFTERMATH: 1914-1920

Historians generally include WWI in the Progressive Era. However, pre-WWI and WWI itself were dramatically different economic eras. Thus, it makes sense to split the period into two distinct segments when examining the effects on the economy.

The US's major trading partners were engulfed in the single largest conflict in global history. Although the US remained neutral at the beginning, it eventually declared war too. Economic growth fluctuated widely, as the trade was curtailed and production shifted to the war effort. When the US did enter the war, the government borrowed and spent heavily.

After the heady growth of the Gilded Age and Progressive Era, the EPI records that the economy's score fell to 81.2%, a C grade. Inflation averaged 10.8% with a depressed average growth rate of 2%. From the time the US entered the war in 1917 until the end of this period, it scored from 66.1% to 78.1%, or four straight years of a D grade.

THE ROARING 20s: 1921-1929

In 1921, newly elected President Harding promised "a return to normalcy." Wartime taxes were reduced, especially in the top tax brackets from 74% to 23%. A surge in economic activity along with higher tariffs led to government surpluses used to retire a third of the national debt. Millions of people emigrated from the countryside to cities. Fields such as automobile manufacturing, glass manufacturing, road construction, electricity, telephones, and others enjoyed enormous growth. It was one of the best periods of growth for virtually all major US industries, with the notable exception of agriculture, which never recovered from the wartime bubble in land prices. But the 1920s still enjoyed one of the best economies in US history. Out of the nine years in this period, seven saw an A grade, including one A+, with an EPI score averaging 96.8%. There was a small deflation of 1.6%, on average, with a small government surplus of 0.9% of GDP. The return to the growth rates of the Gilded and Progressive periods led to its moniker of "The Roaring 20s," and the EPI clearly shows this was the reality.

THE GREAT DEPRESSION: 1930-1940

Black Tuesday generally marks the beginning of one of the worst economic periods in modern world history. In the US, the Federal Reserve and the government made a number of efforts to intervene, to no avail. The Fed's policy led to a contraction of the money supply by as much as one-third. In an attempt to encourage domestic consumption, the government instituted a tariff blockade, sparking a tariff war that resulted in a sharp decline in international trade. To make matters worse, one of the worst droughts in recorded history struck the Midwest, leading to the failure of tens of thousands of farms and businesses.

The government enacted a series of programs aimed at alleviating the effects, including FDR's New Deal and the Federal Deposit Insurance Corporation. To pay for such programs, the government instituted or raised taxes on a number of activities, included doubling income taxes on the wealthy and the creation of a corporation tax.

The Great Depression registered the lowest EPI score ever recorded at 49.5%. This reflects the dramatic change in the economic environment between 1930 and 1933, when the indicator dropped from an A+ score of 104.6% at the end of 1929 to a failing score of 49.5% by the end of 1933. Even with a brief recovery in 1934-1937, the period averages only 77.4%, or a D+. While the average inflation (-1.7%), deficit-to-GDP rate (3.0%), and GDP growth (2.0%) were all manageable numbers, the unemployment rate averaged an astonishing 17.9% for the entire decade, leading to either C or D letter grades for all but two years. History remembers it as a dismal time for the US economy and the EPI shows the harshness of that reality.

WORLD WAR II AND WARTIME CONTROLS: 1941-1947

WWII saw a surge in production as America plunged into the war in Europe and the Pacific. To fill the demand for military supplies, the government organized the economy's production to prioritize war-related production. Consequently, the systemic unemployment of the previous decade evaporated. In fact, because of the labor shortage, women entered the workforce en masse for the first time ever. On the whole, the entire nation concentrated on the war effort. After WWII, a number of issues that had lain dormant during the war surfaced, including rampant inflation, housing shortages, consumer products shortages, and labor disputes.

While the GDP growth rate averaged an astonishing 17.3% during 1941-1943, the last three years of the period saw an abysmal negative rate of -4.3%. Despite those latter years, the GDP growth for the period still averaged an impressive 6.7%. Unemployment rates were extremely low. But the average inflation rate of 7% and the average deficit-to-GDP-ratio of 14.1% depressed the period's score to only 81.8%, or a C- grade. While the economy was growing quickly, the EPI shows that this growth was not supported by higher productivity. Rather, it was fueled by high borrowing and an overheated economy. Consequently, it took decades to reduce the country's tripled national debt.

THE POST-WAR PROSPERITY: 1948-1967

By 1948, though, the country was back on its feet. The next two decades are often remembered as the golden era of American Capitalism. Inflation, unemployment, and budget deficits remained at historic lows even while the economy grew at a respectable rate. Following wartime intervention, the government lessened its involvement in regulating the economy.

After President Truman's term, Presidents Eisenhower, Kennedy, and Johnson adopted looser tax policies, including a reduction of taxes from 91% on the wealthy to 70% and a less drastic cut in corporate taxes. Under President Johnson, the government significantly increased its welfare programs, creating many of the programs that stand today: aid to education, Medicare, conservation, economic development, and national beautification, among others.

This era was indeed one of American prosperity. Aside from the recession year of 1958, the EPI never fell below the B grade level during these twenty years. The average EPI score was 96.9%, a solid A. Low inflation (2.1%), manageable unemployment (4.8%), a low deficit-to-GDP-growth rate (0.2%, despite the costs of President Johnson's initiatives), and a respectable GDP growth rate of 4.1% all aligned to produce a time of economic revival.

STAGFLATION AND MALAISE: 1968-1981

Politically and economically, things soured quickly. The government enacted a series of unpopular and/or ineffective policies, including moving to a fiat money system, wage and price controls, "windfall" taxes on energy, and higher taxes in general. The country also had to grapple with the energy shortages caused by the Organization of the Petroleum Exporting Countries, or OPEC. In addition, the government enacted a number of pro-regulatory stances, including the creation of OSHA (Occupational Safety and Health Administration), the Consumer Product Safety Commission, the Nuclear Regulatory Commission, and others.

Many historians record that the period of post-war prosperity lasted until the recession of 1973. However, our Index records that the economy began deteriorating in the late 1960s as inflation and budget deficits grew even while GDP growth decelerated. After hitting a high of 100.1% in 1965, the EPI dropped slightly the next year to 99.4%, but then fell significantly to 94.6% in 1967, where it hovered for three years before falling further to 88.8% in 1970.

The years 1968-1981 were indeed miserable, as President Carter's Misery Index indicated. Inflation and unemployment were both relatively high at 7.5% and 6.0%, respectively. The deficit as a percent of GDP averaged a remarkable 1.8%, while GDP grew on average by 3.1%. These latter figures would have provided for a good economy, had it not been for inflation and unemployment. As such, the EPI averaged 87.8%, a mid-C grade.

REAGAN REVOLUTION AND THE NEW ECONOMY: 1982-2000

Succeeding presidents reversed or modified many of the previous period's key policies, including tightening of the money supply, a drastic reduction of taxes, deregulation of the economy, and pro-trade stances. However, both Presidents Reagan and George H.W. Bush increased defense spending, including entering the Gulf War, and continued welfare funding.

During the latter years of this period, President Clinton presided over economic growth not witnessed in thirty years. Global trade accelerated, fueled in part by the rise of information technology and a fall in barriers to imports/exports. For the first time in decades, the federal budget ran a surplus.

The overall economy in this period was a relief from the dismal conditions of the 70s, but it was by no means a return to the heydays of the 50s and 60s. The EPI reflected an improvement in economic conditions from a D to a B grade in the late 1980s, followed by a worsening of conditions between 1990 and 1993. By the end of 1994, economic conditions improved strongly as inflation, unemployment, and budget deficits fell and economic growth accelerated. Over the entire time frame, economic conditions trended up with an excellent performance recorded in 1997 through 2000. Also noteworthy is the fact that the federal budget ran surpluses for four straight years beginning in 1998. All in all, the EPI scores this era's economy at just 90.4%, or a B-, despite its solid performance in the late 90s.

THE POST-MILLENNIUM PERIOD: 2001-PRESENT

The economy entered a mild recession in 2000, exacerbated by the events of 9/11. It recovered slightly before plunging into the Great Recession in 2008, as the EPI dipped to 74.5% in 2009s, the lowest score since the Great Depression. Presidents George W. Bush and Barack Obama both took stances of pro-intervention, including a tax stimulus package and industry bailout plans. Despite heavy government involvement, the recession continued for a few years but eventually the recovery in the housing market and the production sector began providing support to the rest of the economy. The economy returned to its pre-recession performance in 2015.

For the fifteen-year-period of 2001-2015, while inflation was manageable at 2.2%, the combined impact of high unemployment (6.5%), a less-than-optimal deficit-to-GDP-growth ratio (5.5%), along with lackluster GDP growth (1.8%) led to the average EPI score of 87.7%, or a C grade.

THE ECONOMIC PERFORMANCE INDEX AND RECESSIONS

A second way to test the EPI's validity is to see if it captures economic recessions. We analyzed annual data from 1890 to 2015, graphing the EPI against all recessions recognized by the National Bureau of Economic Research (NBER). Over the past century, we found that the EPI usually tracks "official"[2] recessions relatively well.

---

[2] The National Bureau of Economic Research defines a recession as a significant decline in economic activity spread across the economy, lasting more than a few months, normally visible in real GDP, real income, employment, industrial production, and wholesale-retail sales (for more information, see the US Business Cycle Expansions and Contractions, http://www.nber.org/cycles.html).

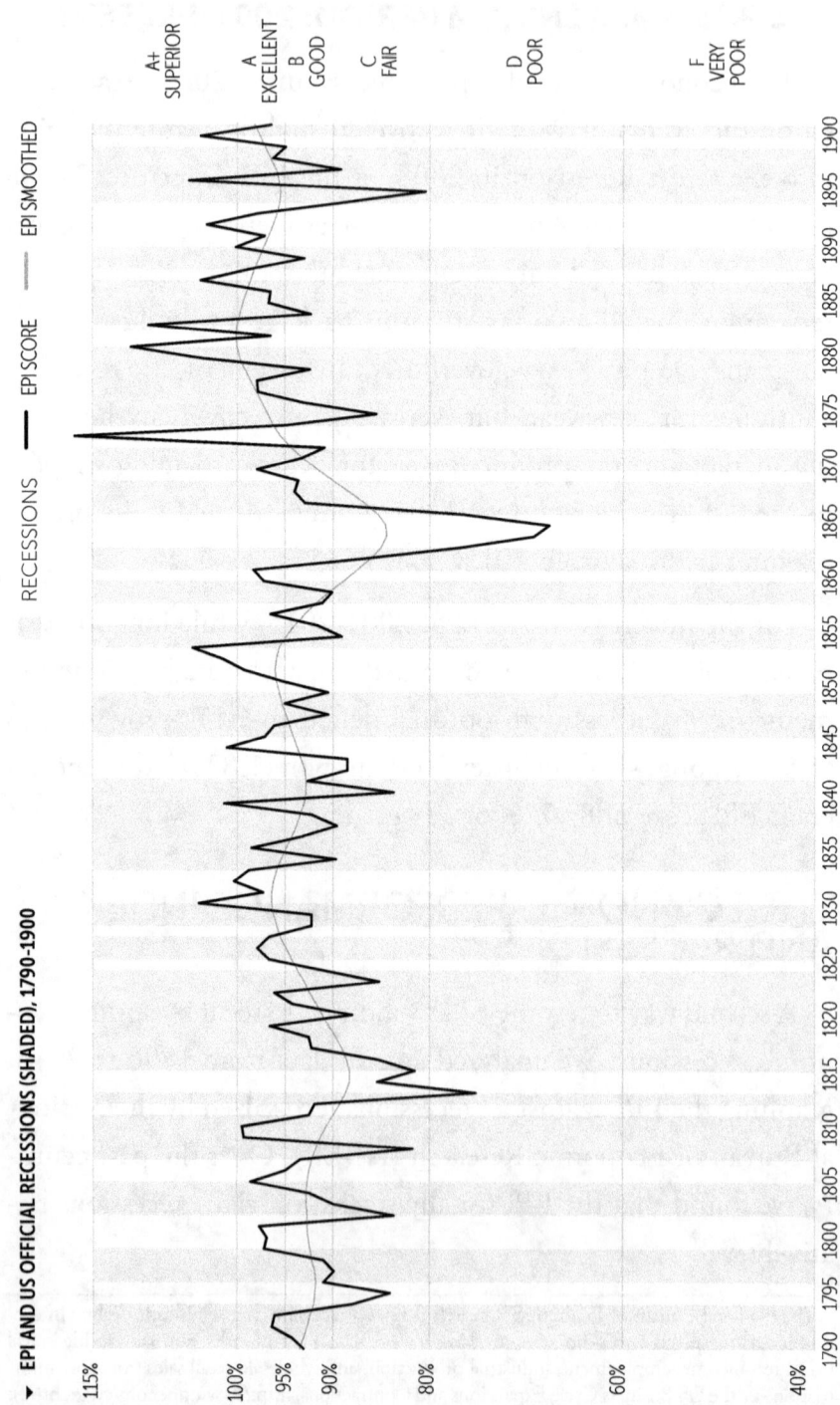

▶ EPI AND US OFFICIAL RECESSIONS (SHADED), 1790-1900

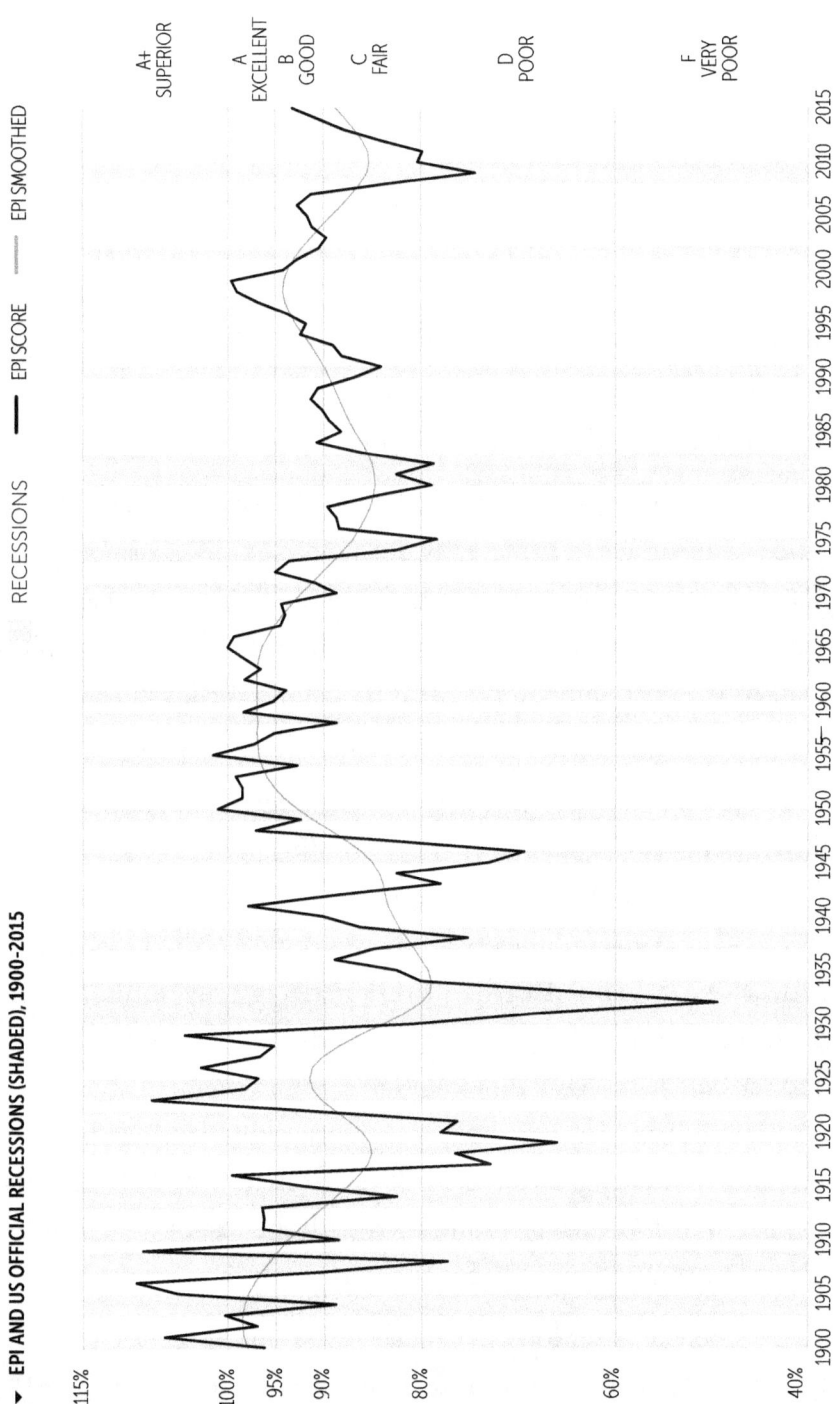

▸ **EPI AND US OFFICIAL RECESSIONS (SHADED), 1900-2015**

RECESSIONS   EPI SCORE   EPI SMOOTHED

An examination of the graph reveals that during all major recessions the EPI fell substantially. Even more surprising, is the fact that the EPI indicates negative changes in the economic environment, on average, two to three quarters *before* the NBER officially announces a recession. While we will not make the claim that the EPI is a leading indicator—i.e. it can be used to foretell a recession before it completely manifests—it does do a great job in revealing the inner workings of the fundamentals of the economy. When the fundamentals are bad, they are reflected in the Index, and then later in the broader picture.

Many people remember the recessions of the mid- and late-1970s. Sure enough, the EPI fell severely during these years, scoring Cs and Ds. The dot com bubble burst in 2000-2001; the EPI began falling even before other experts recognized what was happening. 2008 marked the beginning of the Great Recession. Again, the EPI took a nosedive. In every case of a recession, the EPI captured the reality.

In fact, our Index goes a step further. It reveals economic slowdowns even in cases when there is no officially recognized recession. In 1940 to 1943, for example, GDP growth was at an enviable 15-17% rate and the economy was not officially in recession. But, as we explained earlier, GDP reflects only some aspects of the economy. When we factored in the inflation rate of 6.1% and the deficit-to-GDP ratio of 30.3%, our excitement about how healthy the economy was during this time chills considerably. Despite phenomenal growth, the EPI fell from almost 98% in 1941 to 78.1% in 1943 which, combined with the rest of the economic factors, resulted in a D+ for the year of 1943.

Let's take a closer look at official recessions to see the real story. First, let's score all official recessionary periods using the EPI.

Then, let's rank them by their apples to apples (see table on the next page).

In other indexes, actual recessions can hide behind GDP growth, which can be supported by the government stimulus or it can increase when the recession is almost over. With the EPI, all the fundamentals are laid bare. According to our research, the Great Depression (the recession started in August 1929 with a trough in March 1933) was the worst recession in US history. Now, let's compare that recession with the dot com bubble (March 2001-November 2001). During this official recessionary period, we see the economy was performing at around 92-94%—a solid B! Obviously, not all recessions by name are recessions in reality.

As we said, the major benefit of the Index is its ability to easily compare economic conditions from completely different eras side-by-side. The dot-com bubble of 2001 did burst and many technology-related companies felt it, but the rest of the economy continued to be relatively healthy; plenty of people never realized there was an official recession going on, despite plenty of media reports and attention to the contrary.

The Great Recession was bad—the worst state the economy had been in since WWII. But it was by no means on the scale of the Great Depression in the 1930s. The Great Depression, on the other hand, did not stay as low as long as the economy did during the Civil War.

In other indexes, recessions are "binary events," meaning that, it is either a recession or it is not. There is no room for shades of gray. A period of time may have been "bad"—but how bad, exactly, is "bad"? Only the EPI allows us to compare and contrast recessions.

▼ **OFFICIALLY RECOGNIZED RECESSIONS (NBER DEFINITION) AND THE EPI SCORES, 1790-2015**

	Peak	Trough	Average EPI	Grade
1	August 1929	March 1933	72.4	D
2	August 1918	March 1919	73.3	D
3	February 1945	October 1945	73.8	D
4	January 1980	July 1980	76.4	D+
5	January 1920	July 1921	77.3	D+
6	July 1981	November 1982	79.6	D+
7	December 2007	June 2009	81.6	C-
8	November 1973	March 1975	82.4	C-
9	May 1937	June 1938	82.5	C-
10	January 1893	June 1894	84.6	C
11	July 1990	March 1991	84.6	C
12	May 1907	June 1908	85.3	C
13	April 1865	December 1867	87.7	C
14	December 1969	November 1970	90.3	B-
15	January 1913	December 1914	90.6	B-
16	August 1957	April 1958	92.1	B
17	January 1910	January 1912	92.6	B
18	March 2001	November 2001	93.0	B
19	November 1948	October 1949	94.6	B+
20	April 1960	February 1961	94.8	B+
21	October 1873	March 1879	94.9	B+
22	June 1869	December 1870	95.5	A-
23	March 1887	April 1888	95.8	A-
24	July 1953	May 1954	95.4	A-
25	September 1902	August 1904	96.3	A
26	December 1895	June 1897	96.7	A
27	March 1882	May 1885	98.6	A
28	October 1926	November 1927	98.9	A
29	July 1890	May 1891	100.0	A+
30	June 1899	December 1900	103.6	A+
31	May 1923	July 1924	104.4	A+

THE ECONOMIC PERFORMANCE INDEX AND FINANCIAL MARKETS

The third and final litmus test we administered to the EPI was to graph it against the Dow, NASDAQ, and the S&P 500. By and large, the financial markets reflect not only what is perceived to be happening in the economy, but also what is expected to happen, including anything with regard to policy. If the economy is on an upswing and is believed to continue on doing so, the financial markets will reflect this by going up.

Conversely, if the economy is in the tank and thought to remain there, the markets will also go down and stay there. After putting the EPI and the S&P 500[3] on the same graph, this is the visual we saw (results are very similar for the Dow and the NASDAQ):

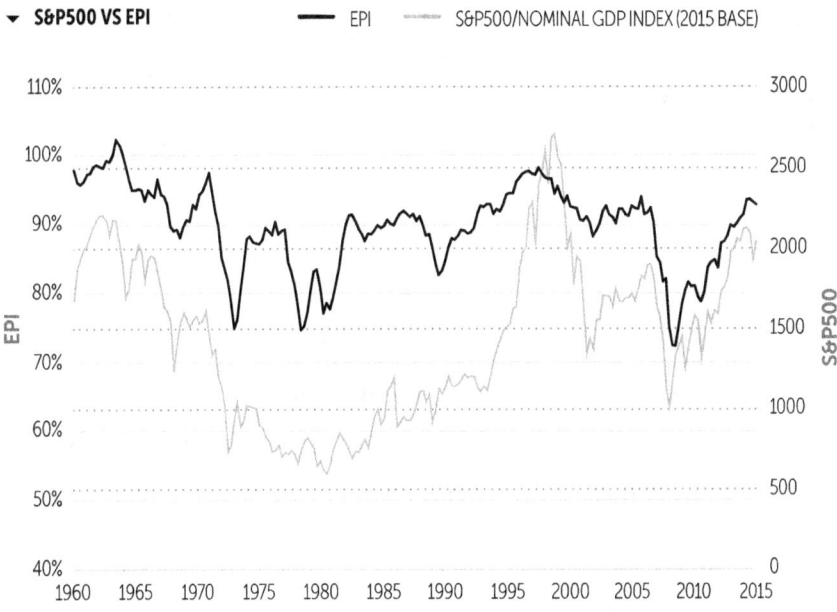

---

[3] The S&P 500 is normalized by nominal GDP to eliminate inflation and GDP growth trends.

As the markets have developed and matured over the last fifty years, they have done an increasingly better job of responding to different economic factors more quickly. Technology and access to more information more quickly have resulted in markets that rise and fall almost in tandem with the economy. The fact that our indicator rises and falls too, shows how accurately it reflects the working fundamentals of the economy.

We calculate correlations between the EPI and major financial indexes during various periods of time to show how well the EPI tracks financial markets:

▼ **THE EPI SHOWS HIGH LEVELS OF CORRELATION WITH FINANCIAL INDEX**

| Period | Years | Correlation with the EPI | | |
		Dow Jones	NASDAQ	S&P500
Post-War Prosperity	1948–1967	-9%	–	-13%
Modern Stagnation	1968–1981	67%	60%	66%
Regan Revolution and the New Economy	1982–2000	81%	74%	80%
The Millennium (pre-Financial Crisis)	2001–2008	52%	52%	62%
The Millennium (The Great Depression)	2010–2015	96%	99%	96%

In short, the fact that the EPI correlates so closely with the financial markets shows that it captures the same key insights just as well (if not better) than the thousands upon thousands of individuals participating in those markets.

PART 2

THE SECRETS
OF THE ECONOMY

HOW'S THE US DOING VS. THE REST OF THE WORLD?

U p to this point, we have discussed the US at length.

But the EPI is not limited strictly the US. In fact, it is not even limited to just advanced economies. Since our Index uses only four basic economic indicators to calculate a country's score, we can score any country's economic performance as long as the methodology for collecting those four numbers is identical across countries.

Fortunately, we have collected the identical data that is available for forty-two countries stretching back to 1980 from the International Monetary Fund Database. It allows us to compare countries' performance against each other for over three decades, from the Cold War through the globalization of the 90s all the way to the end of the Great Recession. These forty-two countries include all advanced economies (including the US, Norway, and Japan), OECD countries (including China, Saudi Arabia, and Argentina), and the twenty biggest countries by GDP (including Brazil and Russia).

Even though these are only 42 out of the world's 195 or so countries, they represent roughly 95% of the world's GDP. Therefore, they can be used as a proxy to represent "the world."

Which brings us to the big question: is the US doing better or worse than the rest of the world?

After scoring and averaging the rest of the world, the chart below represents what we found:

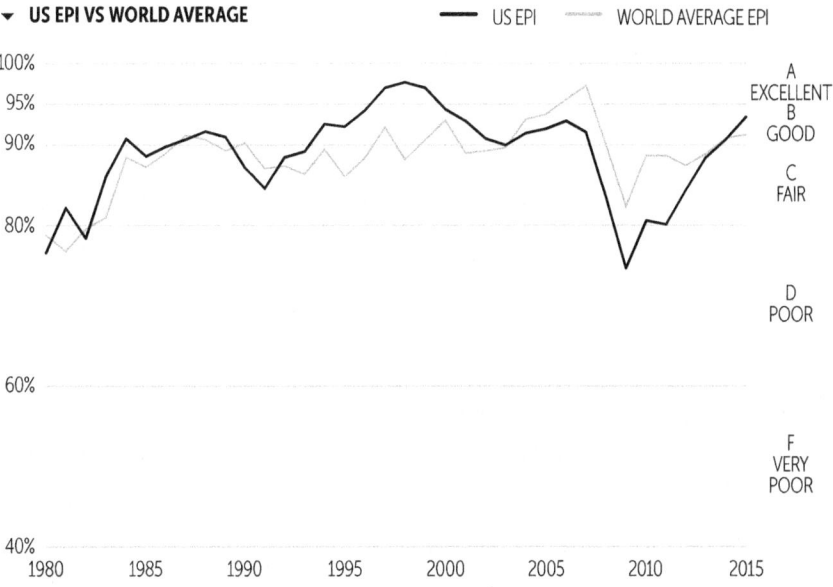

▼ **US EPI VS WORLD AVERAGE** ——— US EPI ∙∙∙∙∙ WORLD AVERAGE EPI

The US outperformed the rest of the world economy in every year leading up to 2004—quite handily in most years. But in 2000, the US's performance began to slip, even as the world's average EPI score started to rise. By 2004, the US was no longer on top: the rest of the world was performing, on average, better than the world's only remaining superpower. In 2009, the US EPI fell to 74.5%, the lowest score since the Great Depression. The world economy turned into the Great Depression, with the world EPI score falling to 82.2%.

The Fed's policy of low interest rates and the government's fiscal support have provided major economic stimulus to the economy since the 2008 crisis. The economy has been showing signs of robust growth and low unemployment levels in the past few years. The Fed began hiking rates in 2015, after strong signs that the economy was on the path to recovery. The housing sector is continuing to recover as well, with housing prices recovering to the pre-crisis levels.

The economy as a whole returned to pre-recession performance in 2015. In 2014, the US and the world economy received almost the same score: 90.5% for the US and 90.7% for the world. But in 2015, the US outperformed the world EPI average scoring with 93.3% vs. 91.1%.

Since we noted that the US's descent began in 2000, we went back to that year to look at the average performance of the world's major economies. If we graph the US's position in the world EPI ranking since 2000, we can see the gradual decline until 2010 and then a fast recovery in the ranking:

▾ **THE US RANK IN THE EPI WORLD RANKING OF ECONOMIC PERFORMANCE, 2000-2015.**
LOWER NUMBER MEANS BETTER PERFORMANCE

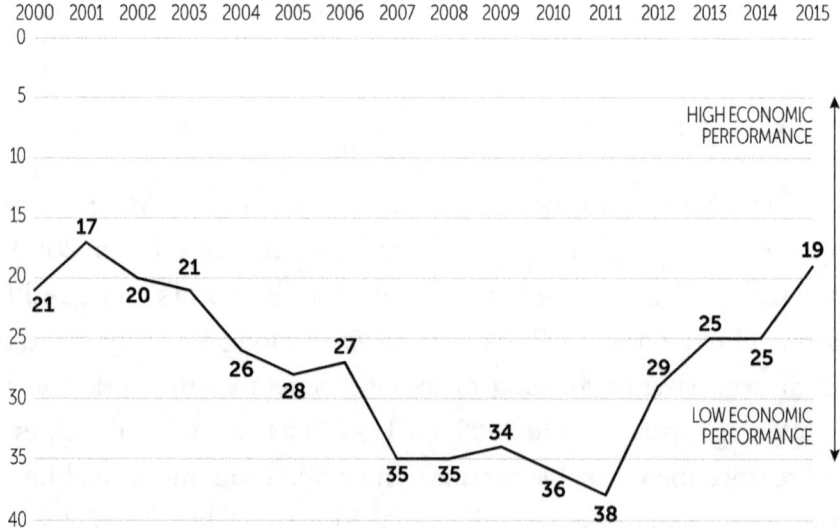

The US ranking went up from the 38th position in 2011, ranking just four spots ahead of dead last, to the 19th position in 2015.

But these forty-two countries include some of the fastest-growing emerging markets in the world; notably, China. Is it really fair to compare the recovering US economy to those economic powerhouses? Perhaps we should break those countries out into small segments so we can compare the US against its peers: other advanced economies not enjoying the rapid growth of emerging markets (see chart below).

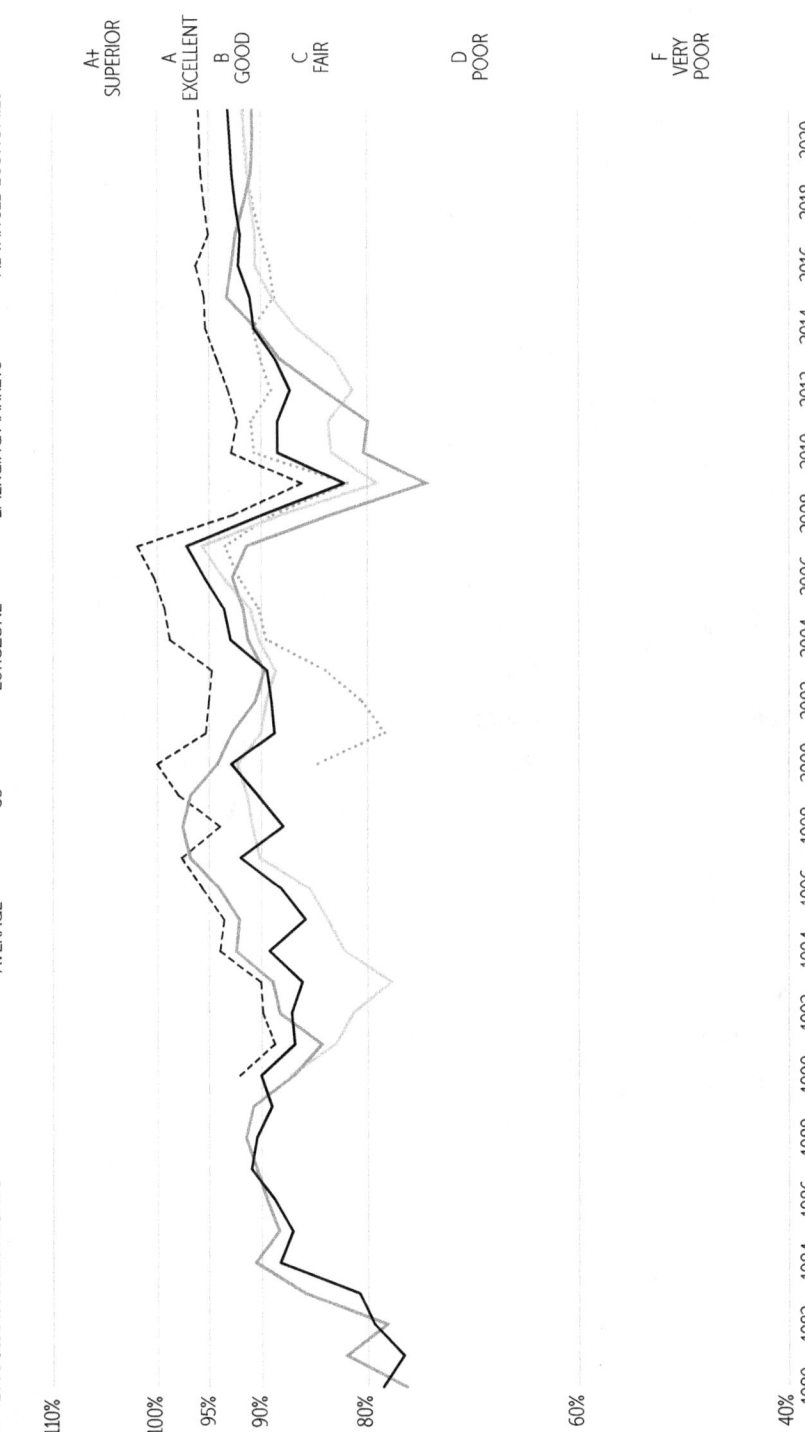

EPI FOR DIFFERENT ZONES

AVERAGE   US   EUROZONE   EMERGING MARKETS   ADVANCED ECONOMIES

When we separate the world's economies into their respective peer groups, we see a similar but still familiar story. The US remains the global leader, outperforming these economic groups in terms of how fast it has been recovering from the slump in 2009. Still, the US was hit the hardest relative to other advanced economies and emerging markets. Currently, the US is outperforming emerging markets and Eurozone economies but is lagging behind other advanced economies overall.

▼ **COUNTRIES INCLUDED IN THE WORLD AVERAGE EPI**

Advanced and Eurozone Economies		Emerging Market Economies
Australia	Austria	Brazil
Canada	Belgium	China
Denmark	Cyprus	Czech Republic
Hong Kong	Estonia	Hungary
Iceland	Finland	Indonesia
Japan	France	Israel
Korea	Germany	Mexico
New Zealand	Greece	Poland
Norway	Ireland	Russia
Singapore	Italy	Taiwan
Sweden	Luxembourg	Turkey
Switzerland	Malta	
United Kingdom	Netherlands	
United States	Portugal	
	Slovak Republic	
	Slovenia	
	Spain	

WAS THE GREAT RECESSION AS BAD AS THE GREAT DEPRESSION?

T he media and even many economists compare the recent global financial crisis that began in 2009 (a.k.a. the Great Recession in the US) to the Great Depression in the 1930s. Some go so far as to say that the Great Recession was, in many aspects, even worse.

Was it?

There are plenty of similarities between the two periods. For one, both were preceded by a robust economy. The Great Depression happened just after the Roaring Twenties, the economy's best performance in the past century. The Great Recession came on the heels of the heyday of the 1990s and a solidly performing economy of the early 2000s. Both downturns were sudden and unexpected.

As we explained previously, while the stock market is not a perfect indicator, it can serve as a proxy to compare the two periods. The graph below shows the Dow Jones's performance during both the Great Depression and the Great Recession, both normalized to 100% in 2006 and 1929, respectively. In other words, the scale

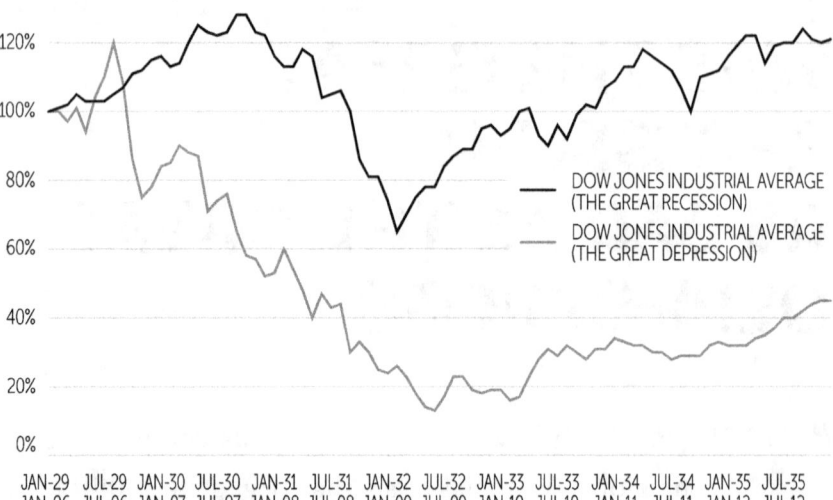

▼ **DOW JONES INDUSTRIAL AVERAGE DYNAMICS DURING
THE GREAT DEPRESSION AND THE GREAT RECESSION
(NORMALIZED TO 100% IN 2006 AND 1929, RESPECTIVELY)**

—— DOW JONES INDUSTRIAL AVERAGE
(THE GREAT RECESSION)

—— DOW JONES INDUSTRIAL AVERAGE
(THE GREAT DEPRESSION)

on the left shows the percent gained or lost relative to its initial value (normalized to 100% for comparison purposes).

Visually, we see that the Dow Jones fell much lower during the Great Depression than it did during the Great Recession. While the recent downturn caused a less than 40% drop in the stock market, the downturn beginning with Black Tuesday eventually resulted in a loss of 85% of the Dow Jones's value. At the end of the same amount of time, in the Great Recession the market recovered to higher than it had been at the beginning; for the Great Depression, the market was still at less than half of its pre-downturn peak.

But again, the stock market is an imperfect indicator, especially in the 1930s. While the EPI reveals a similar story to the stock market graph, there are some important differences.

For one, the economy before Black Tuesday was doing spectacularly at 105% (an A+) before falling to 50% in just three short

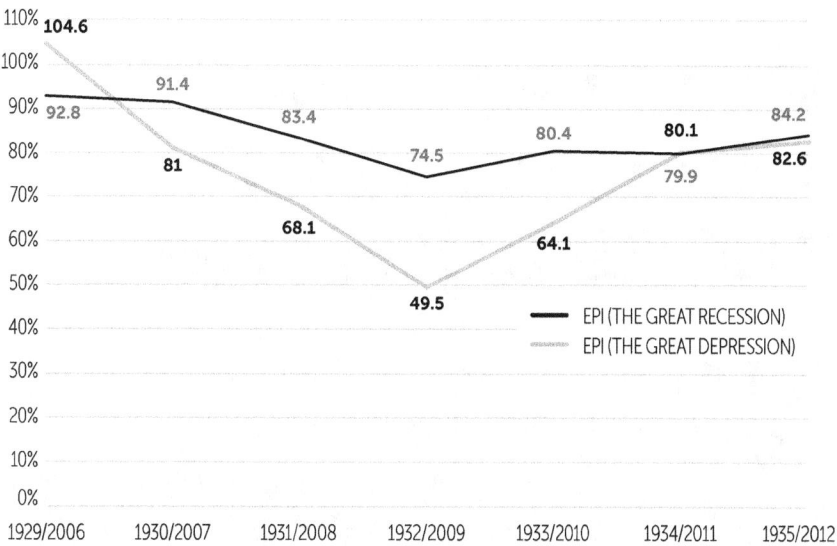

▼ EPI DYNAMICS DURING THE GREAT DEPRESSION
AND THE GREAT RECESSION

years. Not only was the economy's performance effectively cut in half, but this is the lowest ever recorded performance by the EPI in the history of the US. Eventually, the EPI "recovered" to 80%— barely a C grade. During the Great Recession, on the other hand, the economy did not fall as far nor as quickly. It began with the EPI score of 93% (a mid-B) before reaching a low of 74.8% in 2009. At the end of both seven-year periods, the economy was performing about the same, in the 83%-84% range.

To make an explicit comparison: we could surmise that the Great Depression of the 1930s was longer and more severe than the recent Great Recession of 2009.

WERE THE 1950s AND 1960s REALLY THE "GOLDEN YEARS?"

Would you rather live in the America of the 1950-60s or the America of today?

If you're like most people in the US who've lived through both eras, you look back to the 50s and 60s with nostalgia. The Allies had won the WWII, the US emerged as the wealthiest and most powerful nation on earth, and there was a general exuberance in the air. Pent-up demand during the war years led to an economy in which virtually anybody who wanted a job could find one, the economy boomed, American manufacturing dominated global markets, and technological strides turned things that had once been luxuries into everyday goods.

Things were so good as to be unbelievable to the rest of the world. When then-Vice President Nixon told Russian President Nikita Khrushchev that the country had 60 million cars on the road, Khrushchev flatly refused to believe him. When Khrushchev did visit the US, President Eisenhower arranged for him to take a helicopter tour over highways and parking lots, so Khrushchev could see it for himself.

While those decades are called the "Golden Age of American Capitalism," some of the most anti-capitalist regulations and conditions existed. Consumer prices increased dramatically following the removal of WWII-era price controls. The Federal Reserve practiced strong interventionist policies to control inflation and to keep the economy away from major recession. Congress passed a number of indirect taxes on business as well as Social Security taxes, along with personal income taxes at 91% for the top income earners. These are the very things many say would cripple an economy, yet the Post-War Prosperity period is the second-best performing era in US history according to the EPI ranking (see chart below). It comes just after the Gilded Age, with the average EPI score of 96.9%.

How can this be?

Let's look at the EPI breakdown of the period (see table below).

Over these twenty years, inflation was incredibly low (despite the inflation problems at the end of the 40s and the early 50s), averaging at only 2.1%. Except for a brief recession in 1958, the unemployment rate varied from about 3% to 6%, averaging a healthy level of 4.8%. The government deficit was quite low, even showing a surplus for many years; altogether, it was only 0.2% of GDP. Perhaps surprisingly for that time, GDP growth was only 4.1%. While respectable, it's hardly the growth rate you might expect during a Golden Age but still high by current standards.

Looking at the period as a whole though, it performed exceptionally well in the EPI ranking. Out of twenty years, fifteen scored an A or A+. Four scored a B or B+. Even its lowest year, 1958, it scored a C+.

What led to this winning combination of indicators?

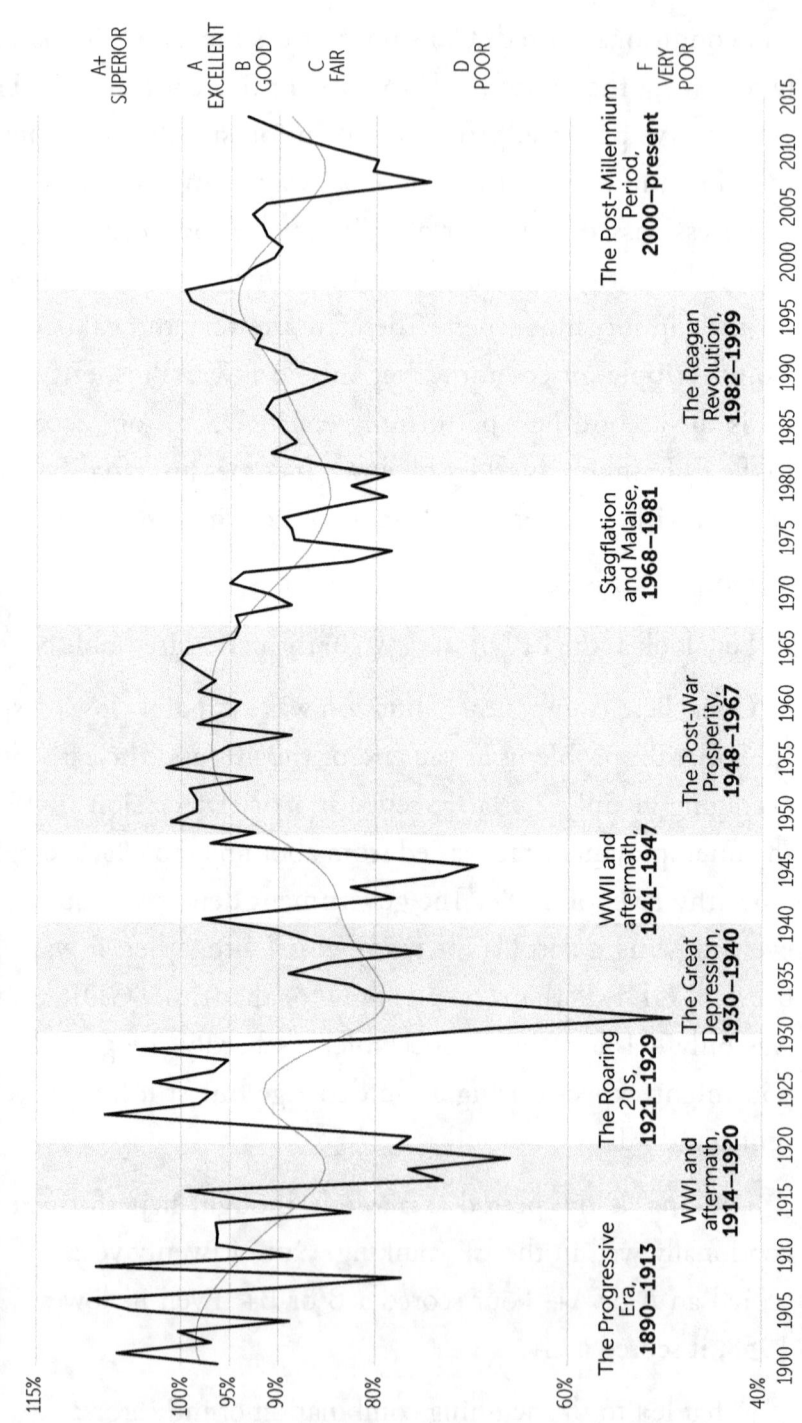

▶ THE EPI SHOWS THE 50s AND 60s AS ONE OF THE BEST TIMES FOR THE ECONOMY IN THE 20TH CENTURY

▼ **EPI FOR THE 1950-60S**

Year End	Inflation (%)	Unemployment (%)	Budget Deficit (% GDP)	GDP Growth (%)	EPI Score (%)	Change from Previous Year	EPI Grade
1948	8.1	3.8	-4.6	4.3	97.1	14.3	A
1949	-1.2	5.9	-0.2	-0.5	92.5	-4.5	B
1950	1.3	5.3	1.1	8.7	101.1	8.5	A+
1951	7.9	3.3	-1.9	7.8	98.5	-2.6	A
1952	1.9	3.0	0.4	3.8	98.5	0.0	A
1953	0.8	2.9	1.7	4.6	99.2	0.7	A+
1954	0.7	5.5	0.3	-0.7	92.8	-6.5	B
1955	-0.4	4.4	0.8	7.1	101.6	8.8	A+
1956	1.5	4.1	-0.9	1.9	97.3	-4.3	A
1957	3.3	4.3	-0.8	2.0	95.2	-2.1	A-
1958	2.8	6.8	0.6	-1.0	88.8	-6.4	C+
1959	0.7	5.5	2.6	7.1	98.4	9.6	A
1960	1.7	5.5	-0.1	2.5	95.3	-3.1	A-
1961	1.0	6.7	0.6	2.3	94.0	-1.3	B
1962	1.0	5.5	1.2	6.1	98.3	4.4	A
1963	1.3	5.7	0.8	4.4	96.6	-1.8	A
1964	1.3	5.2	0.9	5.8	98.4	1.8	A
1965	1.6	4.5	0.2	6.4	100.1	1.7	A+
1966	2.9	3.8	0.5	6.5	99.4	-0.7	A+
1967	3.1	3.8	1.0	2.5	94.6	-4.8	B+
High					101.6		A+
Average	2.1	4.8	0.2	4.1	96.9		A
Low					88.8		C+

The vast increase in productivity—most likely fueled by technological innovation—more than offset consumer price inflation. Additionally, the pent-up demand for consumer goods led to a strong domestic consumer market, while increased manufacturing allowed for building a strong export economy. This was accompanied by a need for laborers, keeping unemployment at a near-optimal rate. And despite the strong social spending programs of Presidents Eisenhower, Truman and Kennedy, the federal government kept the deficit to a minimum. Altogether, these factors led to the greatest period of economic prosperity in living memory:

▼ EPI COMPARISON OF THE BEST ECONOMIC PERIODS IN THE US HISTORY

	Period	Years	Average Score	Grade
1	The Gilded Age	1866-1889	97.5	A
2	Post-War Prosperity	1948-1967	96.9	A
3	The Roaring 20s	1921-1929	96.8	A
4	The Progressive Era (excluding WWI)	1890-1913	96.4	A
7	The Mid Industrial Revolution	1816-1860	94.1	B+

Either because of or in spite of the factors that many would say hold an economy back, the Golden Years really *were* golden.

THE "HIGH TAXES" OF THE GOLDEN YEARS

One topic that seems to trip people up is the fact that taxes were incredibly high during this period—as high as 90%. Many people, including some politicians, use this as a justification to hike taxes. "If high taxes gave us the Golden Years, then high taxes won't hurt us now," goes the thinking.

The fallacy is that although the top marginal tax rate was 90%, almost no one paid that. The true tale is that the average marginal tax rate—that is, the average rate a taxpayer paid on a dollar of earned income—was just 25% in the 1950s[1]. Contrast this to today, where that same rate is now 35%.

Charting Barro and Redlick's study (which includes federal individual income taxes, Social Security payroll tax, and state income taxes), we find the following: while the taxes during the Golden Age of Capitalism were higher than in previous decades, they were nowhere near 90%, and more than 10 points lower than in the 1980s and 1990s.

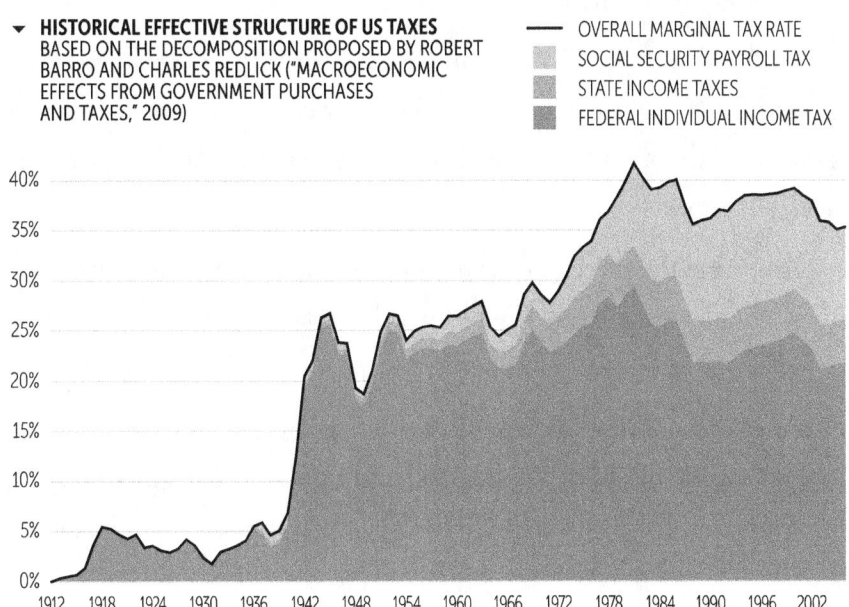

▼ HISTORICAL EFFECTIVE STRUCTURE OF US TAXES
BASED ON THE DECOMPOSITION PROPOSED BY ROBERT
BARRO AND CHARLES REDLICK ("MACROECONOMIC
EFFECTS FROM GOVERNMENT PURCHASES
AND TAXES," 2009)

—— OVERALL MARGINAL TAX RATE
SOCIAL SECURITY PAYROLL TAX
STATE INCOME TAXES
FEDERAL INDIVIDUAL INCOME TAX

Apparently, those years were golden in more ways than one.

---

[1] Robert Barro and Charles Redlick, *Macroeconomic Effects from Government Purchases and Taxes*, 2009

DOES THE ECONOMY GO DOWN AS THE PRICE OF OIL GOES UP?

"More Americans will go on vacation this year, predicts an expert…"

"The economy directly fluctuates with the price of a barrel of oil. We use gas for everything—to transport goods, to drive to work, and to make electricity for our homes and businesses…"

Any time the price of gas goes up, the media immediately begins to speculates how badly it will hurt the economy. In the same way, when oil prices go down, the economy benefits. But does it really?

As the cost of production rises (with firms spending more on intermediary goods) and as consumer spending slows (because of having to divert more of the household budget to gasoline), we can intuitively reason that higher oil prices are bad for the economy. In the same way, we can reason the opposite, that lower oil prices are good for the economy overall. But just how much influence does the price of a barrel of oil have? The cumulative effects are hard to measure.

We cannot conclusively state that we know the full answer, since it would require an enormous amount of research and take up an entire book by itself. However, we can compare the price of oil—and especially price spikes—against the EPI to see how the macro environment reflects it. When we chart the economy's score against the price of oil (in 2015 dollars and against nominal historical prices), this is what we see:

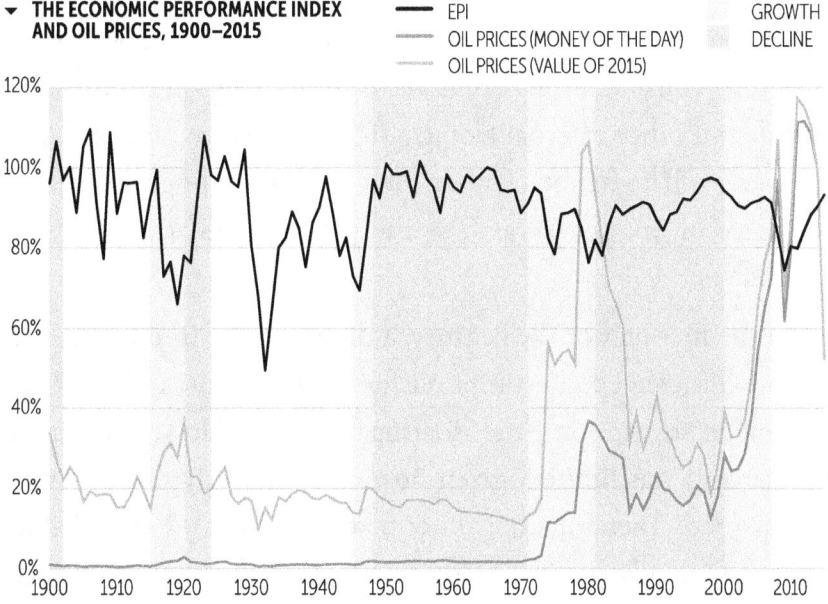

Tracking the EPI, we see that the economy looks like it has an inverse relationship with the price of a barrel of oil. That is, as the price of oil goes up, the economy goes down. But the full story is a bit more complex.

Like prices of other commodities, the price of crude oil widely fluctuates in times of shortage or surplus. The price cycle may extend over several years as supply balances out against demand. From running the numbers, we see that the price of a barrel of crude oil (in 2015 dollars, to account for inflation), has a negative linear relationship against the EPI.

Unsatisfied with that straightforward analysis, we ran a regression analysis for deeper insight. Our results show that, over the past century, an increase in the price of oil by $10 saw a subsequent (and statistically significant) decrease in the EPI by about 1%. So if the price of oil rose from $50 to $100 per barrel, our Index would lose roughly five full percentage points.

Of course, plenty of experts would insist that our analysis should take into consideration a number of other geopolitical, institutional, and other external factors. To address these potential concerns, we will highlight a few key elements that strongly influenced the price of oil, as well as how the EPI captured these external shocks.

In the first half of the century, a dramatic rise in oil prices began with increased consumption for the war effort of WWI and continued to rise until the Roaring Twenties. However, domestic demand was limited, given how comparatively few cars were on the road. Therefore, it did not take long after WWI ended for prices to quickly stabilize. However, during the period oil prices rose, the EPI fell substantially to 66.1% (or a D- grade) before recovering in the 1920s.

Oil prices remained relatively stable, staying within a predictable pricing band, even during WWII. During the post-war prosperity years (a.k.a. the pre-embargo period) of 1948 through the late 1960s, the price was even more stable, with oil hovering between $2.50 and $3.00. When viewed in 2015 dollars, the 20% rise in nominal price over that period just kept up with inflation. During this time of relatively low-cost oil (which, when viewed in real dollars actually declined over the time period), the EPI scores the overall economy at 96.9%—a solid A grade.

But in March of 1971, the control of oil supply shifted from the US to OPEC and the price quickly rose. A little over a year later, the geopolitical situation led to the oil embargo, throttling world supplies and leading to the "first modern stagnation." The nominal price of oil more than quadrupled. As it did, the Index experienced a substantial drop from 95.1% in 1972 to about 78.5% (a D+) just three years later.

In the late 1970s and early 1980s, prices spiked once again with the Iranian Revolution and then the Iraqi invasion of Iran. In just a matter of months, production fell from 6.5 million barrels per day between Iran and Iraq to just a million per day. Oil prices more than doubled. During this entire decade, the economy stayed at about 88% (a C grade).

The 1980s saw oil prices drop precipitously, although not back to pre-embargo levels. Right on cue, the EPI picked back up...before again heading downward in lockstep with the rise in oil prices due to the turmoil in the Persian Gulf and the ensuing Gulf War. From a recent high of 91.5% in 1988, the score slid back down to 84.4% by 1991.

However, with the resumption of oil production, oil prices once again stabilized, setting the stage for the strong economy in the 1990s. But by 1998, global demand (notably in Asia) pushed the price of oil from $18 per barrel to over $100 by 2008. The economy's score fell from 94.3% in 2000 to 83.4% by 2008.

Again, while we cannot responsibly claim that there is a causal relationship between the price of a barrel of oil and the economy's overall performance, we can confidently assert that there is an inverse relationship between the two.

In other words, yes: the economy goes down as the price of oil goes up.

DID GEORGE W. BUSH PRESIDE OVER THE WORST ECONOMY SINCE THE GREAT DEPRESSION?

D o you remember in the presidential debates George W. Bush and Al Gore arguing over how to spend the projected $2.2 trillion budget surplus?

Even as late as January 2001, the Congressional Budget Office (CBO) projected a $3.5 trillion surplus through 2008, assuming policy was left unchanged and the economy went according to its forecast.

Of course, neither of those things happened. The economy imploded, the tech and housing bubbles burst, 9/11 happened, and the US went to war in Afghanistan and then Iraq. Instead of a $3.5 trillion surplus, the federal government had a $5.5 trillion deficit.

Progressives decried the policies and actions of the President, both domestically and internationally. But one of the cries heard the most was that George W. Bush was "presiding over the worst economy since the Great Depression."

Now, we can look back and put their assertion to the test.

Let's look at the EPI from just before the Great Depression to just after George W. Bush's presidency ended:

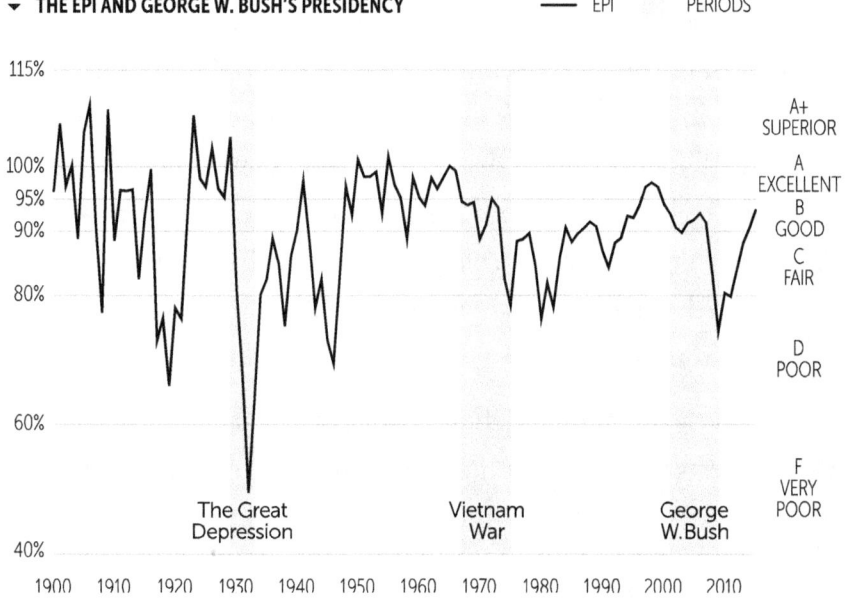

The EPI scores the US economy at 49.5% at the worst point of the Great Depression vs. 74.5% in 2009—just after George W. Bush left office in January. The average performance of the economy during his term was 90.5%, better than the average performance during the Great Depression.

As we discussed in Secret #2, the honor of presiding over the worst economy since the Great Depression actually belongs to President Obama. Perhaps a better question is this: did President Bush *cause* the worst economy since the Great Depression?

No, of course not. No one person, even someone with as much power as the President of the United States can cause a depression any more than they can cause an economic boom. However, there are decisions George W. Bush could have made that might have lessened the impact of the eventual—and some might argue, the inevitable: the Great Recession.

With the bursting of the tech bubble, the economy began what many economists say was an overdue correction. When it comes to unemployment during George W. Bush's term—which rose from 4.7% in 2001 to 9.3% in 2009—there may not have been much he could have done. Likewise, GDP growth fell to -2.8%. Again, with the economic collapse, there's probably little the executive branch (or any branch) could have done to prevent the market correction.

However, the budget deficit is one place where a US president clearly exerts tremendous influence. While the overall budget must be approved by Congress, it is set by the president.

When George W. and Al Gore were arguing about the projected federal surplus, George W. wanted to give the money back to the taxpayers in the form of rebate checks and tax cuts. During the 2000 campaign, he even warned of the dangers of a budget surplus, claiming that Congress would inevitably spend it (though the Paygo rules explicitly prevent such).

One of President Bush's problems was relying on the projections of the CBO, which said that the debt-to-GDP ratio would drop from 34% in 2000 to under 10% by 2010. But how often has the CBO been accurate in their projections?

Graphing projected debt-to-GDP vs. what it actually was, we get this interesting chart:

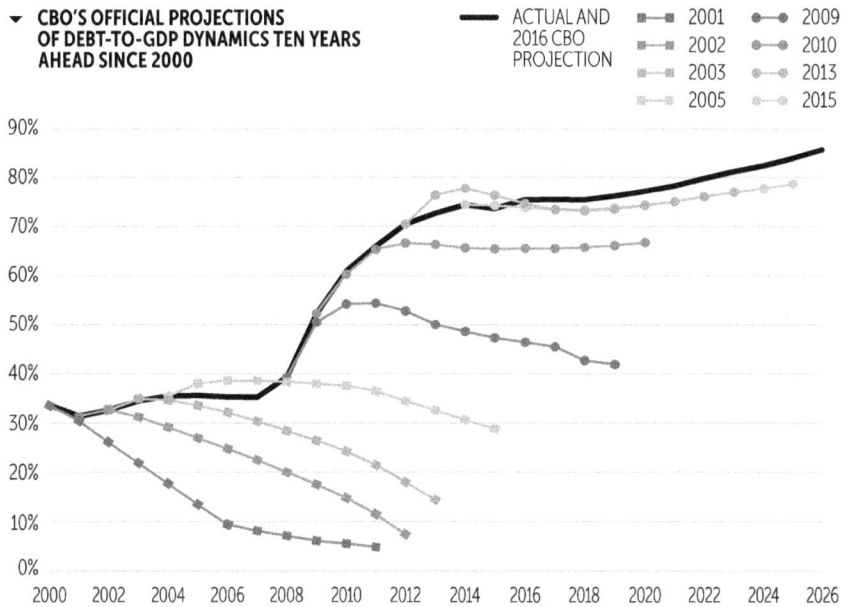

▼ CBO'S OFFICIAL PROJECTIONS OF DEBT-TO-GDP DYNAMICS TEN YEARS AHEAD SINCE 2000

— ACTUAL AND 2016 CBO PROJECTION

2001 2009
2002 2010
2003 2013
2005 2015

Of course, we assume any projection can be wrong. We discussed the limitation of looking at economic forecasts at the beginning of the book. The real issue is how wrong a forecast usually is. In the case of the CBO's recent projections, apparently by a lot.

The takeaway here is that the US federal government is consistently optimistic (even overly optimistic) in its economic projections about debt and GDP. Relying on those numbers, in part, led President Bush to pursue policies like tax rebate checks and two rounds of tax cuts—decisions that reduced federal revenue by $1.6 trillion. Slower-than-expected economic growth trimmed the budget by another $1.4 trillion.

On top of lower revenues, the two wars the president led added tremendously to the debt. By the time he left office, the debt-to-

GDP ratio was nearly 86% by the International Monetary Fund (IMF) definition.

Can we lay the Great Recession at President Bush's feet? Of course not. Much of the groundwork for the eventual recession had been laid years or even decades before his presidency. But can we say that his administration's policies led to a worse recession than the US would have experienced otherwise?

Unequivocally, yes.

DO WARS REALLY HELP THE ECONOMY?

P opular wisdom says that war helps the economy.

People point to WWII pulling the US out of the Great Depression, or that Vietnam was stretched out to jumpstart the economy, or that a lackluster performance was a factor in the Gulf War. The reasoning goes something like: the industrial sector has to manufacture more to supply the war; ergo, an influx of government spending into the private sector will boost the economy.

With the EPI, we can finally compare the performance of the US economy across all major wars. Since we want to consider the effect of war, as independently as possible from other factors, we need to examine not just modern wars but wars before the US became a superpower. We also want to see how wars affected the economy not just during times of prosperity but in times of economic recession. With these goals in mind, we chose nine major wars (restricting it to the years when the US was directly involved) that offer as complete a picture as possible:

1. The War of 1812 (1812-1815)
2. The Mexican-American War (1846-1848)
3. The Civil War (1861-1865)
4. World War I (1917-1918)
5. World War II (1941-1945)
6. The Korean War (1950-1953)

7. The Vietnam War (1964-1975)

8. The Persian Gulf War (1990-1991)

9. The Iraq War (2003-2011)

The graph below shows the US's EPI score with these nine wars highlighted, along with the debt-to-GDP ratio trend line.

Even without examining the underlying Big Four, it is clear that the economy's performance fell substantially during each of the nine wars. Obviously, the economy did not fare better during nor immediately after a major conflict.

Our regression analysis reveals that, historically, the EPI was five percentage points lower during the years of these wars. Additionally, the score falls an extra percentage point for every additional year of war.

Clearly, wars do not help the economy.

The myth persists primarily because GDP often increases during a war. As the government spends more money, domestic production rises. However, as we discussed in the initial chapters of the book, that money almost always comes from government borrowing. As the deficit-to-GDP line in the graph demonstrates, the government almost always borrows money to finance the war. As the government incurs more debt and injects more money into the economy, the inflation rate and budget deficit-to-GDP ratio rise, offsetting the gains in GDP. The most vivid examples are the War of 1812, the Civil War, World War I, and World War II.

In truth, the opposite should be assumed: not only do wars not help the economy, they actually appear to hurt it.

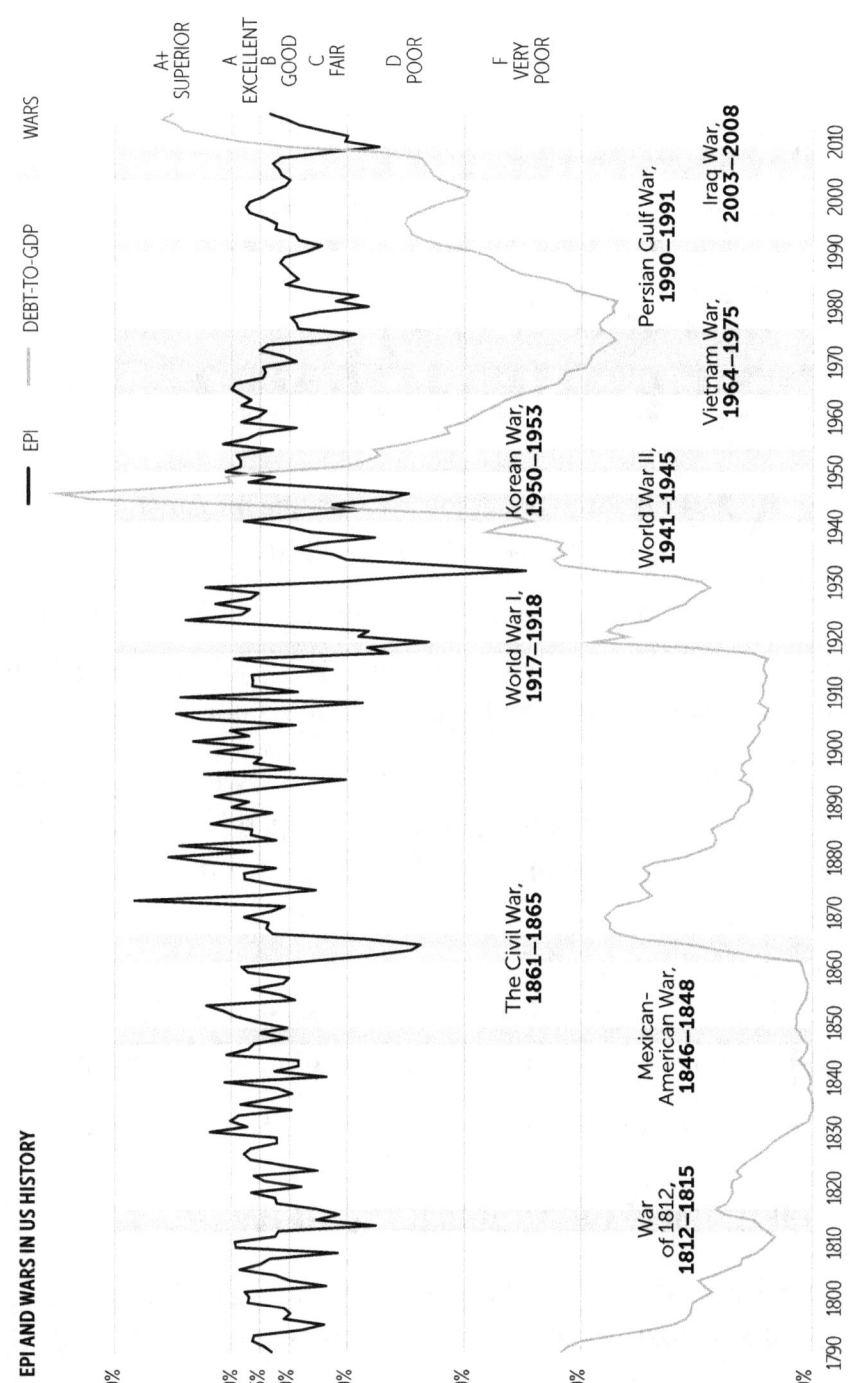

▸ **EPI AND WARS IN US HISTORY**

EPI — DEBT-TO-GDP — WARS

War of 1812, **1812–1815**

Mexican-American War, **1846–1848**

The Civil War, **1861–1865**

World War I, **1917–1918**

World War II, **1941–1945**

Korean War, **1950–1953**

Vietnam War, **1964–1975**

Persian Gulf War, **1990–1991**

Iraq War, **2003–2008**

A+ SUPERIOR

A EXCELLENT

B GOOD

C FAIR

D POOR

F VERY POOR

WHO'S BETTER FOR THE ECONOMY: DEMOCRATS OR REPUBLICANS?

Who does a better job at managing the American economy: Democrats or Republicans?

Whose policies help the country and whose policies hurt it? Who should get credit when things are going well and who should take the blame when the economy slips?

But before we use the EPI to answer the question, we have to figure out how to measure the problem. It is impossible to break down every piece of legislation to see how it affected the performance of the overall economy. We can examine a few key policies, as we do in other secrets, but that doesn't really answer whether one political party does a better job altogether; it only sheds light on that particular piece of legislation—one small piece of a very big puzzle.

So how do we measure the effectiveness of one party's politics?

THE INDEX OF POLITICAL POWER

It stands to reason that the more policy-making positions one party holds, the more policies that party will implement. If one party controls a majority of Congress, for example, then more of that party's policies will likely get passed than the other party's. Therefore, we could measure how many positions each party held, and then use that as a proxy to assume that more of that party's ideas were being enacted.

Obviously, such a measure should include the legislative bodies of the House of Representatives and the Senate. Since the president signs or vetoes legislation into law, that position should be included, too. Even though the Supreme Court can overturn a law, we should not include the judicial body. Many of its decisions are related to social policies rather than economic ones; its impact on the economy, as far as this Index is concerned, is negligible.

However, there is another area outside of legislative control that we should include in this proxy measure: the monetary policy. As we explained earlier, the country's monetary stance is a critical component of the economy's performance. But Congress does not control monetary policy—the Federal Reserve does. By tradition, the Fed follows the decisions of its chairman. In effect, the nation's monetary policy is determined by one individual. Logically, then, we should include the political party of this position, too.

So, our "Index of Political Power" (or IPP) includes four measures: the presidency, the Senate, the House, and the chairman of the Federal Reserve. Now let's assign values so we can measure the balance of power among these positions. For the presidency and the chairman, we assign a value of 1. For each Congressional body, we assign a value of 0.5 (so that, together, Congress adds up to 1). Next, let's assign Republicans positive values (+1) and Democrats negative values (-1).

For example, if the president (-1), both bodies of Congress (-1), and the chairman (-1) are all Democrats, the IPP would register as -3. If all were Republican (+1 each), it would register as +3. If the president (-1) and chairman (-1) were both Democrat but Congress was fully Republican (+1), the IPP would work out to be -1.[1]

If we calculate the IPP for each year since the Fed was established in 1914 and then graph it, we can trace the balance of power between the two political parties:

▼ **INDEX OF POLITICAL POWER (IPP): HIGHER LEVELS REPRESENT MORE REPUBLICAN POWER, LOWER LEVELS REPRESENT MORE DEMOCRAT POWER**
THE IPP COMPRISES FOUR MEASURES: THE PRESIDENCY, THE SENATE, THE HOUSE, AND THE CHAIRMAN OF THE FEDERAL RESERVE

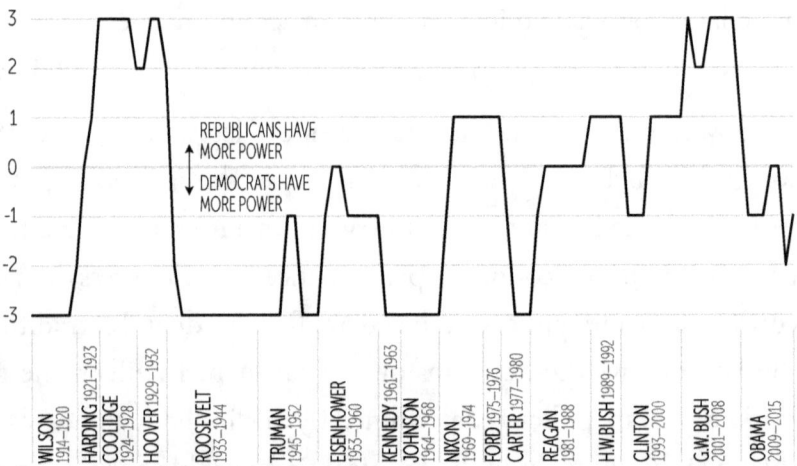

This graph tells us visually what we already know historically. Before the Great Depression, Republicans dominated national politics. But in one of the largest shifts ever in political power, Democrats were overwhelmingly elected after the collapse of the economy. They held power until about the 1970s when the Republicans briefly returned to power during the Nixon and Ford years before turning pro-Democrat again. From the 1980s until 2000, power balanced between the two parties, with the IPP hovering around 0. For the better part of the following decade, Republicans held sway in national pol-

---

[1] Note that even though the Senate and House have respective values of 0.5, in the IPP Congress itself will always have a value of -1 (Democrats control both houses), 0 (each party controls one house), or +1 (Republicans control both houses).

itics under the presidency of George H.W. Bush. However, during the 2008 election, though, power once again balanced around 0.

THE IPP VS. THE EPI

Now that we have a proxy measure of each party's influence, we can compare it against the EPI to see how they scored while in power:

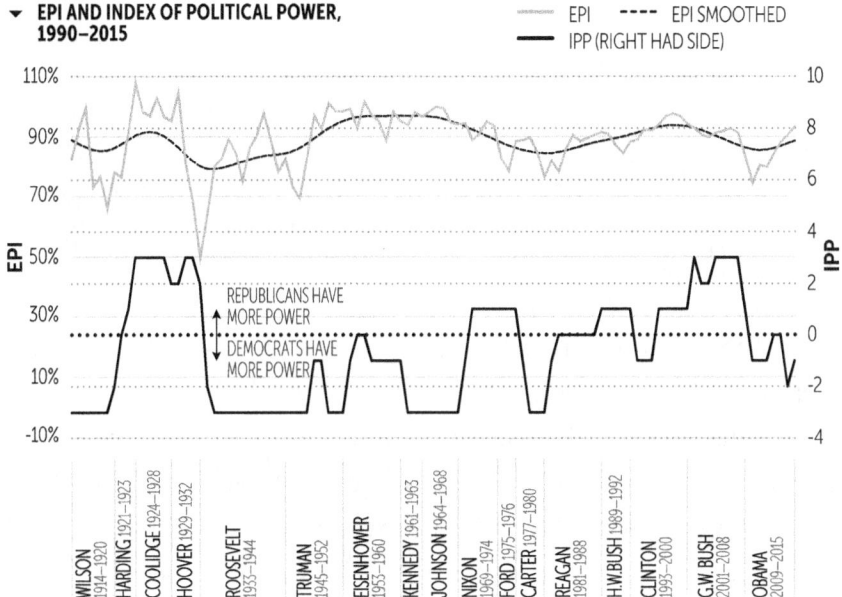

There does not seem to be a clear correlation just from looking at the graph. The economy did quite well under Republican policies in the Roaring Twenties, but also did quite well during the Golden Era in the 1950s and 1960s while Democrats dominated national policies. The economy did well under pro-Republican policies in the early decade of 2000 before sliding into the Great Recession.

Instead of attempting to establish a trend, let's simply look at the EPI score under each combination of political power, i.e. the average score when the IPP was -3, -2, -1, 0, +1, +2, and +3. When we tally and average the EPI score versus each scenario, this is what we see:

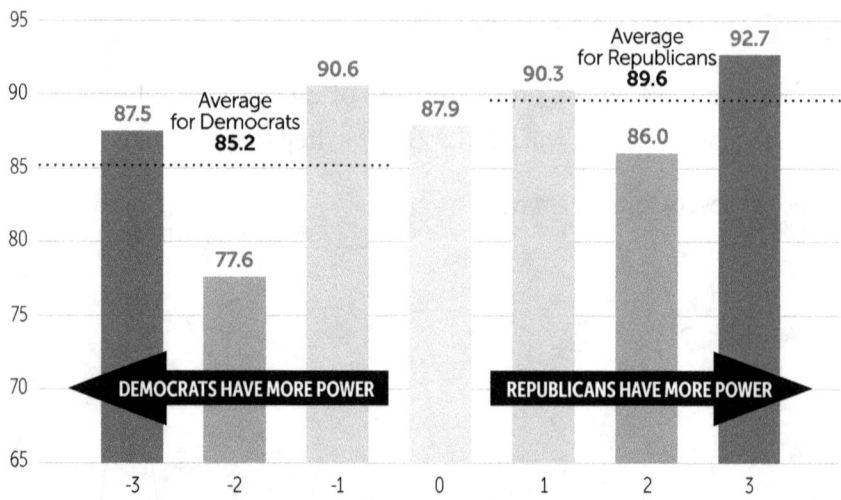

▼ EPI SCORES UNDER VARIOUS LEVELS OF POWER BY REPUBLICANS AND DEMOCRATS MEASURED BY IN INDEX OF POLITICAL POWER (-3 SHOWS THE HOUSE, SENATE, PRESIDENT AND THE FED CHAIRMAN ARE DEMOCRATIC; +3 - SHOWS THE HOUSE, SENATE, PRESIDENT AND THE FED CHAIRMAN ARE REPUBLICAN)

When Republicans held more power—that is, when the IPP was above 0—the average EPI score was 90%. When Democrats held more power—that is, when the IPP was below 0—the average score was 85%. When the balance of power was neutral at 0, the average score was 88%. At the extremes, when each party controlled all four components of the IPP, the difference in performance was only 5% (93% for Republicans vs. 88% for Democrats).

SO DEMOCRATS ARE WORSE FOR THE ECONOMY?

We look at the differences in economic scores between Democrats and Republicans and judge it to be a draw. The Democrats' score may reflect that they had to manage the economy under difficult circumstances, including the Great Depression and the Great Recession. Then again, Republicans enjoyed a booming economy during the Roaring Twenties and the late 90s. If we could control for those shocks, we might find the two parties' positions switched. Moreover, our approach cannot establish causality (whether Republicans or Democrats were the cause of the economy going up or down). All we can view is the correlation (when one party was in power, the EPI score was X%).

However, we could use a regression analysis to look for time connections between one party coming to power and the subsequent performance of the economy. This approach would actually allow us to look for empirical causality. We wanted to isolate economic policies from exogenous shocks, so that we were truly comparing apples to apples. Democrats would not be docked for the Great Depression and WWII, while the Republicans would not get a boost from globalization, etc.

To do this, we subtracted the smoothed trend from the EPI scores. Then, we conducted a regression of the EPI deviation from its trend against the IPP.

In short, if the EPI score was higher than the trend, then economic policies were good in spite of short-term shocks that might have pulled the immediate performance of the economy down, the overall trend of the economy was good. If the EPI score was below the trend, then economic policies were bad in spite of short-term boosts that might have pushed the score up, the general effect of policies was bad.

This way, there could be no disputing whether the economy was up or down because of factors beyond the respective party's control.

Our regression analysis found no statistically significant causality. Which is fine and happens often.

Therefore, we cannot conclude that either party does any better (or any worse) than the other when it comes to managing the economy.

WHICH PRESIDENTS WERE BEST (AND WORST) FOR THE US ECONOMY?

It's easy to rank sports teams. There are a clear set of rules, a clear scoring system, and a transparent record of the teams' past wins and losses.

Ranking US presidents, on the other hand, is nearly impossible. First, what is important? Which topics should be scored and which ignored? And even if something is important enough to consider, how do you assign points? How do you measure the effect of a president's actions in the short-term and the long-term?

Dozens of publications and organizations have attempted to do so, from the *Wall Street Journal* to *History News Network* to the Institute for the Study of the Americas at the University of London. Those serious about the rankings attempt to minimize the bias that such a ranking necessarily includes. Such surveys usually put the larger-than-life American heroes high on the list—such as George Washington, Abraham Lincoln, FDR, JFK, and Thomas Jefferson—and disliked or even disgraced presidents at the bottom, such as Richard Nixon and Jimmy Carter.

But for *The 5-Minute Economist*, the inevitable question is simple: how well did the economy do under their watch? Did presidents' policies improve the performance of the economy or not?

As we've already said, we can't ascribe the failure of the economy to one person anymore than we can credit its success to them. We have to believe, though, that a president's policies and decisions must have *some* effect on the economy. Logically, the longer the president is in office, the greater that effect should be.

Therefore, to rank US presidents, in this study we're going to rank them according to the difference in the EPI score from their first full year in office to their last full year. We offer the rankings of all the presidents in a table at the end of this section, but to begin with, let's focus on post-WWII presidents:

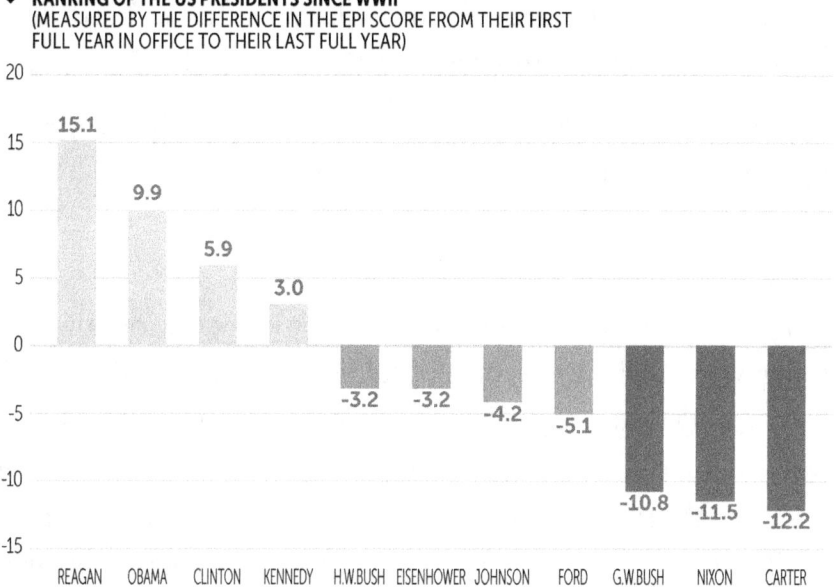

▼ **RANKING OF THE US PRESIDENTS SINCE WWII**
(MEASURED BY THE DIFFERENCE IN THE EPI SCORE FROM THEIR FIRST FULL YEAR IN OFFICE TO THEIR LAST FULL YEAR)

So Ronald Reagan leads the pack with an astounding 15% increase in the EPI from when he took office until he handed the reins to George H.W. Bush. George W. Bush, Richard Nixon, and Jimmy Carter bring up the rear with a cringe-inducing decrease of more than 10%. Let's break down all eleven and see what contributed to how these leaders wound up with the scores they did.

(1) RONALD REAGAN (R) 1981-1989

President Reagan gets an advantage in this particular ranking because the economy was doing so poorly to begin with when he took office; the EPI scored it at 76.4% in 1981. Despite what many fiscal conservatives assert, he presided over a collection of fiscally expansive policies, from defense spending to greater social welfare programs, that tripled the national debt. Combine that with a marked reduction in federal income taxes and it sounds like a recipe for disaster. However, the Federal Reserve tightening of the money supply tamed inflation and GDP growth picked up in the mid-1980s, with unemployment dropping to 5.3% by the end of his term.

The result: an EPI score of 90.8%, making his presidency the best—economically—in recent history.

(2) BARACK OBAMA (D) 2009-2016

Similarly, President Obama gets a boost because of how bad things were when he took office. The global financial crisis was just getting underway and the US economy was performing at 74.5%, worse than when Reagan took office. In spite of a breath-taking spending surge, the economy has scored high at the end of his term. After taking eight years to recover, the US and wider global economies have rebounded. Moderate GDP growth and low unemployment, combined with a stable inflation rate, allow President Obama to leave an economic legacy to rival Reagan's.

(3) BILL CLINTON (D) 1993-2001

You would probably have expected President Clinton to score high on this list. The 1990s were a period of almost unprecedented growth in US history, fueled by a surge in global trade, the rise of the tech sector, and undiminished economic growth in nearly every sector. At the same time, inflation, unemployment, and the federal deficit all fell. If you ranked the presidents by the average EPI score during their term (instead of the change), Clinton actually scores higher than Reagan and Obama. Furthermore, President Clinton's last full year in office was just as the tech bubble was popping and years before the housing crisis.

(4) JOHN F. KENNEDY (D) 1961-1963,
(6) DWIGHT D. EISENHOWER (R) 1953-1961,
AND (7) LYNDON B. JOHNSON (D) 1963-1969

The fourth, sixth and seventh places go to Kennedy, Eisenhower, and Johnson respectively. The span of these terms from 1953 to 1969 encompasses the "golden age of capitalism"— the postwar prosperity years. Growth happened almost magically, jobs abounded, the global demand for American goods kept inflation down yet wages up, and the middle class rose to a new standard of living. The average EPI score during this period was about 96.5%, a solid A, for nearly two decades.

Despite this prosperity, the presidents' rankings aren't that impressive. Kennedy experienced a scant 3.0% increase. Eisenhower and Johnson both lost ground with -3.2% and -4.2% respectively. Although they presided over one of the greatest periods of economic success in US history, individually their impact seems negligible.

(5) GEORGE H. W. BUSH (R) 1989-1993

President George H. W. Bush falls squarely in the middle of these eleven leaders, losing 3.2% from assuming the office from Reagan. Still, he left the economy running at 88.3%, a fine C+ performance as far as the EPI is concerned. He might have performed better, but a slowdown in the economy from its rampant growth in the 80s, combined with a ballooning federal deficit (not helped by the war in the Middle East) left him with an economy that ultimately cost him the presidency.

(9) GEORGE W. BUSH (R) 2001-2009

As we discussed extensively in Secret #5, George W. Bush's policies certainly didn't help the economy avoid the Great Recession and whether the ensuing global financial crisis. Like his father, he took office immediately after a period of fantastic economic growth, so it would have been difficult to leave the White House with the economy in even better shape. However, between his rounds of tax cuts, rebate checks, and funding two international wars plus the war on terror, the debt-to-GDP ratio increased precipitously. When he handed the presidency to Barack Obama, the economy was already slipping into the worst recession since the Great Depression.

(8) GERALD FORD (R) 1974-1977, (10) RICHARD NIXON(R) 1969-1974, AND (11) JIMMY CARTER (D) 1977-1981

After two decades of growth under Kennedy, Eisenhower, and Johnson, the economy slid into a decade of the doldrums under Nixon, Ford, and Carter. Although many historians state the post-war prosperity period lasted until the recession of 1973, the EPI clearly shows the economy began deteriorating in the late 1960s, as inflation and the federal deficit grew while GDP growth slowed.

Historians tend to agree that the political leadership and economic policies of these presidents were particularly weak and misguided. Such examples include Bretton Woods, where the American dollar was unlinked from the gold standard, wage and price controls, the expansion of unsustainable social insurance programs, the unsuccessful "Whip Inflation Now" initiative, "windfall taxes" on energy, and more.

Altogether, this was a period of high inflation, high interest rates, vastly increased government spending, start-and-stall economic growth, and misguided fiscal and economic policies in which each president left the economy worse off than when they found it.

RANKING OF ALL PRESIDENTS

If we're going to judge presidents solely on the difference between when they took office and when they stepped down, though, we need to see all of them to have some context.

Interestingly enough, the president almost universally acknowledged to be the best since the founding fathers, Abraham Lincoln, ranks dead last for average EPI during his office. Obviously, a president's legacy really is about more than just "the economy, stupid."

▼ EPI RANKING OF THE US PRESIDENTS

	President	R/D (F—federalist; I—independent; W—whig)	Years	EPI last year of presidency minus EPI last year of the previous president	Avg EPI during the term	Change in Average EPI
1	Franklin D. Roosevelt: 1933–1945	D	1933–1945	33.1	83.3	7.5
2	Andrew Johnson: 1865–1869	D	1865–1869	26.1	89.2	14.1
3	William Howard Taft: 1909–1913	R	1909–1913	18.9	97.5	0.6
4	John Tyler (Harrison NR): 1841–1845	I	1841–1845	17.3	92.5	0.9
5	Harry S. Truman: 1945–1953	D	1945–1953	15.9	89.1	5.8
6	Ronald Reagan: 1981–1989	R	1981–1989	15.1	87.1	2.1
7	Warren G. Harding: 1921–1923	R	1921–1923	14.2	84.3	1.2
8	Rutherford B. Hayes: 1877–1881	R	1877–1881	13.2	101.1	5.0
9	Millard Fillmore: 1850–1853	W	1850–1853	11.0	98.6	8.2
10	Barack Obama: 2009–2016	D	2009–2016	9.9	84.4	-6.1
11	William McKinley: 1897–1901	R	1897–1901	7.2	97.7	6.9
12	Gerald Ford: 1974–1977	R	1975–1977	5.9	83.5	-7.4
13	Bill Clinton: 1993–2001	D	1993–2001	5.9	94.2	6.5
14	John Adams: 1797–1801	F	1797–1801	5.9	93.6	1.9
15	James Monroe: 1817–1825	D	1817–1825	5.7	91.9	3.2
16	Benjamin Harrison: 1889–1893	R	1889–1893	4.8	99.4	1.6
17	Ulysses S. Grant: 1869–1877	R	1869–1877	4.2	96.2	7.0
18	James Madison: 1809–1817	D	1809–1817	3.7	88.7	-2.7
19	Calvin Coolidge: 1923–1929	R	1923–1929	3.1	99.7	15.4
20	John F. Kennedy: 1961–1963	D	1961–1963	3.0	96.2	0.1
21	James Buchanan: 1857–1861	D	1857–1861	1.8	94.1	-1.3

President	R/D (F—federalist; I—independent; W—whig)	Years	EPI last year of presidency minus EPI last year of the previous president	Avg EPI during the term	Change in Average EPI
22 Andrew Jackson: 1829–1837	D	1829–1837	1.2	96.7	0.9
23 John Quincy Adams: 1825–1829	D	1825–1829	1.2	95.8	3.9
24 George H. W. Bush: 1989–1993	R	1989–1993	-3.2	87.6	0.5
25 Dwight D. Eisenhower: 1953–1961	R	1953–1961	-3.2	96.1	6.9
26 Grover Cleveland: 1885–1889	D	1885–1889	-3.7	97.9	-0.7
27 Lyndon B. Johnson: 1963–1969	D	1963–1969	-4.2	97.2	1.0
28 Zachary Taylor: 1849–1850	W	1849–1850	-4.5	90.4	-4.2
29 Franklin Pierce: 1853–1857	D	1853–1857	-5.0	95.3	-3.3
30 James K. Polk: 1845–1849	D	1845–1849	-5.9	94.6	2.1
31 Grover Cleveland: 1893–1897	D	1893–1897	-8.6	90.8	-8.6
32 Martin Van Buren: 1837–1841	D	1837–1841	-9.7	91.6	-5.1
33 George W. Bush: 2001–2009	R	2001–2009	-10.8	90.5	-3.7
34 Richard Nixon: 1969–1974	R	1969–1975	-11.5	90.9	-6.3
35 Jimmy Carter: 1977–1981	D	1977–1981	-12.2	85.0	1.4
36 Chester A. Arthur (Garfield NR 1881): 1881–1885	R	1881–1885	-14.3	98.6	-2.6
37 Thomas Jefferson: 1801–1809	D	1801–1809	-15.2	91.5	-2.2
38 Woodrow Wilson: 1913–1921	D	1913–1921	-18.2	83.1	-14.4
39 Theodore Roosevelt: 1901–1909	R	1901–1909	-18.9	97.0	-0.7
40 Abraham Lincoln: 1861–1865	R	1861–1865	-30.7	75.1	-19.0
41 Herbert Hoover: 1929–1933	R	1929–1933	-45.8	75.8	-23.9
George Washington: 1789–1797	I	1789–1797		91.8	

WHAT ARE THE BEST (AND WORST) US STATE ECONOMIES?

Although we originally developed the Economic Performance Index to measure national economies, it makes sense to examine US states individually. After all, many states have populations as large as small countries, and most have a gross state product (GSP) and population that rival the GDPs of developed economies.

For example, Alabama has roughly the same number of people as Ireland. Kentucky's population is almost equal to New Zealand's. Illinois and Rwanda, too, are about the same size, population-wise. When we consider economic size, California's economy is about the same size as France's or India's. The GSP of Texas competes with the entire country of Canada, while Virginia is on par with Poland.

Besides sheer size, it also makes sense to look at US states individually because of their relative autonomy. Although the primary driver of state economic performance is driven by the national economy, states have a comparatively large degree of autonomy in managing their own economic and fiscal policies. Moreover, they are diverse geographically, culturally, economically, and density-wise. Those factors make a decided difference in how the economy of each has fared over the past few decades.

When we created a state-appropriate EPI, instead of using national inflation figures we created an average regional inflation (ex. the Northeast vs. West Coast) to reflect local conditions. Budget deficit/surplus was reconstructed by splitting expenditure and revenues between federal, state, and local levels. The other two state-specific factors—unemployment and GSP—were all available in public sources.

The three charts below show maps of the continental US in the 1980s, during the IT and housing market boom in 2000-2007, and after the crisis in 2010-2015, color-coded by their average EPI score: the darker its color, the better their performance.

The overall trend shows that the EPI score improved over time, mainly driven by structurally low inflation and unemployment, while growth rates slowed down after the Great Recession. Inflation rates dropped largely from its peak in the 1980s with an average of more than 5% down to 3% in the early 2000s and below 2% in 2010-2015. GDP growth rates gradually slowed down over time and moved to a "new normal" or structurally lower levels of growth after the 2009 crisis. State deficits have usually reflected the federal-level government policies and have remained elevated after the crisis.

As you can see, the East Coast did particularly well during the 1980s, as well as California and some other West Coast states. In the 1980s, the East Coast states outperformed in their EPI scores mainly due to higher GSP growth rates. Also, higher levels of urbanization on the East Coast kept unemployment levels lower than in the rest of the US.

▼ **EPI PERFORMANCE OF INDIVIDUAL US STATES IN THE 1980S**
(THE DARKER COLOR REFLECTS HIGHER EPI VALUE)

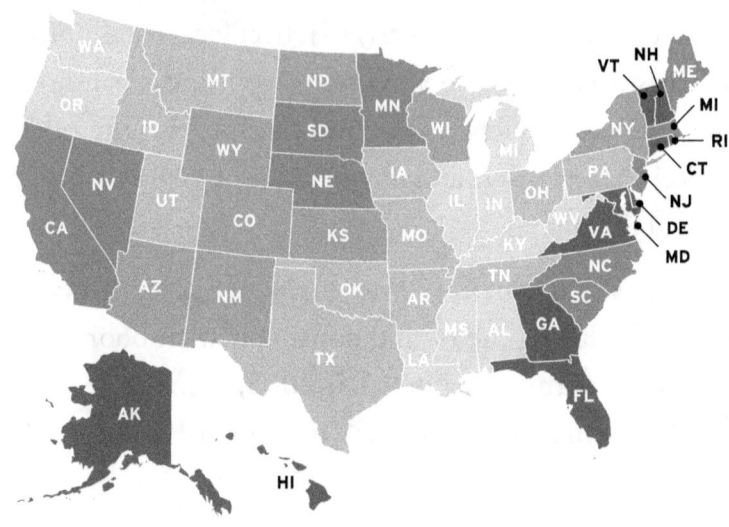

▼ **EPI PERFORMANCE OF INDIVIDUAL US STATES AVERAGED FOR 2000–2007**
(THE DARKER COLOR REFLECTS HIGHER EPI VALUE)

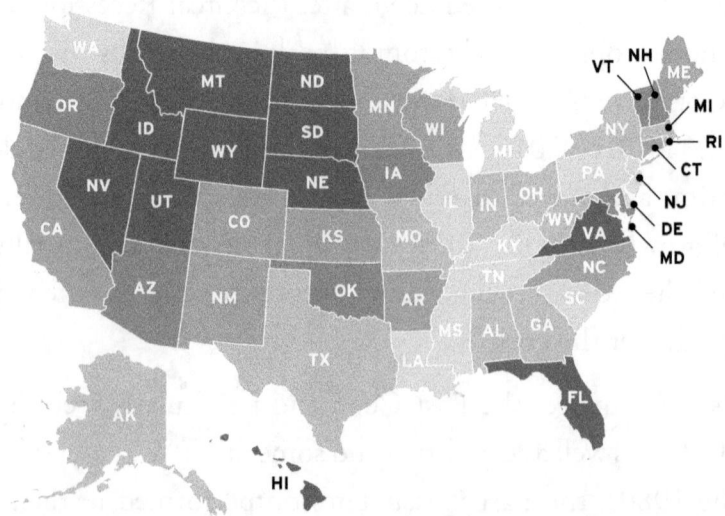

Twenty years later, however, the picture had radically changed. Going into the Great Recession, the Eastern seaboard and California were doing poorly, while the Midwest and the Northwest did spectac-

▾ **EPI PERFORMANCE OF INDIVIDUAL US STATES IN 2010–2015**
(THE DARKER COLOR REFLECTS HIGHER EPI VALUE)

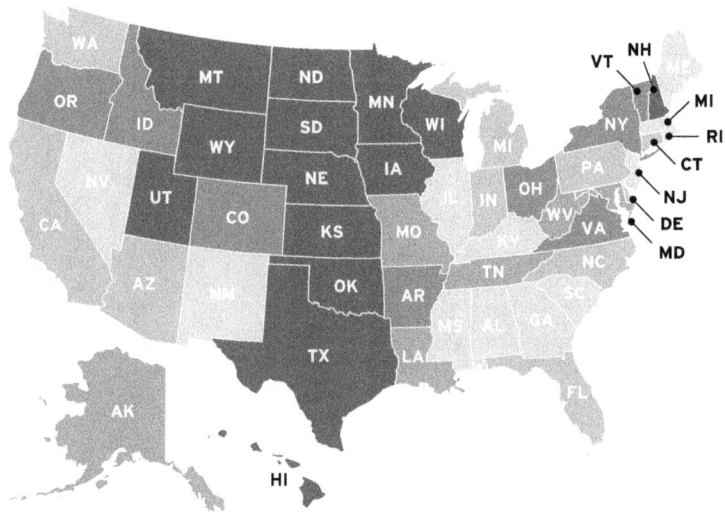

ularly well. One main driver was oil. As prices went up, oil-producing states had larger state surpluses and lower unemployment rates, while net energy importers like California suffered higher fuel costs.

As oil prices continued to increase, oil-producing states continued to grow. The Texas economy moved from 30th in the 1980s to 6th during 2010-2015 in the EPI ranking; Louisiana, from a depressingly low 49th place to the 25th; Oklahoma, from 33rd to being in the top seven.

North Dakota moved from 29th position before the crisis (average for 2000-2007) to the first position in 2010-2015, supported by high oil prices during that time, while other states were in stagnation. Mid-western and western states went through the crisis better, with Nebraska moving from 21st to 2nd place, Wyoming from 23rd to 4th. At the same time, California and Florida's economic performance deteriorated from 19th position to 37th and from 8th to 29th respectively.

▼ TOP 10 US STATES IN THE 2010–2015 EPI RANKING

State Code	State	2010–2015	Rating
ND	North Dakota	100.9	1
NE	Nebraska	91.3	2
SD	South Dakota	90.9	3
WY	Wyoming	89.9	4
MN	Minnesota	89.5	5
TX	Texas	89.5	6
OK	Oklahoma	89.4	7
IA	Iowa	89.1	8
HI	Hawaii	88.8	9
MT	Montana	88.3	10

▼ BOTTOM 10 US STATES IN THE 2010-2015 EPI RANKING

State Code	State	2010–2015	Rating
GA	Georgia	84.2	41
SC	South Carolina	83.7	42
NV	Nevada	83.7	43
KY	Kentucky	83.6	44
IL	Illinois	83.6	45
NJ	New Jersey	83.5	46
MA	Massachusetts	83.4	47
AL	Alabama	83.4	48
RI	Rhode Island	83.2	49
MS	Mississippi	82.5	50

While North and South Dakota don't usually make international news for their economic performance, the two states have consistently had two of the best-performing economies over the last
thirty years, even when oil prices were quite low. Besides a high level of GSP growth (North Dakota reached 20% growth in 2012),

they have experienced quite low unemployment rates over these three periods.

On the flip side, the ten worst-performing economies in 2010-2015 are something of a mirror image of the 1980s.

Nevada, Massachusetts, New Jersey, Rhode Island, Georgia, and South Carolina were some of the top-performers in the 80s. Thirty years later, they're at the bottom of our EPI ranking, plagued by high unemployment and low growth rates.

However, we can expect the story to change over the next decade as oil prices continue to drop, resulting in lower energy costs. This will provide a boost to energy-consuming states like California, Virginia, and Massachusetts, as well as to the national economy as a whole.

DOES IMMIGRATION HELP OR HURT STATE ECONOMIES?

Where do we even begin to discuss immigration?

This fiercely debated subject has pitted Congress against colleagues, the Supreme Court justices against themselves, political parties within themselves and against each other, and even the federal government against state governments.

While some people fear the cultural upset that results from an influx of foreign ideas and customs, most people discuss the economic costs of immigration.

The proponents of immigration point to the fact that foreign-born citizens are more likely to start a business than their US-born counterparts, and especially certain ethnicities, such as Koreans. Advocates also point out how much intellectual property the country owes to immigrants (such as Einstein) and their immediate descendants (such as Steve Jobs). Small business owners also benefit from employing immigrants, many of whom are willing to work for low wages. The US agriculture and construction sectors particularly benefit from lower labor costs.

The dissenters over immigration, on the other hand, point to the costs of illegal immigration. Besides the obvious expenses of border patrol, investigation, and deportation, there are indirect costs of providing healthcare and education for millions of undocumented people in the US who, subsequently, don't pay income taxes.

Of course, the counterargument is that, despite the US having a higher foreign-born population than ever before, the economy is stronger than ever before. It is experiencing respectable GDP growth, lower unemployment, and higher productivity per worker than ever before. That is, it appears the economy might seem to actually do better with more immigrants.

There are too many non-economic factors at play to consider the issue from a national level (national security, for one). Instead, let's look at immigration at the state level.

To use the EPI to measure the effects of immigration, we need to group the fifty states into three categories:

1. Those states with a high percentage of immigrants
2. Those states with a low percentage of immigrants
3. The rest of the states to use as a baseline for comparison

When we chart the percentage of foreign-born individuals, we find that the states with the highest immigration rates are California, New York, New Jersey, Florida, and (perhaps surprisingly) Nevada. That makes historical sense: four of these are coastal states with historically large immigrant populations. The outlier, Nevada, can probably be explained by the fact that the state is sparsely populated and that there are a disproportionately high number of immigrants working in two of the state's largest industries: entertainment (viva Las Vegas) and construction.

▼ **STATES RATING BY IMMIGRATION RATE, 2014 (PERCENT OF FOREIGN BORN-POPULATION)**

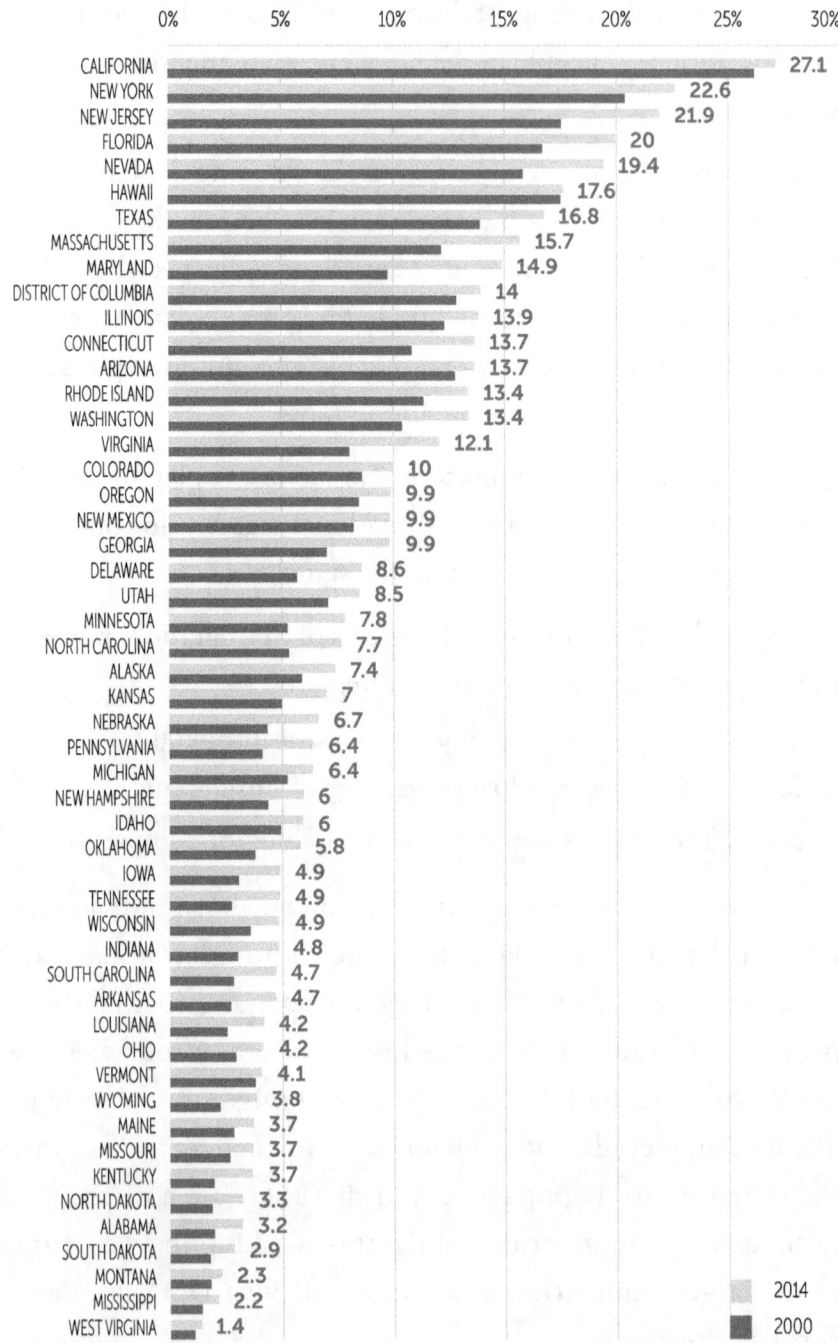

State	2014
CALIFORNIA	27.1
NEW YORK	22.6
NEW JERSEY	21.9
FLORIDA	20
NEVADA	19.4
HAWAII	17.6
TEXAS	16.8
MASSACHUSETTS	15.7
MARYLAND	14.9
DISTRICT OF COLUMBIA	14
ILLINOIS	13.9
CONNECTICUT	13.7
ARIZONA	13.7
RHODE ISLAND	13.4
WASHINGTON	13.4
VIRGINIA	12.1
COLORADO	10
OREGON	9.9
NEW MEXICO	9.9
GEORGIA	9.9
DELAWARE	8.6
UTAH	8.5
MINNESOTA	7.8
NORTH CAROLINA	7.7
ALASKA	7.4
KANSAS	7
NEBRASKA	6.7
PENNSYLVANIA	6.4
MICHIGAN	6.4
NEW HAMPSHIRE	6
IDAHO	6
OKLAHOMA	5.8
IOWA	4.9
TENNESSEE	4.9
WISCONSIN	4.9
INDIANA	4.8
SOUTH CAROLINA	4.7
ARKANSAS	4.7
LOUISIANA	4.2
OHIO	4.2
VERMONT	4.1
WYOMING	3.8
MAINE	3.7
MISSOURI	3.7
KENTUCKY	3.7
NORTH DAKOTA	3.3
ALABAMA	3.2
SOUTH DAKOTA	2.9
MONTANA	2.3
MISSISSIPPI	2.2
WEST VIRGINIA	1.4

2014
2000

The lowest immigration states include West Virginia, North and South Dakota, Montana, Alabama and Mississippi. Again, this makes some intuitive sense. Four of the states are remote, landlocked, and sparsely populated to begin with. While Mississippi is a coastal state, it doesn't have a major seaport (although, curiously, it does have a large agriculture industry; we wouldn't have expected it to have as low of an immigrant population as it does).

Next, we chart the EPI scores of these two groups of states—those with the highest percentage of immigrants vs. those with the lowest—against the scores of the other forty US states and calculate the difference.

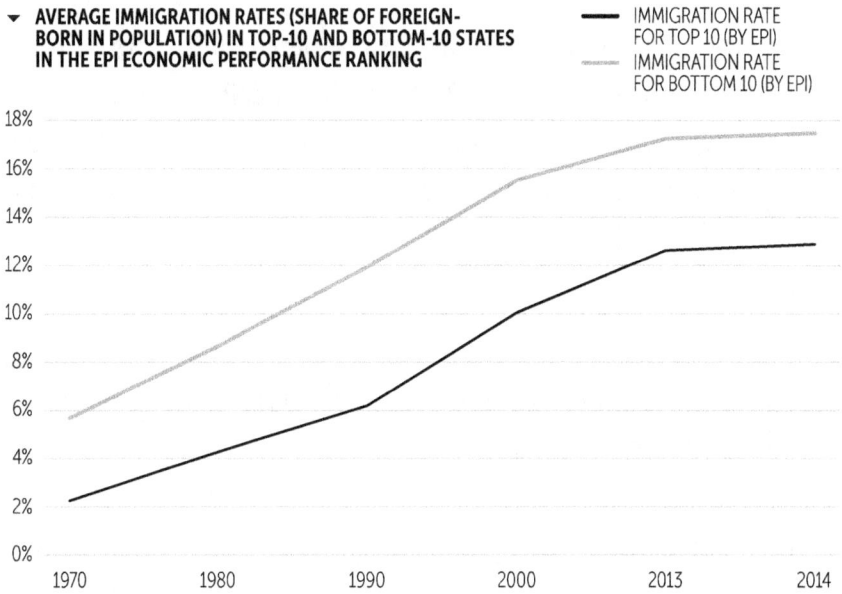

To get the real story, we performed a regression analysis of all fifty states' EPI scores against their immigration rates. The result was a negative (albeit weak) correlation, as you can see below.

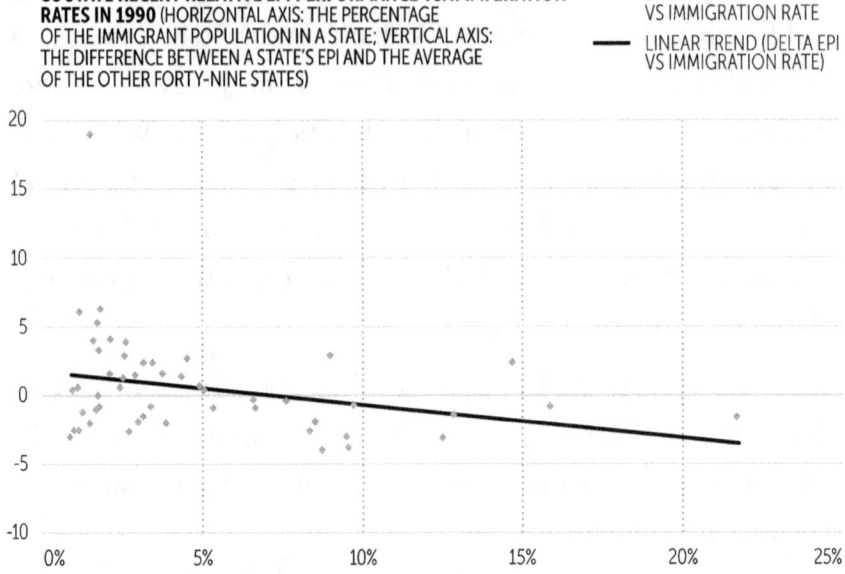

On the horizontal axis, you see the percentage of the immigrant population in a state. On the vertical axis, you see the difference between a state's EPI and the average of the other forty-nine states (that is, how much better or worse a state did against the rest of the US).

Clearly, the graph shows that the more immigrants a state has, the worse its economic performance. In fact, for every additional ten percent of a state's population is foreign-born, its EPI score drops by about 2.4 percent—which, as we've discussed before, represents billions of dollars in economic performance.

Is it beneficial to the country to encourage immigration? Perhaps. Do the costs outweigh the benefits on a state level? Not according to our experiment here.

DOES EDUCATION SPENDING MATTER TO A STATE'S ECONOMY?

W hile most politicians are the first to champion the need for education, when it comes to budget cuts, education is often the first item on the chopping block.

Of course, it's common sense (and a wealth of academic studies support the fact) that the more educated a country is, the better its economy. Everybody knows that. But what about at the state level? It seems fairly obvious that states with high numbers of more educated people (New York, California) do better than states with fewer educated people (Mississippi, Kansas).

But that doesn't really answer the question: does how much a state spend on education affect its economy and economic performance?

It makes sense that states trying to attract skilled jobs like healthcare and technology should encourage education, so that they have a workforce ready to take advantage of those jobs. On the other hand, why not let other states educate their citizens, and then lure those graduates away (as plenty of states do)?

You might also argue that states which rely on low-tech industries such as energy and agriculture don't need a more educated workforce, and so perhaps they waste money by funding higher education. Maybe they should let the states with highly skilled jobs educate students for those positions; those low-tech states could use the funds they save to pay for other programs (or even reduce their respective deficits).

Let's look at the facts (and then at a surprising correlation… or lack thereof).

Obviously, wealthier states can spend more on education than their poorer counterparts. To compare apples to apples, we looked at not how much a state spends on education, but what percentage of the state budget is spent on education. When we chart the twenty best-performing states against the twenty worst-performing states, and then look at how much each spends on education, this is what we find: yes—states that spent more per capita on their education system scored higher on the EPI (see chart below). For every extra one percent spent on total education in the state budget, a state scored about two percentage points higher on the EPI, according to our analysis.

But "education" covers everything from primary education to vocational training to universities. Does one type of education help a state's economy more than others?

To find out, we ran a regression analysis of states' EPI score against two different segments. One was the number of people per capita with a high school diploma or higher; the other was the number of people per capita with a bachelor's degree or higher.

To no one's surprise, the analysis showed that the more people who have at least a high school diploma (if not additional education), the better their respective state's EPI score. For every addi-

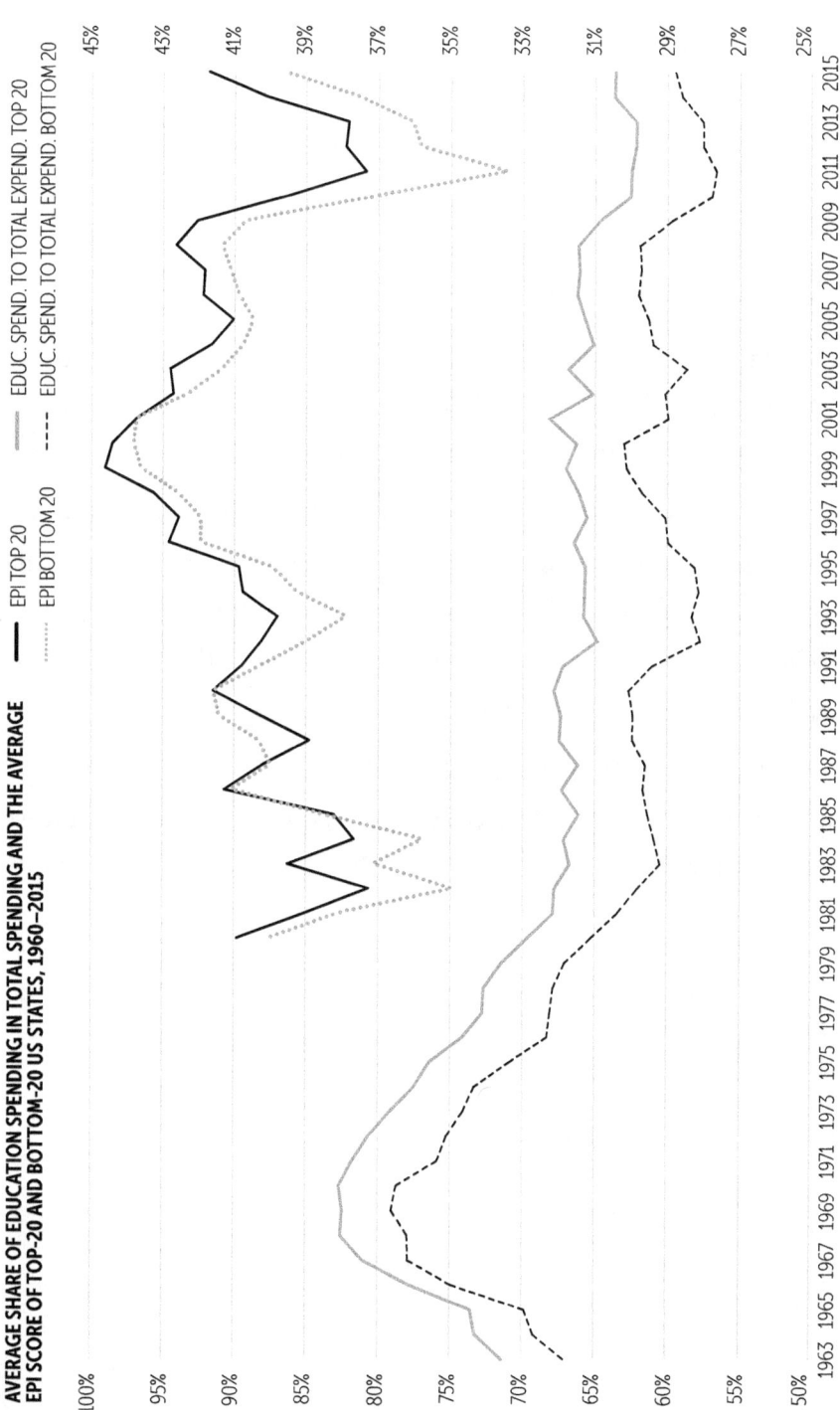

AVERAGE SHARE OF EDUCATION SPENDING IN TOTAL SPENDING AND THE AVERAGE
EPI SCORE OF TOP-20 AND BOTTOM-20 US STATES, 1960–2015

tional ten percent of people who have at least graduated from high school, the state's economy performs about 1.6% better.

Here's the surprise: when we ran the same analysis but only against the number of people per capita who had at least a bachelor's degree, we found a near-zero correlation. In other words, having more college-educated people does not affect a state's economy.

How can we explain this paradoxical phenomenon? We know that more (college) education directly affects the national economy, but it apparently has little effect on individual state economies.

One explanation may be that higher education benefits the whole country. That is, the affect may be cumulative rather than specific (think of a manufacturer headquartered in Minneapolis with factories and distributors all over the nation, then multiply that by the *Fortune* 500).

Whatever the true reason, EPI underscores how important basic education is to each state's economy: the more people with at least a high school diploma in your state, the better the state's economy.

THE TEXAS MODEL VS. CALIFORNIA—WHICH WORKS BETTER?

In many ways, California and Texas are quite alike. They are two of the largest states in the US by population and by sheer size. They both have large immigrant populations, long coastlines, a border with Mexico, and abundant energy reserves.

Politically, though, they represent opposite sides of the spectrum. California, famously liberal; Texas, fiercely conservative. Consequently, they have quite dissimilar public policies. California ranks in the top five states for highest state and local taxes, while Texas ranks in the bottom five. While Texas encourages energy extraction, California actively legislates against it (despite having the largest shale oil reserve in the nation). Hand in hand with this, the West Coast state has some of the most onerous business regulations in the nation, while the Midwestern state is decidedly business-friendly.

In fact, during 2013, these radio ads played throughout California: "Building a business is tough, but I hear building a business in California is next-to-impossible. This is Texas Governor Rick Perry, and I have a message for California businesses: come check out Texas."

As such, the states employ different strategies of taxation, as the chart below shows.

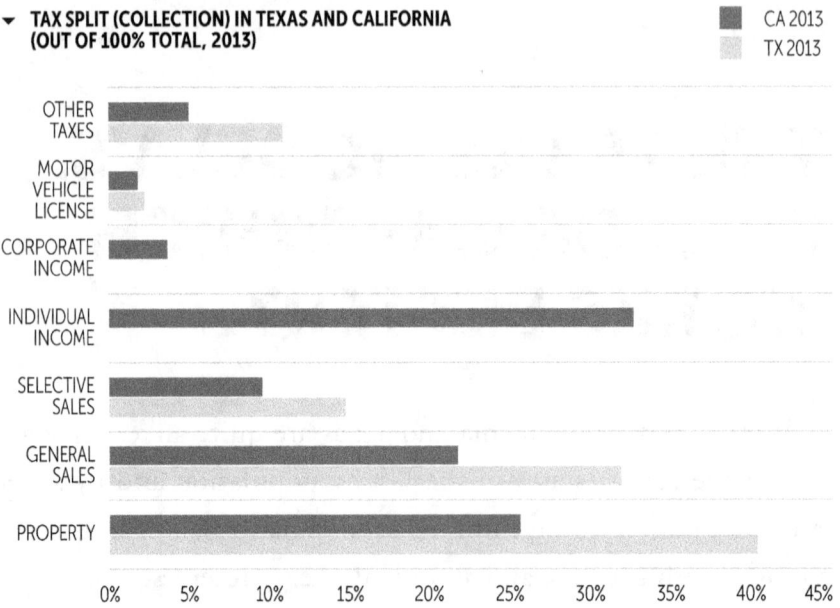

TAX SPLIT (COLLECTION) IN TEXAS AND CALIFORNIA (OUT OF 100% TOTAL, 2013)

CA 2013
TX 2013

California does indeed have far higher corporate and individual income taxes than its cowboy counterpart, but that doesn't mean Texas taxes less. It actually has higher sales and property taxes as well as selective taxes (e.g. cigarettes, gasoline, liquor) than its coastal cousin.

But do the two radically different approaches produce radically different results? Let's see.

On the chart below, the EPI scores for both states somewhat track each other. Some years, Texas is ahead, while others, California. When we calculate the average EPI score from 1980 to 2015, the final tally stands with California at 88.0% and Texas only marginally better at 89.7%—both solid B grades.

Furthermore, we have to take into account each state's disproportionate economic impact. Texas is among the top oil-producing states in the nation. The rising prices of oil and natural gas have driven a large part of the Lone Star State's growth in the past decade. With the recent decline of energy prices, though, the state's EPI is decreasing, too.

▼ THE EPI FOR CALIFORNIA AND TEXAS, 1978–2015   —— CA
                                                        ---- TX

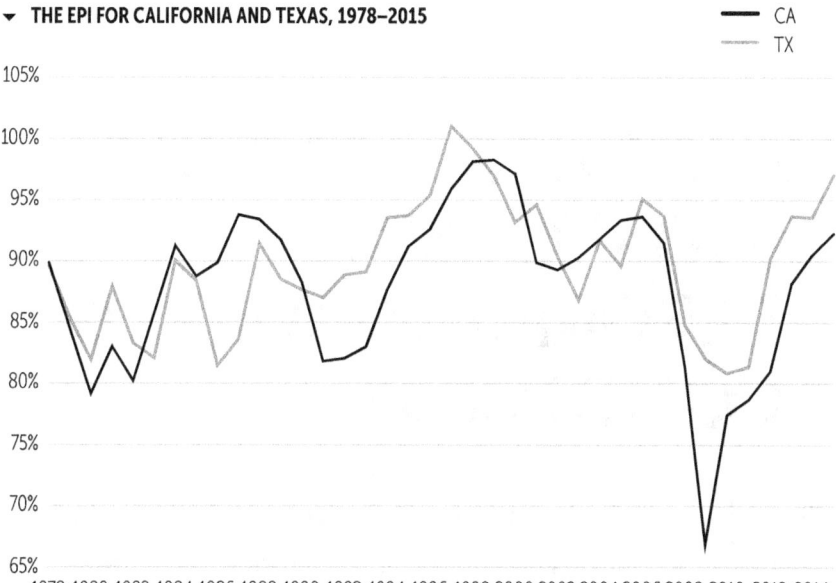

California was hit harder by the burst of the housing bubble than Texas in 2009. Although Texas property taxes are higher, its real estate and rental-and-leasing sectors make up only about 8% of its Gross State Product (GSP). California, on the other hand, derives about 16% of its GSP from those same sectors. Inevitably, the housing crash hurt the West Coast state harder than it did Texas.

Both states have diversified their industries, though. California's income taxes have risen, thanks to the economic recovery and the state's high personal income taxes in the past few years. Texas has made a concerted effort to diversify in healthcare and technology, so the recent downturn in oil prices hasn't affected it as badly as a similar downturn in 1986 (when its EPI dropped from 90% to 81.5% in just two years).

So, despite quite different public policies and methods of taxation, both states perform admirably well—really, no better nor worse than the other.

WHAT ARE THE BEST (AND WORST) PERFORMING WORLD ECONOMIES?

In Secret #1 we discussed the economic performance of the US vis-à-vis the rest of the world. Even though we do not have the Big Four that compose the EPI, we do have data from forty-two of the world's biggest economies, representing roughly 95% of the world's GDP. But in Secret #1, we did not reveal the scores of those countries—only the US's rank among them.

Here, in Secret #13, we reveal the best—and worst—performers on the global stage right now. After gathering data from 2015, running the calculations, and scoring and averaging the EPI of each of the forty-two countries, this is what we found: the top five performers in 2015 were Singapore, Norway, Iceland, China, and Luxemburg. The bottom five were Greece, Russia, Brazil, Spain, and Cyprus.

The chart below provides just a snapshot in time. Is it really fair to rank countries by just their most recent performance in 2015? Shouldn't we look at their average performance, perhaps after the Great Recession as well as before?

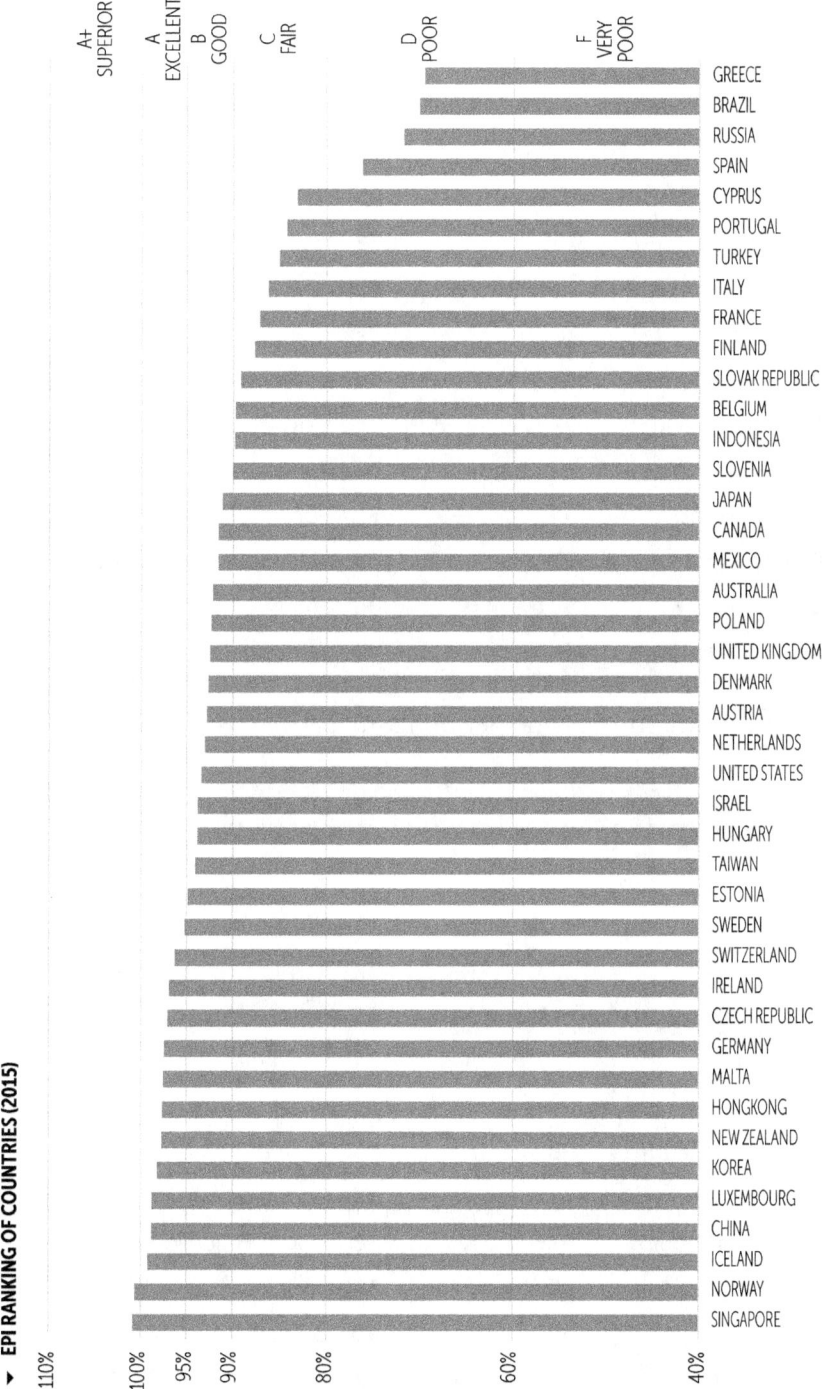

EPI RANKING OF COUNTRIES (2015)

If we look at the top and bottom rankings of the average EPI scores from 2008 to 2015, we find this:

▼ 2010-2015 AVERAGE EPI RANKING. TOP-10 AND BOTTOM-10 COUNTRIES

Rank	Country	EPI Score (Average 2008–15)	Grade	Rank	Country	EPI Score (Average 2008–15)	Grade
1	Norway	106.9	A+	32	Hungary	84.1	C
2	Singapore	104.3	A+	33	Italy	84.0	C
3	China	100.6	A+	34	Iceland	84.0	C
4	Korea	98.1	A	35	Cyprus	83.6	C
5	Switzerland	97.8	A	36	Slovak Republic	83.1	C
6	HongKong	97.8	A	37	Turkey	82.9	C-
7	Luxembourg	94.5	B+	38	Portugal	78.7	D+
8	Taiwan	93.1	B	39	Ireland	77.5	D+
9	Germany	92.6	B	40	Spain	69.2	D
10	Sweden	91.7	B	41	Greece	67.2	D

If we extend the time period from 2000 to the present, we still see a similar picture:

▼ 2008-2015 AVERAGE EPI RANKING. TOP-10 AND BOTTOM-10 COUNTRIES

Rank	Country	EPI Score (Average 2008–12)	Grade	Rank	Country	EPI Score (Average 2008–12)	Grade
1	Norway	108.4	A+	32	Italy	86.0	C
2	Singapore	106.8	A+	33	Malta	84.4	C
3	China	101.8	A+	34	Hungary	84.3	C
4	Korea	99.4	A+	35	Brazil	84.0	C
5	Switzerland	98.3	A	36	Poland	83.4	C
6	HongKong	97.6	A	37	Portugal	83.3	C
7	Luxembourg	97.6	A	38	Slovak Republic	80.5	D+
8	New Zealand	95.2	A-	39	Spain	79.7	D+
9	Taiwan	94.4	B+	40	Greece	75.7	D+
10	Denmark	94.1	B+	41	Turkey	73.1	D

In all three time periods—2015, 2008-2015, and 2000-2015—
we find some common countries ranked at or near the top. For
instance, Norway has been number one in all three views. Intuitively, this makes sense. It is a major oil exporter with universally admired macroeconomic policies. Despite falling oil prices, it
still performs well due to its large fiscal buffers. Two other European countries also performed well: Switzerland and Luxembourg.
Both have "safe-haven" economies with well-developed and prudent economic policies.

The Asian Pacific Rim has somewhat dominated the three lists,
with Singapore, China, Korea, Hong Kong, and Taiwan in the top
five or top ten in all three cases. Again, this matches what most
people would expect: these Asian countries have had extraordi-
nary growth rates while keeping inflation tamed.

Similarly, the countries at the bottom of the list should not
come as a surprise: hard-hit by the global crisis Eurozone countries—notably, Portugal, Ireland, Greece, and Spain (or "PIGS,"
as they came to be known). The substantial fiscal stimuli the countries implemented in the beginning of the global financial crisis did
not help recovery. In fact, they led to higher debt levels and only
seemed to intensify the problems. From a financial crisis, the situation transformed into a political crisis, and then into a sovereign
debt crisis. From these core countries, the crisis also spread to other European countries such as Hungary, the Slovak Republic, and
Poland, which have recovered from the crisis in the past few years.

Once again, we want to point out how the EPI can be used
to objectively quantify an economic situation where, for most people, they only have fragmented information and/or a subjective

opinion by which to evaluate. In the media, all four of the Euro-zone's PIGS were lumped into one category. However, our Index clearly shows a substantial gap in their performance.

In other words, the EPI helps us see not just that things are bad, but allows us to measure just *how* bad they are; not just that things are good, but *how* good. For example, Spain scored 76.1% vs. Greece at 69.5%—a clear comparison of how bad things in Greece were. Norway has enjoyed a great economy in recent years, but using the EPI we can see that it has enjoyed a whopping 108.4% average since 2000, putting it on par with the Gilded Age and the Roaring Twenties.

IS CHINA OUTPERFORMING THE US?

After the Cold War, the world's only remaining super-power was the US. For two decades, the US has reigned unchallenged as the world's largest economy, its largest market, its most productive workforce, and its largest man-ufacturer.

However, one country has emerged as a serious contender to challenge the US's global dominance. The real question many people have on their mind is not how the US is performing against the world average, but against its biggest rival for "the number one spot."

China.

While we cannot speak to many of the concerns we hear ex-pressed about China, we can shed light on its economic perfor-mance versus the US's. We could begin by comparing the easiest and/or most commonly used of all economic indicators: GDP.

In 1980, China's GDP was about $303 billion, or roughly 10% of the US's $2.9 trillion economy. Since that time, Chi-na has enjoyed one of most impressive sustained growth rates ever recorded. By 2015, its economy weighed at $11 trillion—

▼ **GDP DYNAMICS OF THE US AND CHINA SINCE 1980
(TOTAL NOMINAL GDP IN USD)**

—— CHINA
—— US

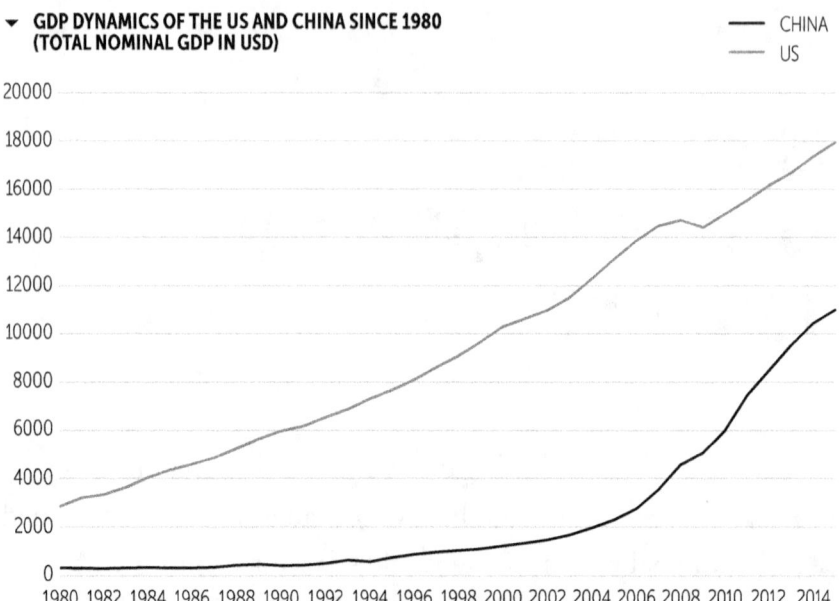

about 61% of the US's $18 trillion. While that sounds impressive, China will have to sustain its growth rate for many, many years to come (a difficult task for any emerging market economy) before the US is seriously challenged for the title of "world's largest economy."

One of the main concerns we read and hear about is the trade imbalance, i.e. the US imports more from China than it exports. If that were true, then the current account balance for each country should mirror each other. That is, for every US dollar spent on imports, there is a US dollar made on a Chinese export. We graph the two countries' account balances below.

Beginning in 1995, we can see that it does appear that the two countries' account balances mirror each other. The US experienced a net deficit while China had a net surplus. Furthermore, the countries' import/export balances rose and fell in near

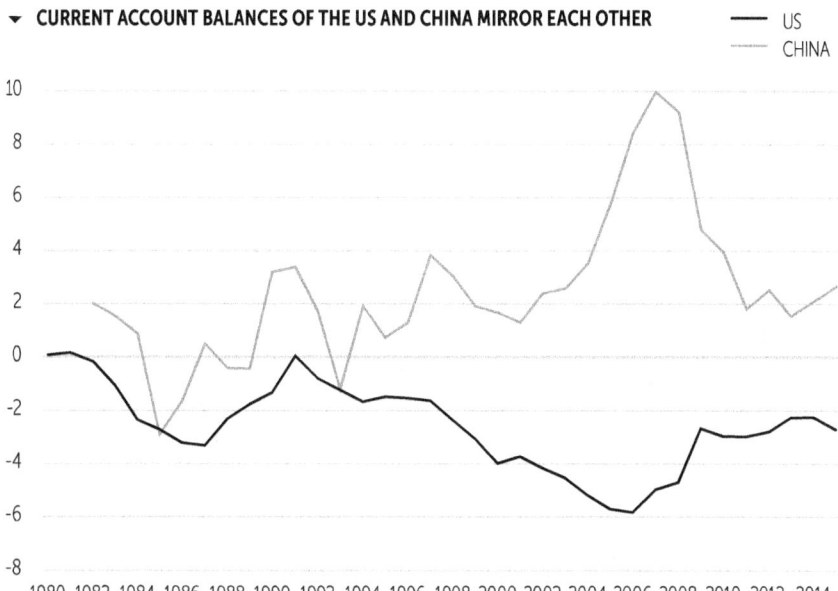

▼ CURRENT ACCOUNT BALANCES OF THE US AND CHINA MIRROR EACH OTHER ——— US ········ CHINA

tandem. This does give credence to the idea that China's gain is the US's loss.

Moreover, many people argue that the loss is more than economic. Plenty of pundits, politicians, and economists have claimed that China's economic competitiveness was rooted in an undervalued exchange rate, in artificially high savings and investment rates, and in substandard working conditions. According to these voices, all of this has played a major role in the US's loss of competitiveness and was a significant factor in its decline. Were that true, then we should see that correlation reflected in both countries' EPI scores over the past few decades.

Let's focus on the US's performance first. From 1984 until 2007, its EPI score was roughly in the low 90s. With the Great Recession, of course, its score plummeted to around the low 80s.

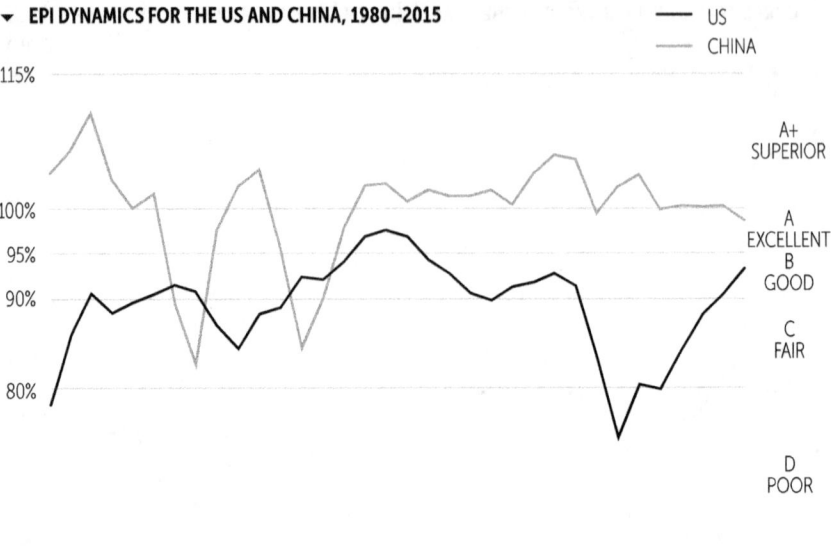

EPI DYNAMICS FOR THE US AND CHINA, 1980–2015

China, on the other hand, experienced wild swings, going from an A+ to a C a few times, until about 1997. Instead of dropping again, its performance became relatively stable, consistently scoring around 100%, if not better.

If the US's loss is China's gain, then at some point the two economies' scores should somewhat mirror each other. From the graph of their EPI scores, there is no indicator that this is the case. While the two countries certainly do not perform independently of each other, there is not a strong economic interdependence, either.

Let's look at the underlying numbers to see the two countries' Big Four since 2000.

The average inflation rates for both countries over those sixteen years were on par with each other at about 2.2–2.3%. The US's unemployment rate averaged 6.3%, which was only 2.3 percent-

▾ **CHINA EPI COMPONENTS, 2000–2015**

Year	Inflation (%)	Unemployment (%)	Budget Deficit (%)	GDP (%)	EPI
2000	0.4	3.1	2.8	8.4	102.1
2001	0.7	3.6	2.6	8.3	101.4
2002	-0.8	4.0	2.9	9.1	101.4
2003	1.2	4.3	2.4	10.0	102.1
2004	3.9	4.2	1.5	10.1	100.5
2005	1.8	4.2	1.4	11.3	103.9
2006	1.5	4.1	1.1	12.7	106.0
2007	4.8	4.0	-0.1	14.2	105.5
2008	5.9	4.2	0.0	9.6	99.5
2009	-0.7	4.3	1.8	9.2	102.4
2010	3.3	4.1	-0.6	10.6	103.8
2011	5.4	4.1	0.1	9.5	99.9
2012	2.6	4.1	0.7	7.7	100.3
2013	2.6	4.1	0.8	7.7	100.2
2014	2.0	4.1	0.9	7.3	100.3
2015	1.4	4.1	2.7	6.9	98.7
Average	2.3	4.0	1.3	9.5	101.7

age points higher than China's. From just these two indicators, the two countries performed similarly. However, the paths begin to diverge when we look at their budget deficits. The US ran a deficit more than four times that of China—5.3% vs. 1.3% respectively. But the key difference in the two countries' scores was in their GDP growth rates. For sixteen years, the US experienced a lackluster average of 1.9%, versus China's 9.5% average.

It is beyond the scope of this book to evaluate the political policies of China. However, we can say that, based on the EPI, we conclude that China's performance is primarily rooted in a pru-

▼ **THE US EPI COMPONENTS, 2000–2015**

Year	Inflation (%)	Unemployment (%)	Budget Deficit (%)	GDP (%)	EPI
2000	3.4	4.0	2.5	4.1	94.3
2001	2.8	4.7	0.6	1.0	92.8
2002	1.6	5.8	3.8	1.8	90.6
2003	2.3	6.0	4.7	2.8	89.8
2004	2.7	5.5	4.3	3.8	91.3
2005	3.4	5.1	3.1	3.3	91.8
2006	3.2	4.6	2.0	2.7	92.8
2007	2.9	4.6	2.9	1.8	91.4
2008	3.8	5.8	6.7	-0.3	83.4
2009	-0.3	9.3	13.2	-2.8	74.5
2010	1.6	9.6	10.9	2.5	80.4
2011	3.1	8.9	9.6	1.6	79.9
2012	2.1	8.1	7.9	2.2	84.2
2013	1.5	7.4	4.4	1.5	88.2
2014	1.6	6.2	4.1	2.4	90.5
2015	0.1	5.3	3.7	2.4	93.3
Average	2.2	6.3	5.3	1.9	88.1

dent set of policies and stable economic performance that have allowed for high growth while maintaining low inflation and a low budget deficit.

So, is China outperforming the US? Yes, the EPI shows that China's economic performance has been better in the past decade.

SECRET #15

HOW WELL DOES THE PUBLIC KNOW WHAT'S GOING ON IN THE ECONOMY?

How well is the economy doing?

That's a different question from how well people *think* the economy is doing.

The public's perception of the economy's health is quite important and, to a degree, even drives the economy. When people believe things are looking up, they feel more expansive: they spend more individually, company leaders make plans to expand facilities, and consumers are more likely to take out loans for houses and cars. On the flip side, when people are afraid that things aren't doing so well, they're more financially conservative. They save more, stay with their current home or automobile for a little longer, and scale back their business plans.

So you see how important it is that people's perception matches the reality. If people are getting ready to spend their savings while the economy is going down, they could suffer financial setbacks when a recession does hit. On the other hand, if the economy has pulled out of the recession, yet people still feel like things aren't stable, then they miss opportunities they otherwise would have seized.

Of course, how people perceive the economy comes from the information they gather. Domestic and international media, internet forums, news from inside their social networks, the price of energy and commodities, interest rates on their mortgage and checking accounts, and thousands of other factors all influence the average person's view on how well things are going. Some pundits say that the media, especially, unduly influences people's perceptions by reporting sensational news stories, instead of painting an accurate picture of the economy.

So just how well does the typical American sift through all of these sources to settle on how things are faring? To chart people's perception of the economy, we turned to the Michigan Consumer Sentiment Index (MCSI)[1]. This telephone survey has interviewed US households since 1964 about their recent purchases and plans for future purchases. The premise of the survey is that the more confident people are about the economy, the more they will spend and plan to spend. The less optimistic they are, the less they'll buy and the more they'll plan to conserve their money.

When charted against the EPI below (with official recessions marked for convenience), this is what we found: the two graphs follow each quite closely (with a pairwise correlation of more than 80%). This means that the average US household actually has quite a good grasp on how the economy is faring. You might expect that when things are really bad (i.e., an economic recession), people would perceive that things were really bad. By the same token, when things are going quite well (i.e., the EPI score is at an A), people's opinion would consequently optimistic.

---

[1] We also used the Consumer Confidence Index and found quite similar results.

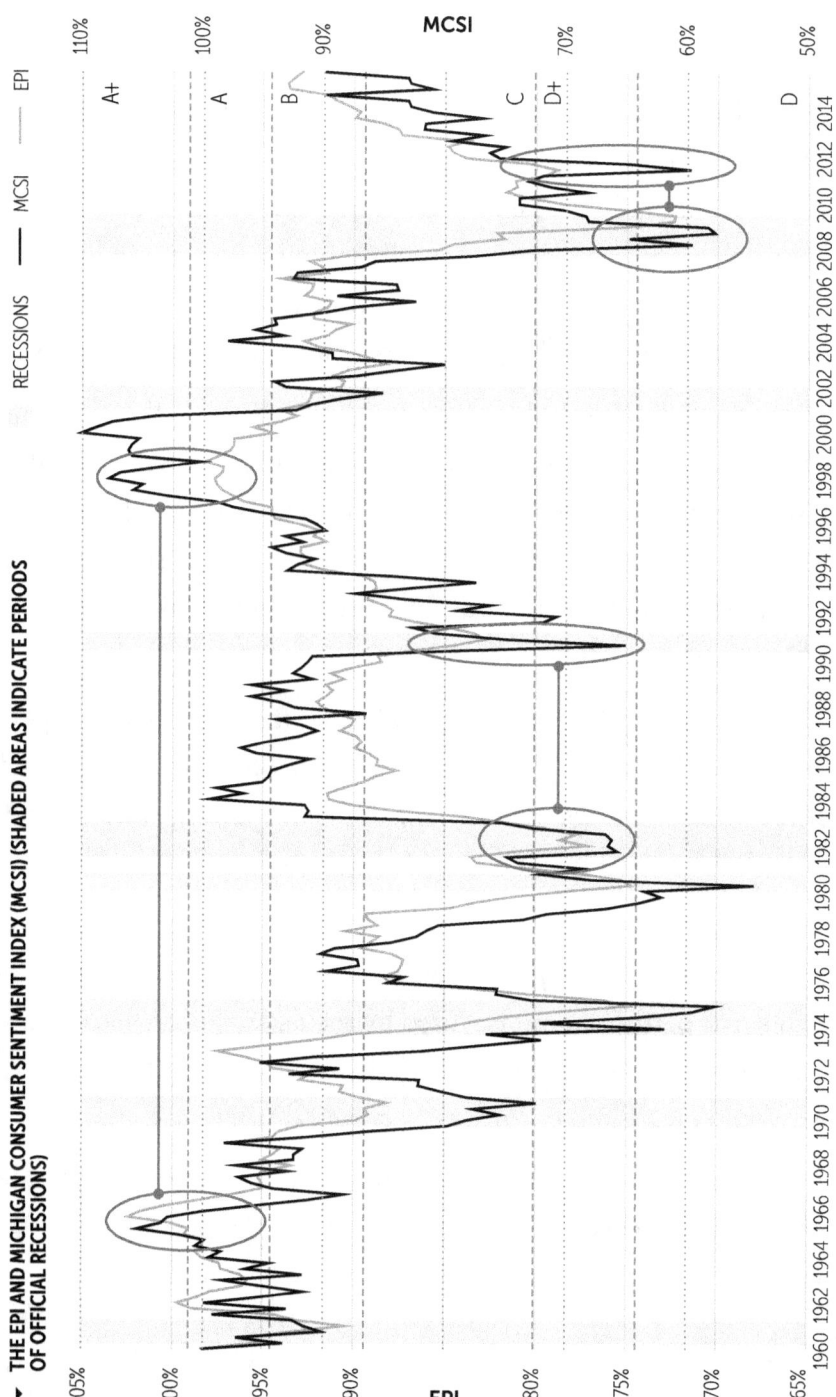

THE EPI AND MICHIGAN CONSUMER SENTIMENT INDEX (MCSI) (SHADED AREAS INDICATE PERIODS OF OFFICIAL RECESSIONS)

RECESSIONS —— MCSI ------- EPI

But what about during the interim? What about when the economy is at a B or a C? It's harder to see how things are doing when the news is mixed: interest rates are down but exports are up, or the price of gas has fallen but people are being laid off by the thousands. It's easy to say things are great when all signs point to things being great, but what about when things are only fair? Even then—or, as we were surprised to find, even more so— the average American has a firm grip on the economy's health.

In fact, US household opinion actually deviated from its true performance during economic extremes. That is, when the economy was in a recession, the MSCI showed that people actually believed it was worse than it was. Conversely, when the economy was doing quite well, the public thought it was doing even better than that.

Public perception also seems to lag behind the economy's performance. When going into a recession, people's opinions stayed cheerier than things actually were. When coming out of one, households stayed pessimistic.

When we graphed the difference between how people thought the economy was doing (as measured by the MSCI) and the economy's true performance (as scored by the EPI), this is what the deviation looked like: as you can see below, the biggest differences between perception and reality occurred during recessions.

The good news is that when things are bad, they're probably not as bad as everyone thinks. The bad news is that when things are good, they're not quite as good as people believe.

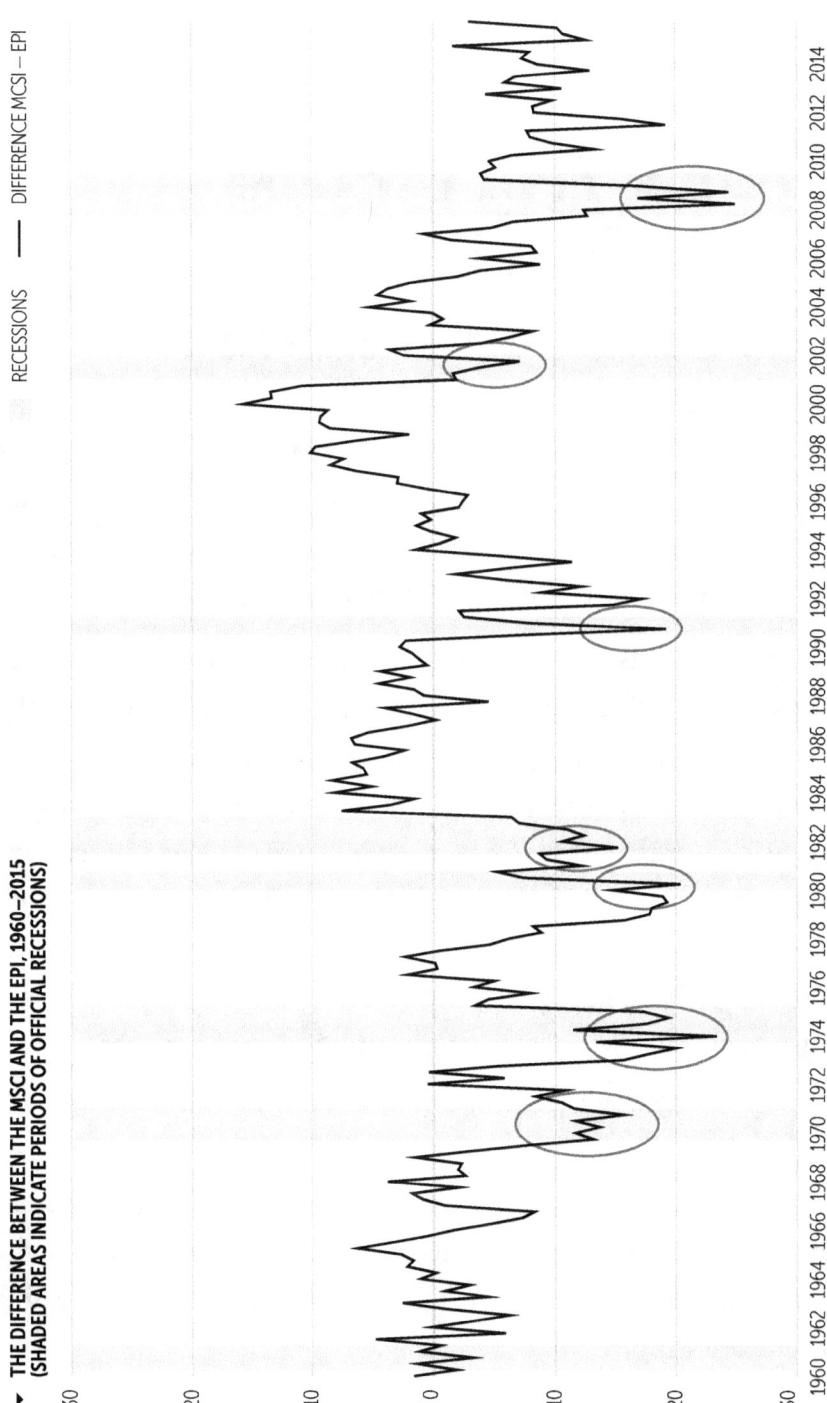

THE DIFFERENCE BETWEEN THE MSCI AND THE EPI, 1960–2015
(SHADED AREAS INDICATE PERIODS OF OFFICIAL RECESSIONS)

RECESSIONS — DIFFERENCE MCSI – EPI

DOES THE MEDIA ACCURATELY REPORT ECONOMIC NEWS?

Few Americans would say that they completely trust the media. Most people believe that the media in general has an inherent bias, and plenty of people believe different media sources outright mislead their audience.

Despite this distrust, a majority of Americans still get most of their economic news from the media. As we discussed in the previous secret, a person's perception of how well the economy is fairing directly influences their financial decisions. If they think things are bad, they'll make more conservative financial decisions. If they believe things are good, they're more likely to spend money and make long-term financial commitments. As a consequence, it's vital that we know just how much we can trust the public's major source of economic information.

The best broad measure we have of how the media reports on the economy is the News Heard of Recent Changes in Business Conditions score, developed by the University of Michigan and published since 1965. (For brevity's sake, let's call it the "News Index.")

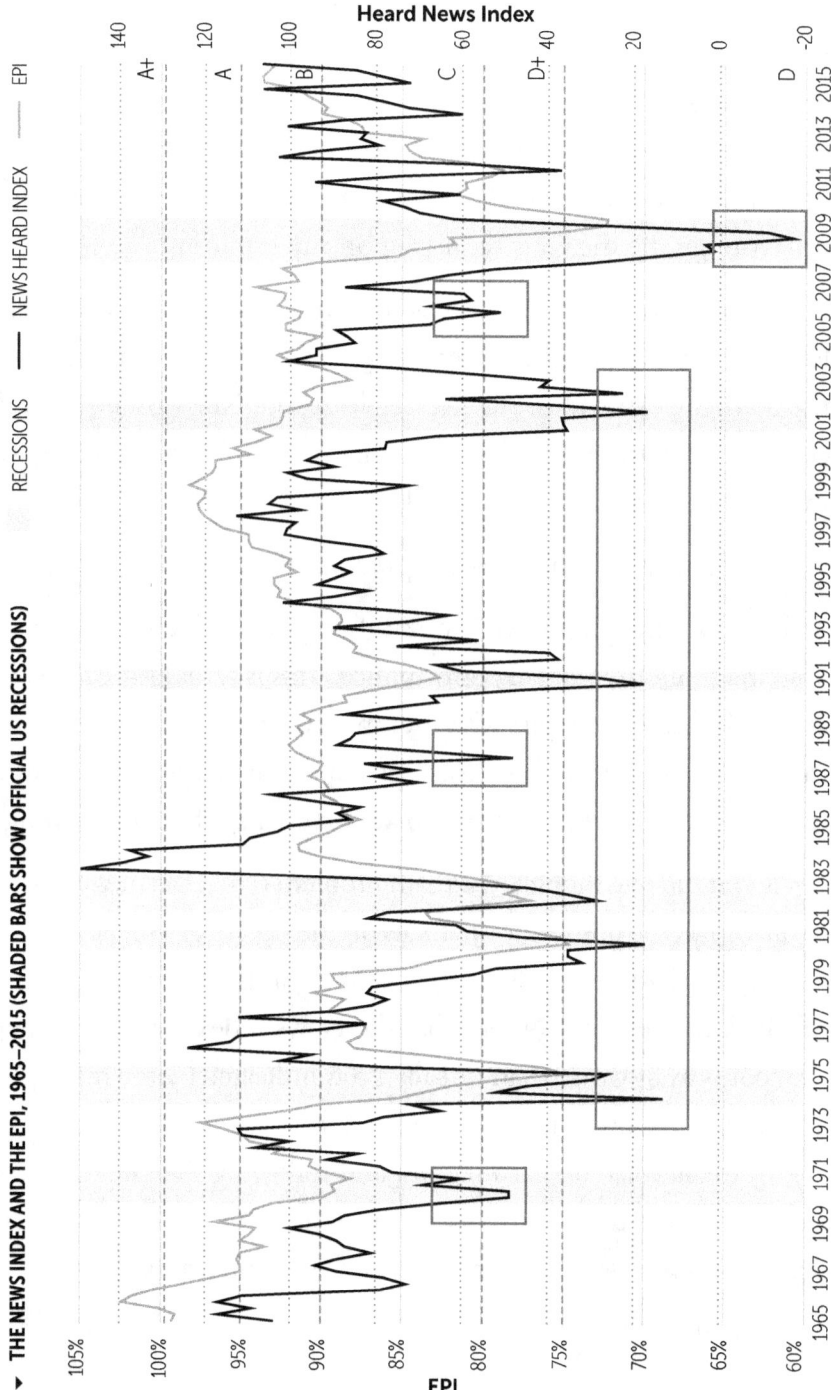

▶ THE NEWS INDEX AND THE EPI, 1965–2015 (SHADED BARS SHOW OFFICIAL US RECESSIONS)

The News Index uses surveys to gauge how much favorable, unfavorable, or neutral (no mentions) respondents have recently heard about the economy from all media sources. The idea is that the more good news people hear, the more positive the media coverage is on the economy. The more bad news they hear, the more unfavorably the media is reporting on the economy.

What we would hope to see is that the News Index closely follows the EPI. The further away from the EPI it is, the less accurate the media's portrayal is. At the very least, the News Index should correlate with the EPI, otherwise what the media portrays doesn't match the economic reality at all.

Let's look at the chart on the previous page.

Just from the graph, we can tell that, yes, the News Index follows the economy's actual performance. This is actually great news, as it indicates that, despite whatever misgivings you may have about the media, on the whole—from the conservative right to the progressive left—it does a decent job at portraying what's happening.

As you can see, though, the main problem is that the media tends to downplay the positive (or to focus on the negative, whichever way you say it: "bad news sells," right?). The graph's shaded bars show official US recessions. Notice that the News Index always portrays the economy as worse than it really is (as indicated by the highlight boxes). On the other hand, sometimes the media oversells a recovery. In the late 1970s, early 1980s, and following the Great Recession, according to the number of media reports, the economy appeared much rosier than it really was. Is this intentional?

Unlikely.

The News Index surveys individuals whose news sources run the entire gamut of media sources, both domestic and international, and from the entire spectrum of readership. For all of them to collude to intentionally report economic conditions as better or worse than they really are does seem implausible.

We suspect there's a simpler answer: it's hard to distinguish between the severity of news. The News Index counts how often people hear "unfavorable" news reports—not "bad news" vs. "very bad news" or "hopeful news" vs. "great news."

Still, our regression analysis (not shown here) shows that since 2010, the News Index has more closely followed the EPI. Hopefully, that means that the media is actually getting *more* accurate in tying the amount of economic news covered to the actual health of the overall economy.

IS IT GREAT TO BE AN OIL-PRODUCING US STATE?

Ever since the oil crises of the 1970s, many people find security—even pride—in the fact that their state has oil, coal, gas, or other energy resources. This is especially true when commodity prices are high and energy-producing states see a boom in related construction and production. It means higher employment, higher GDP growth, and more tax revenue.

But what about when the price of oil drops, as has been the case since the end of 2014 to present? Does the windfall make up for the shortcomings? Does the decline in employment, revenue, and commerce dramatically affect the state's economic performance? Does it help more than it hurts?

Basically, is it great to be an oil-producing state?

In 2006, the US imported more than half of the energy it used. Even while doing so, oil extraction technologies continued to develop, such as hydraulic fracturing ("fracking") and horizontal drilling, spurred in part by the peak price of oil in 2008. Today, the US is the world's largest supplier of natural gas and is poised to become the largest oil producer in the entire world. Such technological advances have completely altered the global market for energy-producers.

This should be good news for the US and particularly for oil-producing US states, right? As oil technology makes extraction easier and more profitable, shouldn't it affect states with large oil and natural gas reserves, such as California, Colorado, Oklahoma, and others?

Let's find out.

We need to compare the EPI score of states that are large oil-producers against states that aren't. It's fairly easy to pick the oil-rich states: just ten states supply more than 90% of crude oil in the US—Texas alone provided more than one-third of the US's oil supply in 2015. Additionally, US oil production has almost tripled since 2009. Here's the breakdown of where that comes from:

▼ TOP US OIL-PRODUCING STATES (2015)

	Crude Oil Production	Annual, mn barrels	% of US total
	US total	**3,442**	**100%**
1	Texas	1,262	37%
2	North Dakota	429	12%
3	California	202	6%
4	Alaska	176	5%
5	North Slope	170	5%
6	Oklahoma	158	5%
7	New Mexico	149	4%
8	Colorado	119	3%
9	Other states	778	23%

The economies of Alaska and Oklahoma are quite dependent on the price of oil. Alaska, for example, derives as much as 90% of its state operating budget from taxes on crude oil production. It should be especially sensitive to changes in oil prices. While California produces more oil than Alaska or Oklahoma, it's so large and diverse that oil production accounts for a relatively small proportion of the state's total economy. Although we include California in our group of oil-producers, we'll focus on the other four: Texas, North Dakota, Alaska, and Oklahoma.

For comparison, we'll need a group of non-oil producing states from different regions (e.g., the South, the Midwest, etc.) to accurately represent other state economies. For this analysis, we chose 19 states. As such, we now have two comparison groups: the five major oil-producers we just mentioned vs. nineteen states with virtually no energy production. To represent the effects of oil production itself, we use the energy industry's standard price of West Texas Intermediate (WTI) per barrel of oil.

The next two charts show the EPI scores of these two groups against the US average EPI (that is, the other twenty-five states). If being an oil-producer is a good thing, then our oil-producing states should have spectacular economies when oil prices are high and they're raking in the money. On the other hand, if being an oil-producer doesn't really affect the economy, then oil producers shouldn't fare substantially better during those times than non-oil producing states.

Let's first chart the EPI score of oil-producing states against the performance of the rest of the US (chart below). On the right-hand side, you see the difference between the EPI for the Top-5 oil producing states and the US average EPI (that is, how much better or worse the oil-producers did against the rest of the US).

When WTI oil prices were close to $20 per barrel in the 1980s and 1990s, these states should have been consistently lower than

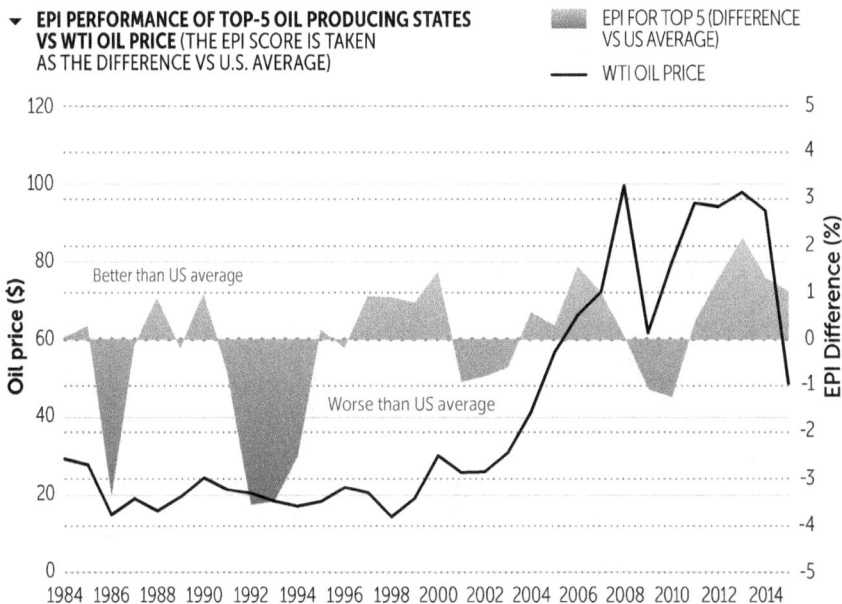

EPI PERFORMANCE OF TOP-5 OIL PRODUCING STATES VS WTI OIL PRICE (THE EPI SCORE IS TAKEN AS THE DIFFERENCE VS U.S. AVERAGE)

EPI FOR TOP 5 (DIFFERENCE VS US AVERAGE)

WTI OIL PRICE

the US average. Instead, they seem to fluctuate around the average; sometimes better, sometimes worse. When oil prices rose upwards of $90, they should have seen economic booms. Instead, we see the same effect: sometimes better and sometimes worse, but more or less in pace with the rest of the pack.

Before even looking at the next chart, we can see that there doesn't seem to be a high correlation between the price of oil and the EPI of oil-producing states. These states scored higher EPI grades than the average US states in the mid-1980s, but they performed just as badly during the late-1990s—and the price of WTI was virtually the same.

Obviously, being an oil-producing state didn't help them any more than the average US state. But before we conclude, let's compare the performance of nineteen non-oil-producing economies against oil prices.

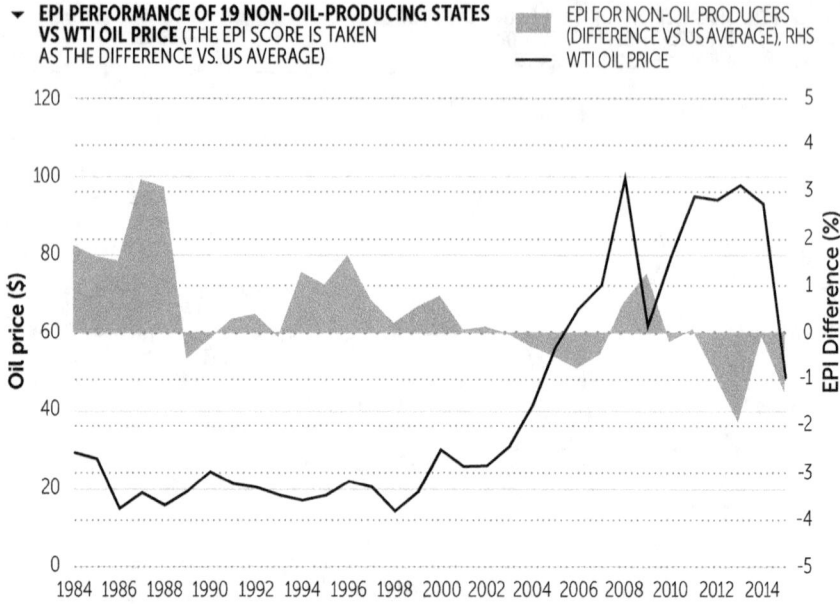

▼ **EPI PERFORMANCE OF 19 NON-OIL-PRODUCING STATES VS WTI OIL PRICE** (THE EPI SCORE IS TAKEN AS THE DIFFERENCE VS. US AVERAGE)

▬ EPI FOR NON-OIL PRODUCERS (DIFFERENCE VS US AVERAGE), RHS
— WTI OIL PRICE

For our nineteen states with virtually no crude oil production, we might conclude that *not* being an oil-producer hurt them in the early 2000s as the price of a barrel of oil rose... but then again, there were troughs when they didn't do well, despite a relatively stable price. Sometimes they did better than the average state, sometimes worse.

So it's hard to tell from these two graphs how being an oil producer or not affects a state's economy. To be accurate, we have to run a regression analysis.

When we study the EPI scores of our two groups—producers and non-producers—against the price of WTI, this is where we find that the price of WTI correlates with the EPI of our two groups. When the price of oil is lower, non-oil producers fare better than the average state, while oil-producers fare worse. As the price of oil rises, though, these two groups switch places. Our energy-rich states have better EPI scores than average, while the other group pays a toll.

Still, the connection is weak, at best, according to our econometric tests. This means that data does not strongly support the idea of better performance of one group over another when oil prices go up. In other words, a high price of oil helps oil-producing states—but only a little bit. A low price hurts—but again, only a little bit.

While even a small change in a state's EPI score can represent hundreds of millions of dollars and a materially better economy, what we've looked at here doesn't support the myth that oil production is a windfall for a state's economic performance. As we've gathered from secrets elsewhere, the key to a good economy isn't just its resources but long-term economic growth (grounded in a diversified economy), low unemployment, and sensible fiscal policies.

In short, it doesn't matter if a state has oil reserves or not—it can still create the conditions for a great economy.

APPENDIX I

COUNTRY REPORTS

Data and forecasts were taken from the IMF's
April 2016 World Economic Outlook database.

AUSTRALIA

Gradual Improvement

AUSTRALIA'S ECONOMIC PERFORMANCE HAS IMPROVED IN THE PAST FEW YEARS. IN 2016, THE EPI PROJECTS AUSTRALIA TO HAVE A PERFORMANCE SCORE OF 92%, OR A SOLID B GRADE. WHILE THE ECONOMY IS IMPROVING, IT STILL FACES SOME CHALLENGES AS THE MINING INVESTMENT BOOM IS WINDING DOWN, IN ADDITION TO FACING LOWER GLOBAL COMMODITY PRICES.

WORLD RANK

25

EPI GRADE

B VERY GOOD

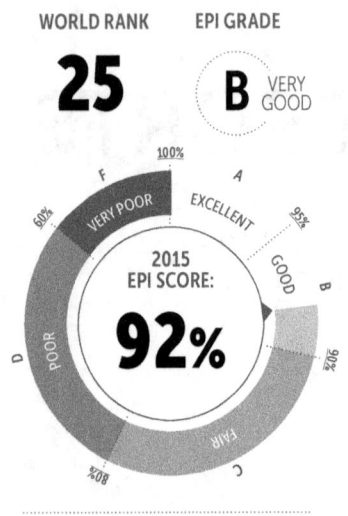

2015 EPI SCORE: **92%**

Its GDP growth of 2.5% in 2015 was relatively modest and is expected to stay around this level in 2016. This is due, in part, to a particularly weak final domestic demand and a decline in public and private investment. Also, because of the lower commodity prices, there are lower tax revenues from iron ore exports going to the government. For the same reason, inflation is low and is projected to be 2.1% in 2016.

The government is on the sustainable path of winding down a fiscal stimulus. Last year's budget deficit comes in at only 2.9% of GDP with projections of reaching a balanced budget by 2020. Despite this, fiscal consolidation has become more difficult in the current environment and public debt is rising (albeit from a quite low starting point).

The main economic drag on Australia's EPI score is its unemployment. It is expected to stay high, close to 6%, in the next few years. Still, this unemployment level is below the average for many advanced economies, especially the European ones.

By 2021, Australia's EPI score will continue to improve, but only gradually: from a current 92.0%, or a B level to 94.8%, or a B+ level. Less investment in mining and a sharp fall in revenue from commodity exports pose the primary macroeconomic challenges, and will slow GDP growth. As such, the major positive drivers will be a continued fiscal deficit reduction and lower unemployment levels. In such an environment though, inflation will likely start picking up, probably reaching 2.5% by 2021 as monetary policy continues to be loose.

▼ EPI COMPONENTS (2015)

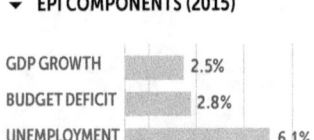

GDP GROWTH	2.5%
BUDGET DEFICIT	2.8%
UNEMPLOYMENT	6.1%
INFLATION	1.5%

1%   3%   5%   7%

▼ ECONOMIC PERFORMANCE INDEX (2000–2020)

AUSTRALIA — UNITED STATES

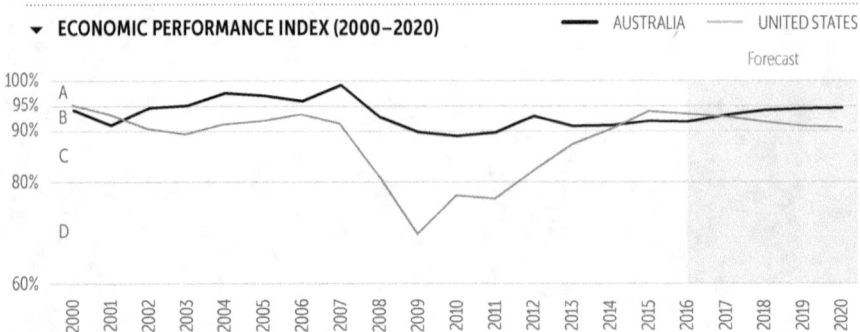

Forecast

AUSTRIA

Conservative Policies

AUSTRIA HAS RELATIVELY STRONG MACROECONOMIC FUNDAMENTALS BUT A FURTHER ECONOMIC SLOWDOWN IN THE EURO AREA CREATES CHALLENGES FOR THE COUNTRY. IN 2016, THE EPI PROJECTS AUSTRIA TO HAVE AN EPI SCORE OF 91.8%, OR A B GRADE.

Austria is one of the richest countries in the world in terms of GDP per capita, with a well-developed social market economy and high standards of living. Germany has historically been the main trading partner of Austria, but since Austria became a member state of the EU, it has gained closer ties to other EU economies, reducing its economic dependence on Germany.

Austria's GDP is projected to accelerate to 1.2% in 2016 versus 0.9% in 2015, driven by the recovery of countries in the EU and in Germany, in particular. Inflation is likely to start picking up, despite low oil prices. Due to conservative fiscal policies, the budget deficit is projected to be 1.7% in 2016. Its unemployment level of 5.7% is low by European standards.

The 5-Minute Economist projects Austria's EPI score to stay at a B level by 2021, with gradually increasing inflation compensated by improved GDP growth.

WORLD RANK 21

EPI GRADE B VERY GOOD

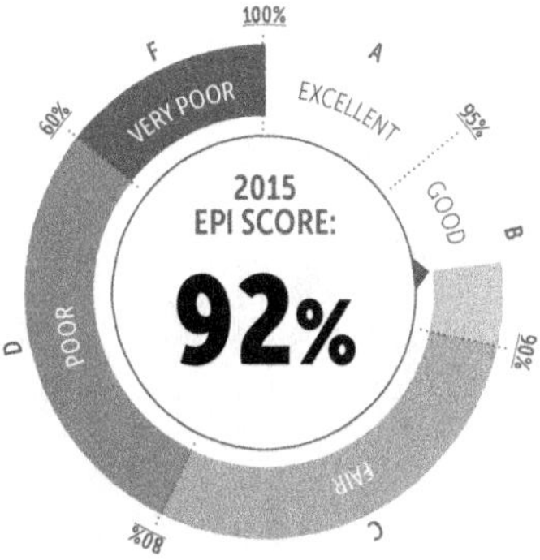

EPI COMPONENTS (2015)

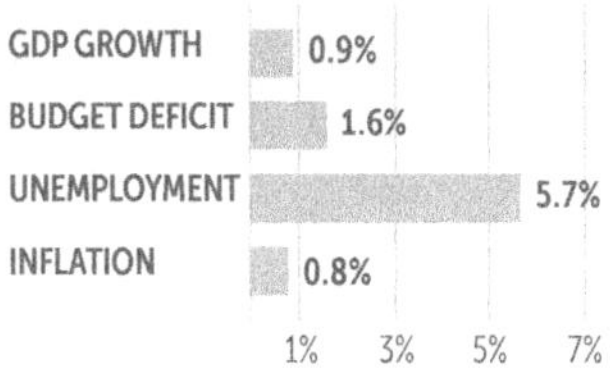

ECONOMIC PERFORMANCE INDEX (2000–2020)

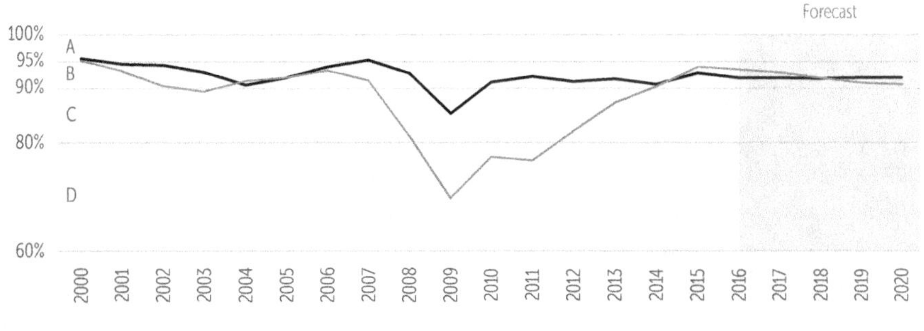

BELGIUM

Lagging The Eurozone

BELGIUM'S ECONOMIC PERFORMANCE HAS BEEN IMPROVING IN THE PAST FEW YEARS AND THE EPI GRADES ITS CURRENT ECONOMIC PERFORMANCE AT A C+ LEVEL, WITH THE EPI SCORE PROJECTED TO BE 88.9% IN 2016. THE ECONOMY HAS SHOWN CONSIDERABLE RESILIENCE BUT THE OUTLOOK IS WEIGHED DOWN BY WEAK DEMAND IN EUROPE.

WORLD RANK

31

EPI GRADE

C+ FAIR

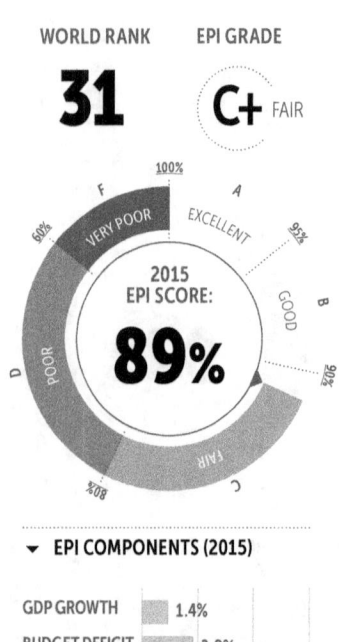

2015 EPI SCORE: **89%**

The relatively subdued economic outlook will be affected by still-muted external demand from the rest of Europe, persistently high unemployment, wage restraint and fiscal consolidation. Belgium's recovery has been continuing, mainly driven by domestic demand, but still remained modest with real GDP growing by 1.4% in 2015, up from 0% in 2013. The unemployment level of 8.3% is still high. Fiscal adjustment is expected to resume after a pause in 2014, with the budget deficit reduced from 3.1% in 2014 to 2.8% in 2015. Inflation remains very low, driven by low commodity prices and the disinflationary environment in Europe.

The 5-Minute Economist projects Belgium's EPI score to continue improving only gradually in the medium term from almost 89.7% or a C+ level currently to 90.3% or a solid B- level by 2021. The major drivers for improvement in the EPI score the medium term are projected to be continued fiscal deficit reduction as well as lower unemployment levels. Improvements in economic growth rates are unlikely, with GDP projected to stay flat at 1.4% in the medium term. Inflation is likely to start picking up in this environment and reach 1.5% by 2021, once monetary conditions in the Eurozone normalize.

▼ EPI COMPONENTS (2015)

GDP GROWTH	1.4%
BUDGET DEFICIT	2.8%
UNEMPLOYMENT	8.3%
INFLATION	0.6%

3% 6% 9%

▼ ECONOMIC PERFORMANCE INDEX (2000–2020)   ── BELGIUM   ── UNITED STATES

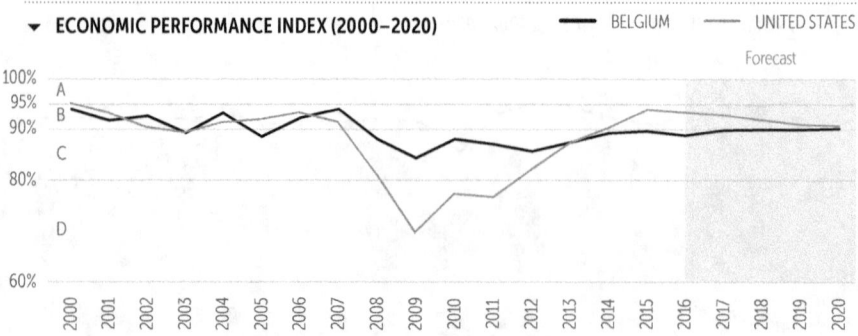

BRAZIL

Continued Recession

THE ECONOMIC RECESSION IS LIKELY TO CONTINUE IN 2016, DRIVEN BY POLITICAL NOISE AND A LOW INVESTORS' CONFIDENCE LEVEL. THE PERFORMANCE OF BRAZIL'S ECONOMY HAS BEEN POOR, WITH THE EPI SCORE PROJECTED TO BE 69.6%, OR A D GRADE, IN 2016.

During 2015, the Brazilian economy slipped into a recession, inflation and unemployment soared, and Brazil lost its investment-grade sovereign credit rating. The Brazilian real lost more than half of its value in the past two years, pushing inflation to 9.0% in 2015, making the recession more severe.

Still, inflation is likely to slow down to 6.1% in 2017, but will stay elevated. The fiscal position of the government has been negatively affected by the low GDP growth, pushing the budget deficit to 8.7% in 2016. Unemployment is projected to increase from 6.8% in 2015 to 9.2% in 2016, driven by the second-year recession in the economy. Real wages have started going down, driven by high unemployment rates and elevated inflation.

Brazil's policy makers have struggling to control the increasing inflation without further constraining the weak economy. The government faced renewed pressure to moderate austerity proposals aimed at bolstering public accounts and avoiding further credit downgrades. The recent impeachment proceedings and the corruption scandal have also been hindering approval of economic policies in the parliament.

The 5-Minute Economist projects Brazil's EPI score to improve gradually to about 81.6%, or a C- level, by 2021, with gradually improving GDP growth and decreasing inflation and unemployment rates.

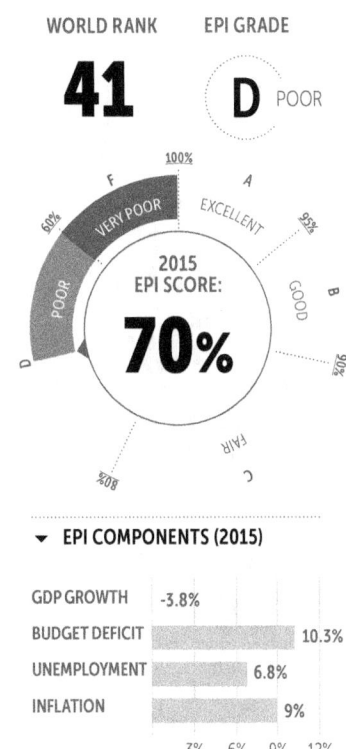

WORLD RANK **41**

EPI GRADE **D** POOR

2015 EPI SCORE: **70%**

▼ **EPI COMPONENTS (2015)**

GDP GROWTH	-3.8%
BUDGET DEFICIT	10.3%
UNEMPLOYMENT	6.8%
INFLATION	9%

3%   6%   9%   12%

▼ **ECONOMIC PERFORMANCE INDEX (2000–2020)**   — BRAZIL   — UNITED STATES

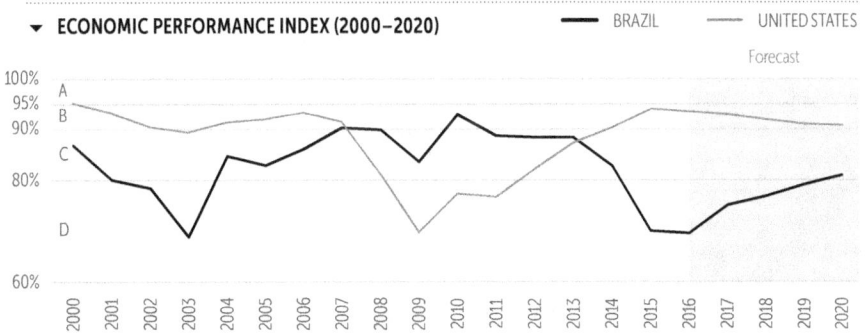

Forecast

CANADA

Very Oil-Dependent

AS A MAJOR OIL- EXPORTER, CANADA WAS HIT HARD BY LOW OIL PRICES, WITH GDP GROWTH SLOWING DOWN AND THE CANADIAN DOLLAR LOSING ABOUT A THIRD OF ITS VALUE. IN 2016, THE EPI PROJECTS CANADA TO HAVE A PERFORMANCE SCORE OF 90.4%, OR A B- GRADE.

WORLD RANK

27

EPI GRADE

B VERY GOOD

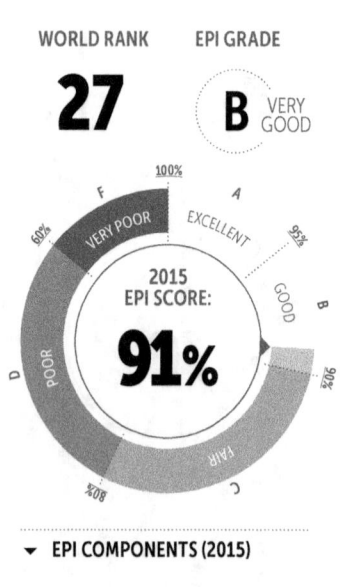

2015 EPI SCORE:

91%

The energy sector contributes significantly to Canada's economy, with the oil, gas and mining sector accounting for more than one quarter of the value of the country's GDP. Valued at $259 billion in 2014, natural resources account for more than half of Canada's merchandise exports. The US (78%), the UK (5%) and China (4%) are the three main destinations of all natural resources exports. The US is the destination of 97% of energy exports, 66% of forest products exports and 52% of minerals and metals exports.

GDP growth slowed from 2.5% in 2014 to 1.2% in 2015 and is projected to be 1.5% in 2016, mainly because of a large investment drop in the energy industries. Still, Canada's economic fundamentals remain strong, with the country's strong commitment to an open- market. The newly elected government is likely to use fiscal stimulus to decrease the pain of the oil shock. But the budget deficit is still projected to remain close to 2.4% in 2016. Unemployment is projected to be 7.3% and inflation to be low at 1.3% in 2016.

The 5-Minute Economist projects Canada's EPI score to stay at a B level by 2021, with gradually increasing inflation compensated by improved GDP growth.

▼ **EPI COMPONENTS (2015)**

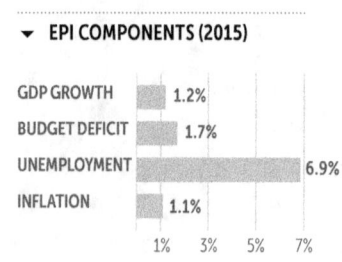

GDP GROWTH	1.2%
BUDGET DEFICIT	1.7%
UNEMPLOYMENT	6.9%
INFLATION	1.1%

1%   3%   5%   7%

▼ **ECONOMIC PERFORMANCE INDEX (2000–2020)**   —— CANADA   —— UNITED STATES

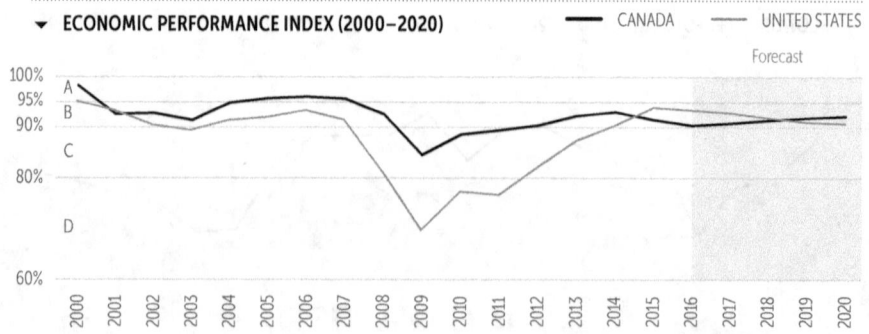

Forecast

CHINA

A New Normal

CHINA'S ECONOMIC PERFORMANCE HAS BEEN EXCELLENT IN THE PAST FEW YEARS AND THE EPI GRADES ITS CURRENT ECONOMIC PERFORMANCE AT A LEVEL, WITH THE EPI SCORE PROJECTED TO BE CLOSE TO 97.6% IN 2016. CHINA IS TRANSITIONING TO A "NEW NORMAL" GROWTH MODEL, WITH LOWER YET MORE SUSTAINABLE GROWTH RATES OF THE ECONOMY AND CREDIT.

China's "hard landing" remains a risk but the government's monetary and fiscal stimuli are likely to ensure that the slowdown is gradual. Lower growth would eventually lead to lower corporate profits and lower dividends, negatively affecting stock prices. The stock market crash in the second half of 2015 was a reason for investors to re-price the growth potential of the Chinese economy.

GDP growth is projected to decelerate to 6.5% in 2016 after peaking at 10.6% in 2010 due to slower investment, especially in real estate. The labor market has remained resilient despite slower growth, as the economy pivots toward the more labor-intensive service sector. The official unemployment rate is likely to remain flat at 4.1%, despite the economic slowdown. Fiscal policy has been accommodative and continues to be impacted by off-budget activity, with the budget deficit projected to increase to 3.1% of GDP this year from 2.7% in 2015. Inflation is projected to be 1.8% this year, on the back of lower commodity prices.

The 5-Minute Economist projects China's EPI score to gradually decelerate in the medium term from 98.7%, or A level currently, to 96.7%, still a solid A level, by 2021. The major drivers for the slowdown in the EPI score in the medium term are projected to be lower GDP growth, which is projected to stabilize at 6% by 2021, and some acceleration in inflation to 3%. Changes in the unemployment rate are unlikely, and the budget deficit is likely to stay close to 2.2% a year.

WORLD RANK

4

EPI GRADE

A+ XLNT

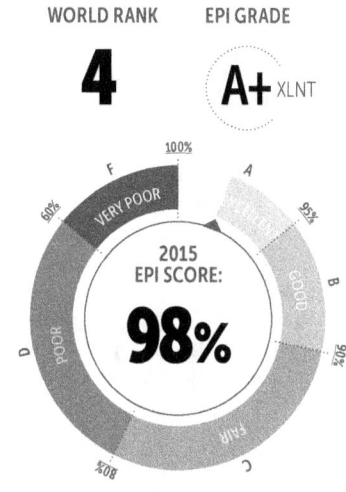

2015 EPI SCORE:

98%

▼ EPI COMPONENTS (2015)

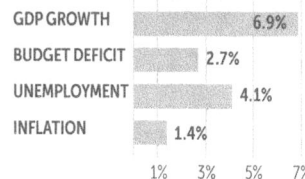

GDP GROWTH	6.9%
BUDGET DEFICIT	2.7%
UNEMPLOYMENT	4.1%
INFLATION	1.4%

1%   3%   5%   7%

▼ ECONOMIC PERFORMANCE INDEX (2000–2020)   ▬▬ CHINA   ┈┈┈ UNITED STATES

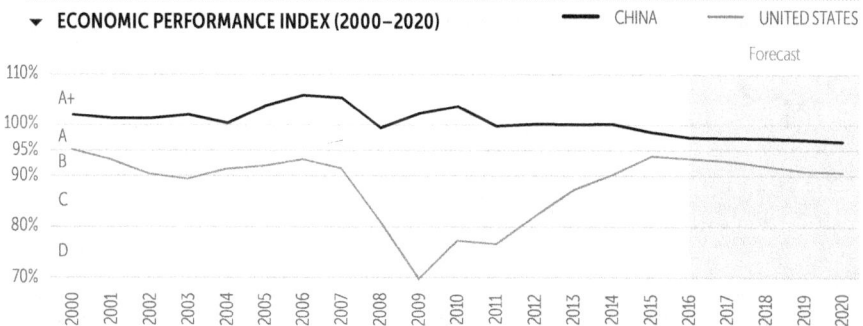

CYPRUS

Getting Out
Of the Crisis

THE CYPRIOT ECONOMY SHOWS SIGNS OF A GRADUAL RECOVERY AFTER ITS DEEP CRISIS
AND THE EPI GRADES ITS CURRENT ECONOMIC PERFORMANCE AT C LEVEL, WITH
THE EPI SCORE PROJECTED TO BE CLOSE TO 86.9% IN 2016, UP FROM THE BOTTOM
OF 73.4%, OR D LEVEL, IN 2013.

WORLD RANK   **EPI GRADE**

38   C- FAIR

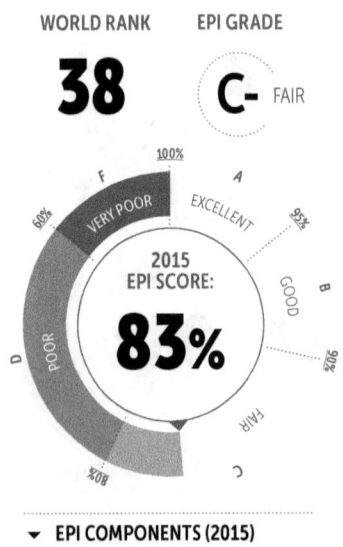

2015
EPI SCORE:
83%

After the large banking crisis and the government
bail-out of major banks, the debt-to-GDP ratio is likely
to peak at about 100% of GDP and decline gradually
in the medium term, driven by fiscal surpluses and
gradual improvement in GDP growth rates.

GDP growth is projected to turn back into positive
territory this year after a cumulative drop by 10% since
2012. The main driver of growth remains the tourism
industry, which accounts for around 7% of gross value
added. Despite the trend reversal, unemployment
of 15.3% remains high, especially compared to the pre-
crisis average of 4.4% in the period 2000-09. Fiscal
adjustment is expected to resume after a pause in 2015,
with a budget deficit increase to 1.7% of GDP in 2015, —
still small by international standards. Inflation remains
negative, driven by the lower demand in the economy
and the disinflationary environment in Europe.

The 5-Minute Economist projects Cyprus' EPI
score to continue improving in the medium term from
almost 83.1%, or a C- level, currently to 93.2%, or a solid
B level, by 2021. The major drivers for improvement
in the EPI score in the medium term are projected to be
a continued turn of fiscal deficit into surplus, a decrease
in the level of unemployment, and the resumption
of economic growth. Inflation is likely to start picking
up in this environment and reach almost 2% by 2021.

▼ **EPI COMPONENTS (2015)**

GDP GROWTH	1.6%
BUDGET DEFICIT	1.7%
UNEMPLOYMENT	15.3%
INFLATION	-1.5%

4%   8%   12%   16%

▼ **ECONOMIC PERFORMANCE INDEX (2000–2020)**   —— CYPRUS   —— UNITED STATES

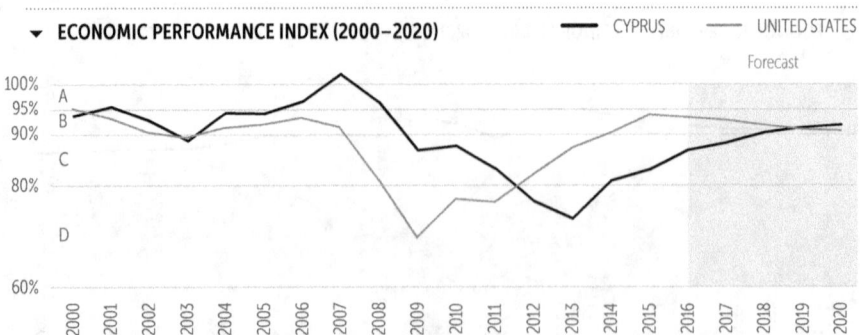

CZECH REPUBLIC

Gaining Momentum

THE CZECH REPUBLIC'S ECONOMY IS GAINING MOMENTUM DUE TO IMPROVING DOMESTIC DEMAND AND STRONG EXPORTS. THE EPI GRADES ITS CURRENT ECONOMIC PERFORMANCE AT A SOLID A LEVEL, WITH THE EPI SCORE PROJECTED TO BE CLOSE TO 95.2% IN 2016.

This is a strong improvement from its C level grade in 2012–2013 and a B level in 2014. Both exports and domestic demand are performing well, and the recovery in domestic demand is broad-based. The Czech Republic's recovery has been continuing, with GDP growth projected to decelerate to 2.5% in 2016, down from 4.2% in 2015. Employment continues to shrink, reaching its lowest rate since the onset of the 2008 crisis and is contributing to a welcomed recovery in real wages. Following substantial fiscal adjustment during 2011–2013, the budget deficit is projected to decline to 1.6% in 2016. Inflation remains low, driven by low commodity prices and the disinflationary environment in Europe.

The 5-Minute Economist projects the Czech Republic's EPI score to start declining gradually in the medium term from almost 96.9%, or an A level, currently to 94.1%, or a B+ level, by 2021, mainly driven by growth slowdown and a gradual pick-up in inflation, despite lower budget deficit and unemployment rates.

WORLD RANK   **EPI GRADE**

11   **A** XLNT

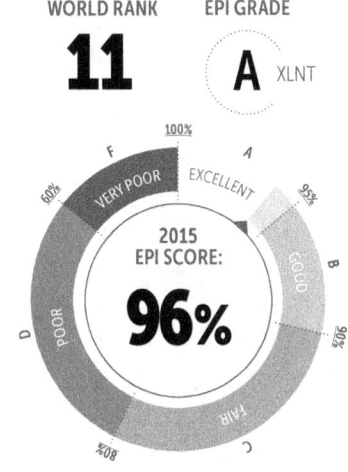

2015
EPI SCORE:

96%

▼ **EPI COMPONENTS (2015)**

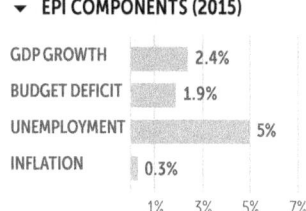

GDP GROWTH — 2.4%
BUDGET DEFICIT — 1.9%
UNEMPLOYMENT — 5%
INFLATION — 0.3%

1% 3% 5% 7%

▼ **ECONOMIC PERFORMANCE INDEX (2000–2020)**   ━━ CZECH REPUBLIC   ─── UNITED STATES
Forecast

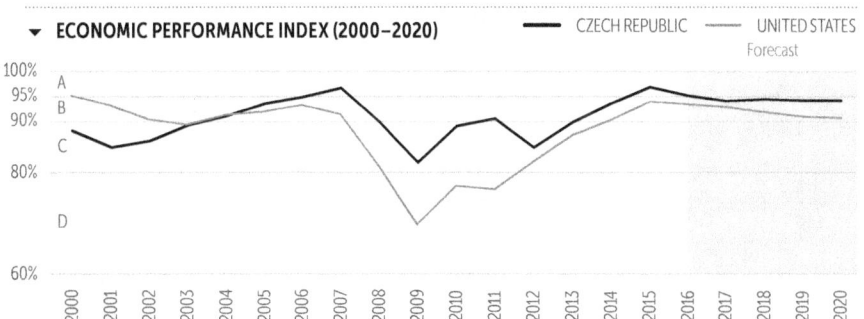

DENMARK

Slow Improvements

DENMARK'S ECONOMIC PERFORMANCE HAS BEEN GOOD, WITH THE EPI SCORE PROJECTED
TO BE CLOSE TO 92.0%, OR A B LEVEL, IN 2016. ECONOMIC CONDITIONS HAVE IMPROVED
STEADILY OVER THE PAST TWO YEARS, WITH DOMESTIC DEMAND STRENGTHENING
AND EXPORTS IMPROVING.

WORLD RANK

22

EPI GRADE

B GOOD

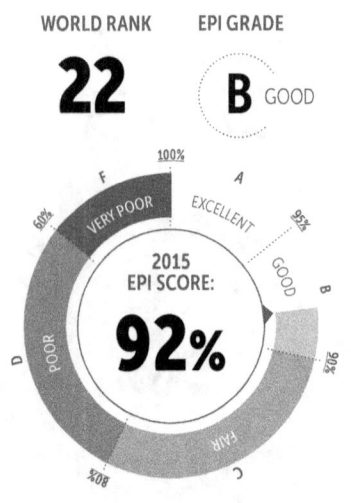

2015
EPI SCORE:

92%

Denmark is a net exporter of food and energy and has had a balance of payments surplus since the 1990's. Denmark's main exports are industrial production and agricultural products, but cheaper oil has had a negative, though still limited, effect on the economy so far. Unemployment at 6% remains elevated, which is typical for European economies. The general government deficit turned from a surplus of 1.5% in 2014 to a deficit of 2.0% of GDP in 2015 and is projected to be 2.8% in 2016. The government's fiscal consolidation plans are aimed at keeping the deficit within 3% of GDP, in line with the EU's demands. Inflation is projected to be 0.8% in 2016, in line with the low inflationary environment in the EU overall.

The 5-Minute Economist projects Denmark's EPI score to remain at a B level by 2021.

▼ **EPI COMPONENTS (2015)**

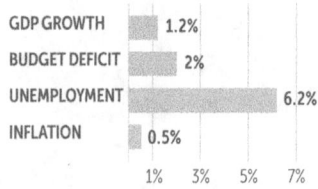

GDP GROWTH	1.2%
BUDGET DEFICIT	2%
UNEMPLOYMENT	6.2%
INFLATION	0.5%

▼ **ECONOMIC PERFORMANCE INDEX (2000–2020)**   DENMARK   UNITED STATES

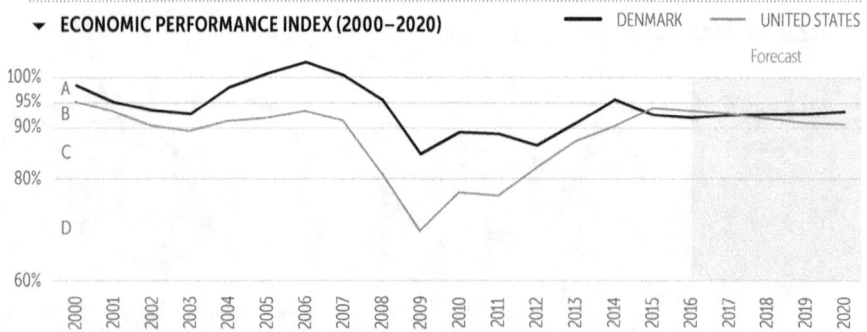

ESTONIA

Remains Resilient

THE EPI GRADES ESTONIA'S CURRENT ECONOMIC PERFORMANCE AT A B+ LEVEL, WITH THE EPI SCORE PROJECTED TO BE CLOSE TO 94.3% IN 2016, A STRONG IMPROVEMENT FROM ITS B- LEVEL IN 2012. ESTONIA'S LOW GOVERNMENT DEBT OF LESS THAN 10% OF GDP AND STRONG FISCAL POSITION OF THE GOVERNMENT, ALONG WITH A CONSISTENT TRACK RECORD OF STRUCTURAL REFORMS, SUPPORTS FURTHER INCOME CONVERGENCE TOWARD THE EUROPEAN UNION AVERAGES.

Estonia's recovery has been on track, with GDP growth projected to be 2.2% in 2016, up from 1.1% in 2015. Unemployment continues to decline, reaching its lowest rate since the onset of the 2008 crisis. Following substantial fiscal adjustment in 2014, the government is projected to have small budget surplus in 2016. Inflation remains low, driven by low commodity prices and the disinflationary environment in Europe.

The 5-Minute Economist projects Estonia's EPI score to remain at current levels in the medium term with only a gradual improvement to 95.6% or an A- level by 2021, driven by economic growth acceleration and a lower unemployment rate, despite a gradual pick-up in inflation.

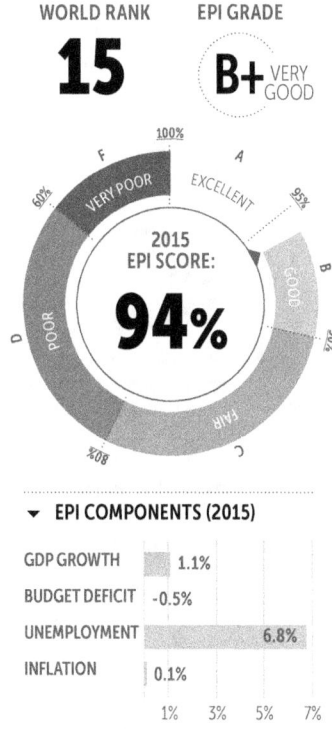

WORLD RANK
15

EPI GRADE
B+ VERY GOOD

2015 EPI SCORE:
94%

▼ EPI COMPONENTS (2015)

GDP GROWTH	1.1%
BUDGET DEFICIT	-0.5%
UNEMPLOYMENT	6.8%
INFLATION	0.1%

1%   3%   5%   7%

▼ ECONOMIC PERFORMANCE INDEX (2000–2020)

ESTONIA ⸻ UNITED STATES

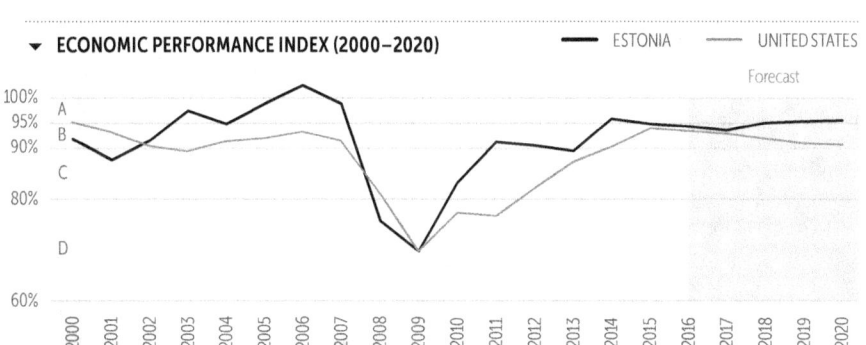

FINLAND

Still Under Pressure

FOLLOWING A STRONG ECONOMIC PERFORMANCE IN THE EARLY 2000S, FINLAND HAS SUFFERED A UNIQUE CONFLUENCE OF CYCLICAL AND STRUCTURAL SHOCKS SINCE THE GLOBAL FINANCIAL CRISIS IN 2008. THE EPI GRADES FINLAND'S CURRENT ECONOMIC PERFORMANCE AT A C LEVEL, WITH THE EPI SCORE PROJECTED TO BE CLOSE TO 88.4% IN 2016.

WORLD RANK

33

EPI GRADE

C FAIR

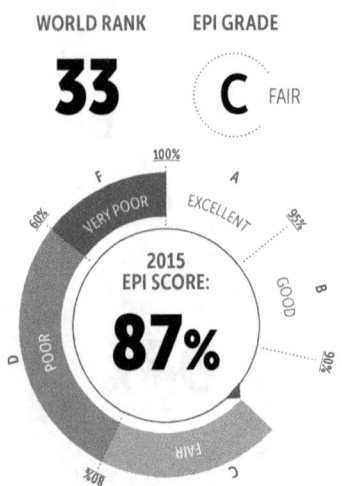

2015 EPI SCORE:

87%

Weak external demand, along with the parallel declines of Nokia and the paper industry, have reduced exports. Additional external factors, primarily the recession in Russia, have taken further tolls on exports.

GDP is projected to increase by 0.9% in 2016, partly driven by higher private consumption growth as inflation remains low and "mortgage amortization holidays" are being offered by major banks to households. The unemployment level increased to 9.3% in 2015 from 8.7% the year before. The government is providing some fiscal stimulus and kept the budget deficit at 3.4% in 2015. Inflation remains at zero, driven by low commodity prices and the disinflationary environment in Europe.

The 5-Minute Economist projects Finland's EPI score to improve from the current levels only gradually in the medium term to 91.6%, or a B level, by 2021, driven by economic growth acceleration and a lower unemployment rate, despite a gradual pick-up in inflation.

▼ **EPI COMPONENTS (2015)**

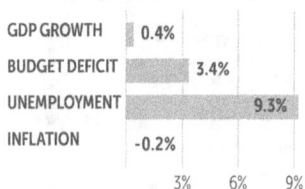

GDP GROWTH	0.4%
BUDGET DEFICIT	3.4%
UNEMPLOYMENT	9.3%
INFLATION	-0.2%

▼ **ECONOMIC PERFORMANCE INDEX (2000–2020)** ⸺ FINLAND ⸺ UNITED STATES

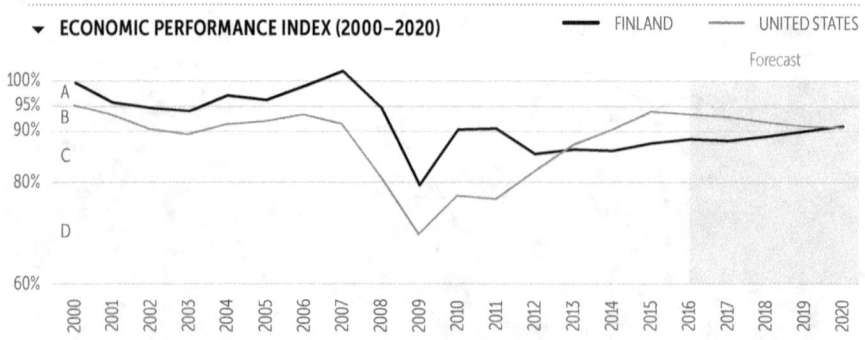

FRANCE

Short-term Recovery

THE FRENCH ECONOMY IS RECOVERING, BUT ITS GROWTH POTENTIAL STILL APPEARS MUCH WEAKER THAN BEFORE THE 2008 CRISIS. THE EPI GRADES FRANCE'S CURRENT ECONOMIC PERFORMANCE AT A C LEVEL, WITH THE EPI SCORE PROJECTED TO BE 87.2% IN 2016. DESPITE A SOLID SHORT-TERM RECOVERY, STRUCTURAL RIGIDITIES CONTINUE TO WEIGH ON MEDIUM-TERM PROSPECTS.

After almost four years of near-stagnation, GDP growth is projected to rise to 1.1% in 2016, supported by a highly accommodative external environment, in particular sharply lower oil prices, a depreciated euro, and interest rates at historic lows. The initial rebound has been driven by household consumption, with exports expecting to pick up as well, however, investment has not yet responded and unemployment remains stubbornly high above 10%.

High government spending has been at the heart of France's fiscal problems for many years, with government spending reaching 57% of GDP in 2015, about 10% of GDP above the euro area average. While the growth of government and health care spending have been recently contained, local government spending has continued to expand, and social spending is the highest in the OECD. Nevertheless, the government has been reducing its fiscal deficit, following EU rules and it is projected to be below 3.4% in 2016.

Negative effects of the Brexit are likely to start materializing quickly. Renegotiation of trade and immigration agreements with the EU will determine the effects of the separation on France, the UK's closest neighbor, and on the EU overall.

The 5-Minute Economist projects France's EPI score to improve only gradually in the medium term from almost 87.1%, or a C level, currently to 90.6%, or a B- level, by 2021, driven by economic growth acceleration and a lower unemployment rate, despite a gradual pick-up in inflation. The fiscal deficit is likely to be brought narrowly below 3% of GDP in 2017.

WORLD RANK

34

EPI GRADE

C FAIR

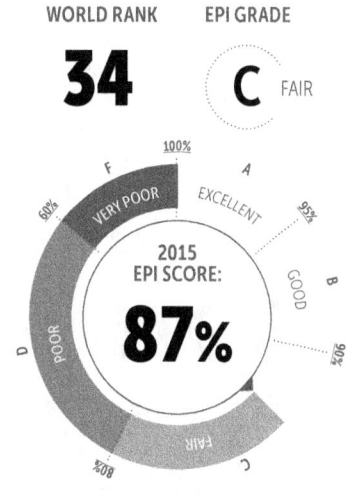

2015
EPI SCORE:

87%

▼ **EPI COMPONENTS (2015)**

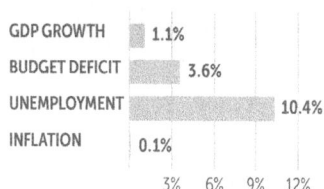

GDP GROWTH	1.1%
BUDGET DEFICIT	3.6%
UNEMPLOYMENT	10.4%
INFLATION	0.1%

3% 6% 9% 12%

▼ **ECONOMIC PERFORMANCE INDEX (2000–2020)** ━━ FRANCE ─── UNITED STATES

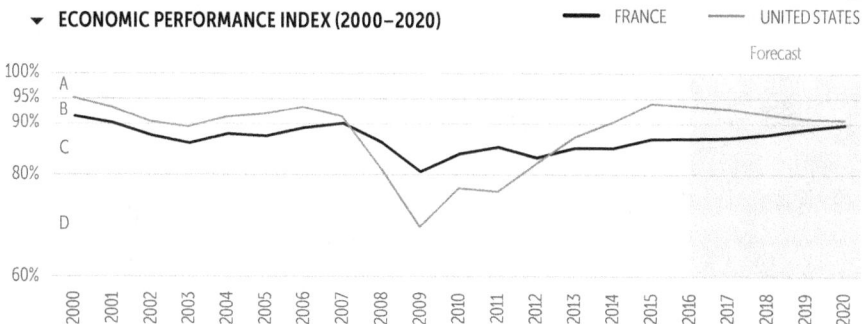

GERMANY

Remains Solid

GROWTH IN GERMANY IS EXPECTED TO CONTINUE, LIFTED BY THE DOUBLE STIMULUS OF LOW ENERGY PRICES AND QUANTITATIVE EASING BY THE ECB. THE EPI GRADES GERMANY'S CURRENT ECONOMIC PERFORMANCE AT AN A LEVEL, WITH THE EPI SCORE PROJECTED TO BE CLOSE TO 96.5% IN 2016.

WORLD RANK

10

EPI GRADE

A XLNT

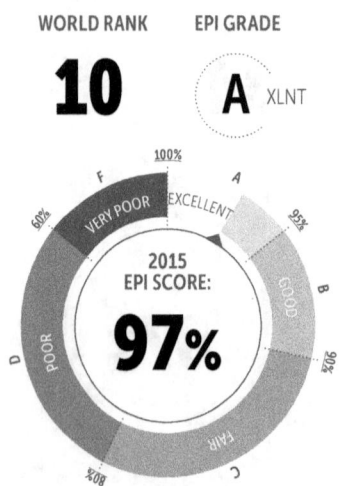

2015
EPI SCORE:

97%

GDP growth is projected to remain around 1.5% in 2016, with private consumption most likely being the largest contributor to growth, underpinned by a strong increase in real disposable income. Exports are also expected to support the momentum, while inflation should remain subdued in the medium term. The unemployment level remains below 5% and the government runs a small budget surplus.

On June 23, 2016, British voters decided to vote to "Leave" the European Union. Renegotiation of trade and immigration agreements with the EU will determine the effects of the separation both on the UK and the European Union.

The 5-Minute Economist projects Germany's EPI score to decline only slightly in the medium term from 97.3%, or an A level, currently to 95.1%, or an A- level, by 2021, mainly driven by a gradual pick-up in inflation.

▾ **EPI COMPONENTS (2015)**

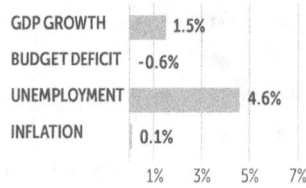

GDP GROWTH	1.5%
BUDGET DEFICIT	-0.6%
UNEMPLOYMENT	4.6%
INFLATION	0.1%

1%   3%   5%   7%

▾ **ECONOMIC PERFORMANCE INDEX (2000–2020)** ⸺ GERMANY ⸺ UNITED STATES

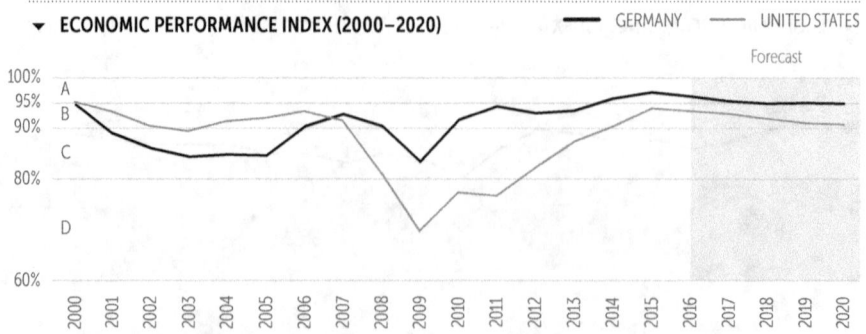

GREECE

In crisis, again

THE GREEK ECONOMY IS STILL IN RECESSION AND THE EPI GRADES GREECE'S CURRENT ECONOMIC PERFORMANCE AT A D LEVEL, WITH THE EPI SCORE PROJECTED TO BE CLOSE TO 68% IN 2016.

Greece has been going through a deep financial and sovereign debt crisis that led to a multi-year recession, when the country's real GDP shrank almost by 30% in real terms between 2008-2013. The EPI score in Greece reached 59%, or an F level, in 2011, the lowest score among euro zone countries in the past decade. The so-called troika of international creditors—International Monetary Fund, European Central Bank, and European Commission—provided the biggest financial program in the world to the Greek government that included both sovereign debt restructuring and large bank recapitalization.

The 5-Minute Economist forecasts that Greece's economy will struggle to grow under the new three-year program as fiscal austerity measures, that include higher taxes and government spending cuts, would weight on growth compounding popular dissatisfaction. There is a high risk that Greece would leave the euro zone in the next few years but these are not our expectations, as Europe wants to make sure that Greece pays back its debt and continues structural reforms.

WORLD RANK | EPI GRADE

42 | **D** POOR

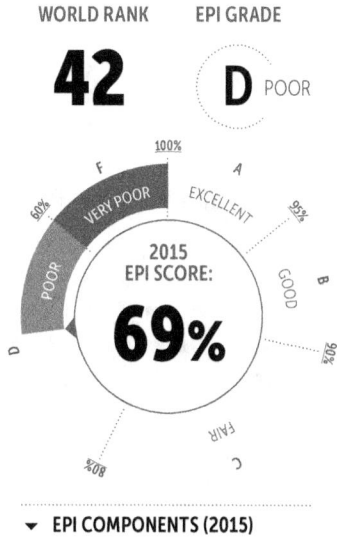

2015
EPI SCORE:

69%

▼ **EPI COMPONENTS (2015)**

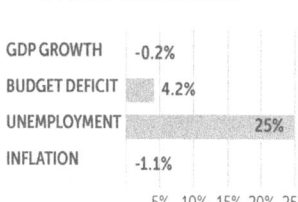

GDP GROWTH	-0.2%
BUDGET DEFICIT	4.2%
UNEMPLOYMENT	25%
INFLATION	-1.1%

5% 10% 15% 20% 25%

▼ **ECONOMIC PERFORMANCE INDEX (2000–2020)** ⎯ GREECE ⎯ UNITED STATES

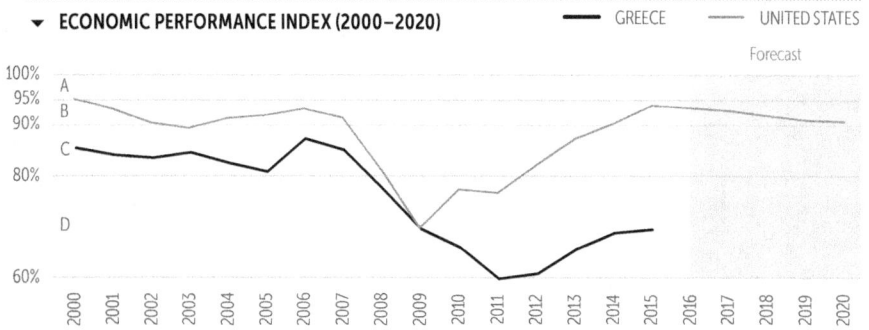

HONG KONG

The Shadow Of China

HONG KONG'S ECONOMIC PERFORMANCE HAS BEEN EXCELLENT, WITH THE EPI SCORE PROJECTED TO BE 97.9%, OR AN A LEVEL, IN 2016. HIGH ECONOMIC GROWTH RATES AND IMPROVED TRADE ALLOWED THE GOVERNMENT TO HAVE FISCAL SURPLUSES AND LOW UNEMPLOYMENT LEVELS.

WORLD RANK

8

EPI GRADE

A XLNT

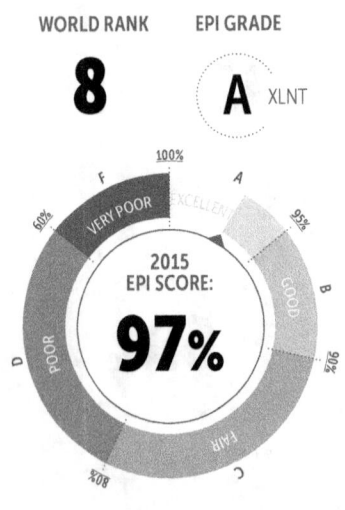

2015 EPI SCORE: **97%**

Hong Kong's economy is characterized by its low taxation, almost free port trade, and well-established international financial markets. The economy is highly dependent on international trade and finance, with the value of trade close to four times the country's GDP. Hong Kong is strongly integrated with China through trade, tourism, and financial links, leaving it vulnerable to renewed global financial market volatility or a slowdown in the Chinese economy.

GDP growth rate is projected to be 2.2% in 2016, due to increased investment and trade with China. Hong Kong has also had an abundant supply of labor from nearby regions but high demand for labor has been keeping the unemployment rate close to 3%. A skilled labor force coupled with the adoption of modern Western business methods has ensured that opportunities for external trade and investment were maximized. Inflation is projected to be 2.5% in 2016, as low global inflation will likely limit external price pressures and local cost increases will likely be restrained.

The government maintains the policy of low government spending by having no armed forces, minimal outlays for foreign affairs and modest recurrent social welfare spending, all of which allowed the accumulation of large reserves with minimal foreign debt.

The 5-Minute Economist projects Hong Kong's EPI score to improve to 99.2% by 2021, driven by improved GDP growth and continued fiscal surpluses.

▾ **EPI COMPONENTS (2015)**

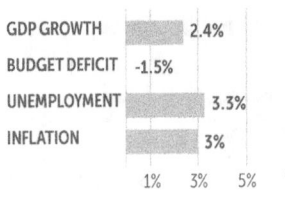

GDP GROWTH	2.4%
BUDGET DEFICIT	-1.5%
UNEMPLOYMENT	3.3%
INFLATION	3%

1% 3% 5% 7%

▾ **ECONOMIC PERFORMANCE INDEX (2000–2020)**   ━━ HONG KONG   ━━ UNITED STATES

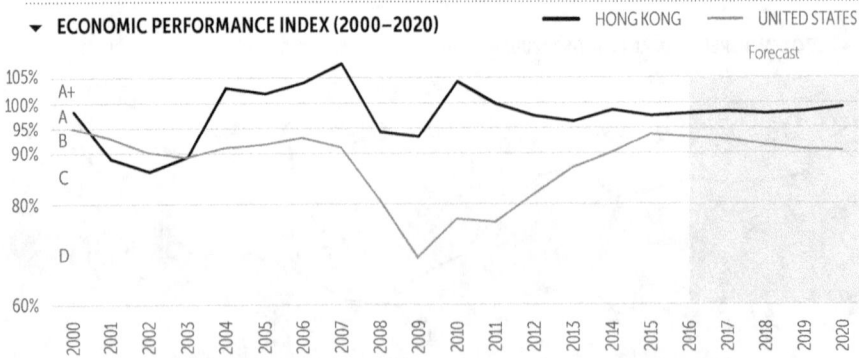

Forecast

HUNGARY

Strong Growth

THE HUNGARIAN ECONOMY IS GROWING AT A STRONG PACE SUPPORTED BY LOOSE MONETARY POLICIES AND IMPROVED MARKET SENTIMENT, DESPITE WEAK ECONOMIC ACTIVITY IN THE EURO AREA. THE EPI GRADES HUNGARY'S CURRENT ECONOMIC PERFORMANCE AT A SOLID B LEVEL, WITH THE EPI SCORE PROJECTED TO BE CLOSE TO 93.0% IN 2016.

A surge in investment and private consumption boosted GDP growth to 2.9% in 2015 and to an expected 2.3% in 2016, despite weak economic activity in the euro area. The unemployment level remains elevated at 6.9% and the government is providing some fiscal stimulus, with a projected budget deficit of 2.1% in 2016. Inflation remains at zero, driven by low commodity prices and the disinflationary environment in Europe.

The 5-Minute Economist projects Hungary's EPI score to decline slightly in the medium term from almost 93.8% currently to 91.7% by 2021 but still stay at the solid B level, mainly driven by a gradual pick-up in inflation. GDP growth is likely to slow down as well, as the government fiscal support would be gradually decreased along with its budget deficit.

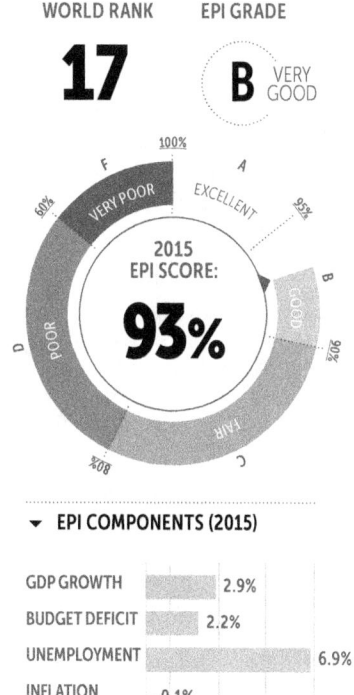

WORLD RANK

17

EPI GRADE

B VERY GOOD

2015
EPI SCORE:

93%

▼ EPI COMPONENTS (2015)

GDP GROWTH	2.9%
BUDGET DEFICIT	2.2%
UNEMPLOYMENT	6.9%
INFLATION	-0.1%

1%   3%   5%   7%

▼ ECONOMIC PERFORMANCE INDEX (2000–2020) ━━ HUNGARY ── UNITED STATES

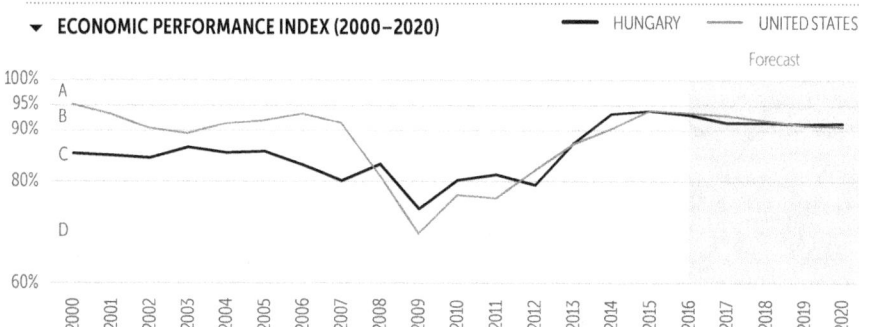

Forecast

ICELAND

Temporary Boost

THE ICELANDIC ECONOMY IS GROWING AT A STRONG PACE, SHOWING EXCELLENT ECONOMIC PERFORMANCE, DESPITE WEAK ECONOMIC ACTIVITY IN THE EURO AREA. THE EPI GRADES ICELAND'S CURRENT ECONOMIC PERFORMANCE AT A SOLID A+ LEVEL, WITH THE EPI SCORE PROJECTED TO BE 97.9% IN 2016.

WORLD RANK

3

EPI GRADE

A+ XLNT

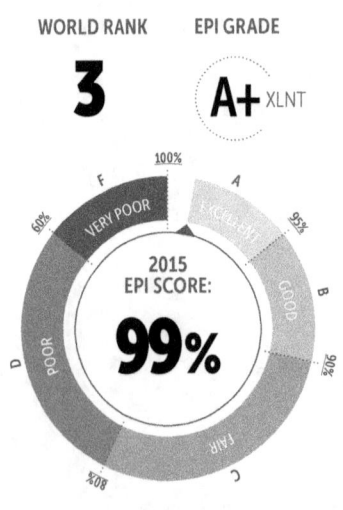

2015 EPI SCORE: **99%**

GDP growth is projected to be 4.2% in 2016, driven by internal consumption and investment, while relatively weak demand from key export markets in the EU will mean a small negative contribution from the external sector. After peaking at 12.7% in 2008 during the financial crisis and a sharp currency depreciation, inflation decreased and is projected to be close to 2.6% in 2016. Unemployment levels are low and close to 3.8%. A multi-year fiscal consolidation program has reduced the deficit from 13.1% of GDP in 2008 to a projected surplus of 0.1% in 2016, as the government raises revenue from the stability tax as part of its capital-account liberalization strategy.

The 5-Minute Economist projects Iceland's EPI score to decline to about 94.9% by 2021 but will remain at the A/A-level. GDP growth is likely to slow down from its currently high levels and a pick-up in inflation is likely to follow. The government is projected to run close to a balanced budget and the unemployment level is likely to stay around 4%.

▼ EPI COMPONENTS (2015)

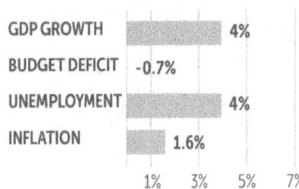

GDP GROWTH	4%
BUDGET DEFICIT	-0.7%
UNEMPLOYMENT	4%
INFLATION	1.6%

1%   3%   5%   7%

▼ ECONOMIC PERFORMANCE INDEX (2000–2020)

— ICELAND   — UNITED STATES

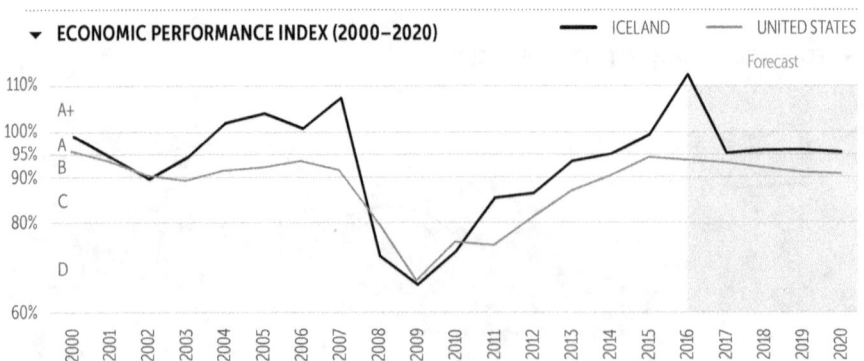

INDONESIA

Strong Growth

THE INDONESIAN ECONOMY IS GROWING AT A STRONG PACE WITH PRUDENT FISCAL AND MONETARY POLICIES, BUT ELEVATED INFLATION PUTS PRESSURES ON THE OVERALL ECONOMIC PERFORMANCE. THE EPI GRADES INDONESIA'S CURRENT ECONOMIC PERFORMANCE AT A C+ LEVEL, WITH THE EPI SCORE PROJECTED TO BE CLOSE TO 92.0% IN 2016.

GDP growth is projected to reach 4.9% in 2016, mainly driven by private consumption. Inflation remains close to 5.9%, despite the disinflationary effects of lower commodity prices. Import-substitution policies, such as the imposition of higher tariffs across a range of consumer goods, as well as the currency weakness, have also created inflationary pressures in 2015-2016. The budget deficit is projected to stay close to 2.8% of GDP, despite the government's expansionary policies. Unemployment has been on a declining path and is projected to be below 6% in 2016.

The 5-Minute Economist projects Indonesia's EPI score to increase gradually in the medium term from almost 89.7% currently to about 93.7%, or a B level, by 2021. Economic growth is likely to accelerate, with the main contribution to economic growth coming from private consumption, supported by the rising number of formal-sector jobs, the expansion of the so-cial- welfare net, and some loosening of monetary policy. Inflation is likely to slow down slightly, but the budget deficit and unemployment are likely to stay close to their current levels.

WORLD RANK

30

EPI GRADE

C+ FAIR

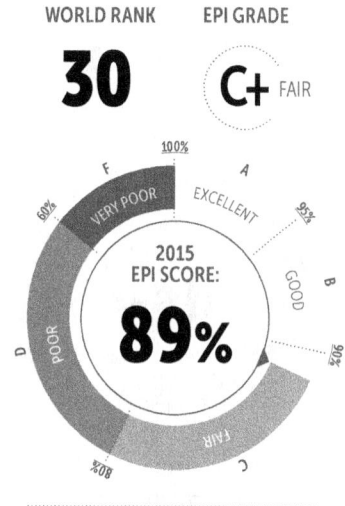

2015 EPI SCORE:

89%

▼ **EPI COMPONENTS (2015)**

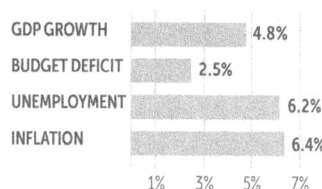

GDP GROWTH	4.8%
BUDGET DEFICIT	2.5%
UNEMPLOYMENT	6.2%
INFLATION	6.4%

1%   3%   5%   7%

▼ **ECONOMIC PERFORMANCE INDEX (2000–2020)**

—— INDONESIA —— UNITED STATES

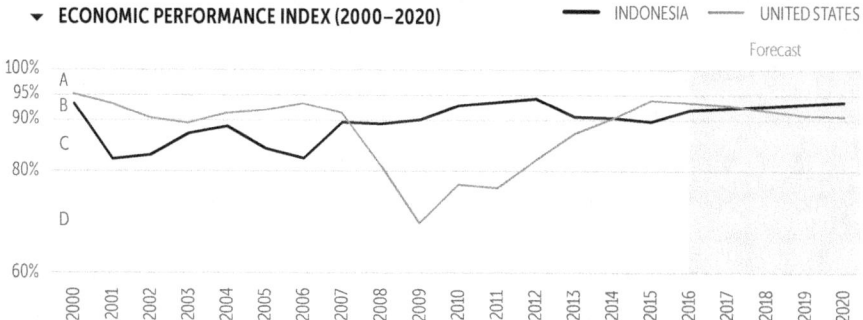

IRELAND

Life After Crisis

IRELAND HAS BEEN RECOVERING AFTER A MAJOR ECONOMIC AND BANKING CRISIS
IN 2009-2010. THE EPI GRADES IRELAND'S CURRENT ECONOMIC PERFORMANCE
AT A B LEVEL, WITH THE EPI SCORE PROJECTED TO BE 96.8% IN 2015.

WORLD RANK

12

EPI GRADE

A XLNT

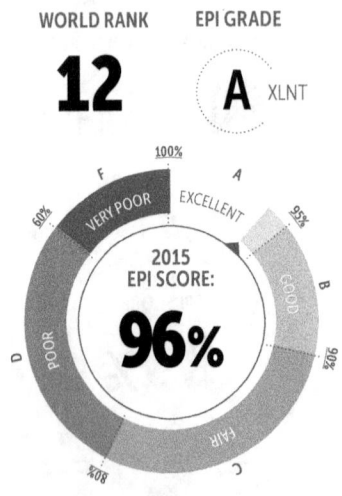

2015 EPI SCORE:

96%

A combination of GDP drop, increased unemployment, and a high bank recanalization cost that the government had to pay translated into its EPI score of 52%, or an F level, in 2010. A prolonged period of fiscal austerity since 2009 helped to reduce the fiscal deficit from a peak of 32.2% of GDP in 2010 to 0.4% in 2016. GDP growth is projected to be close to 5.0% in 2016, as conditions stabilize domestically and in the Eurozone. Inflation is still small and in line with the Eurozone average, but the unemployment level of 8.3% remains high.

The 5-Minute Economist projects Ireland's EPI score to remain roughly at the same level in the medium term, showing a solid B level economic performance. Economic growth is likely to decelerate after the initial effects of recovery fade out. Inflation is projected to start picking up from the currently low levels. The government is projected to run close to a balanced budget and the unemployment rate is likely to drop below 7% in the medium term.

▼ **EPI COMPONENTS (2015)**

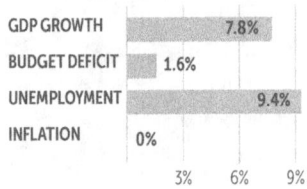

GDP GROWTH	7.8%
BUDGET DEFICIT	1.6%
UNEMPLOYMENT	9.4%
INFLATION	0%

▼ **ECONOMIC PERFORMANCE INDEX (2000–2020)** ———— IRELAND ———— UNITED STATES

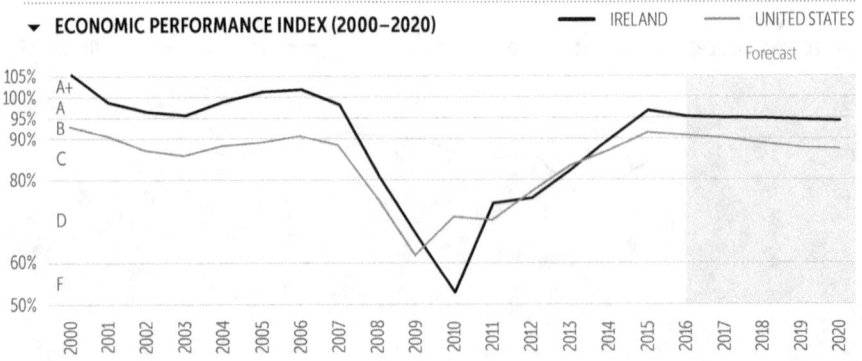

ISRAEL

Stable Growth

ISRAEL'S ECONOMY IS PERFORMING WELL AND THE EPI GRADES ITS CURRENT ECONOMIC PERFORMANCE AT A SOLID B LEVEL, WITH THE EPI SCORE PROJECTED TO BE 93.6% IN 2016.

GDP growth is expected to stay around 2.8% in 2016, as the result of strong private consumption growth, driven by rapid employment growth and near-zero interest rates. Inflation was slightly negative in 2015, driven by lower commodity prices, a stronger shekel, and tax cuts as well as structural factors such as higher competition in local markets that pushed prices down in many sectors. Unemployment remains stable at around 5.3% and the government is keeping the budget deficit below 4% of GDP.

The 5-Minute Economist projects Israel's EPI score to remain roughly at the same level in the medium term, showing a solid B-level economic performance.

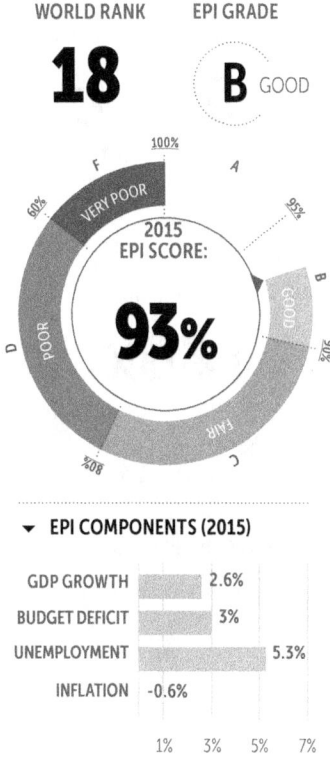

WORLD RANK **18**

EPI GRADE **B** GOOD

2015 EPI SCORE: **93%**

▼ EPI COMPONENTS (2015)

GDP GROWTH	2.6%
BUDGET DEFICIT	3%
UNEMPLOYMENT	5.3%
INFLATION	-0.6%

1%   3%   5%   7%

▼ ECONOMIC PERFORMANCE INDEX (2000–2020)   —— ISRAEL   —— UNITED STATES

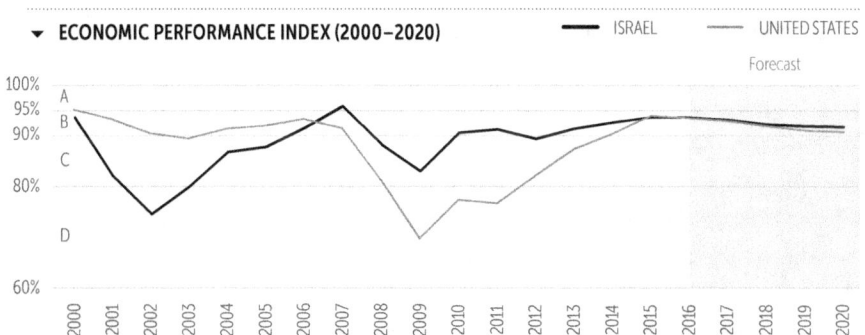

ITALY

Trying To Get Out Of Stagnation

ITALY'S ECONOMY IS EMERGING SLOWLY FROM A HURTING RECESSION WHILE THE ECB'S QUANTITATIVE EASING AND RECENT REFORM EFFORTS PUSHED MARKET CONFIDENCE INDICATORS TO A REBOUND. THE EPI GRADES ITALY'S CURRENT ECONOMIC PERFORMANCE AT A C LEVEL, WITH THE EPI SCORE PROJECTED TO BE 86.1% IN 2016.

WORLD RANK

35

EPI GRADE

C FAIR

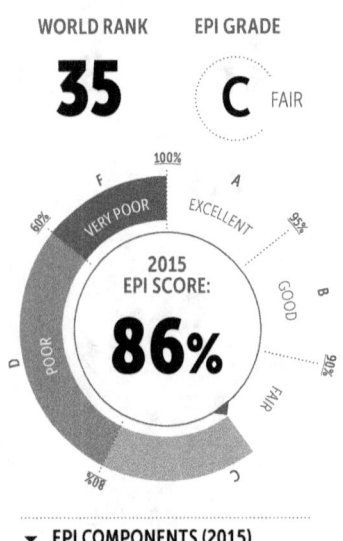

2015 EPI SCORE:

86%

Unemployment of 11.9% remains a concern and has been declining only very gradually in the past few years. Incomplete implementation of previous reforms, together with depressed demand and weakened balance sheets, have been dragging down growth. Real activity and investment are still far from their pre-crisis levels, and medium-term growth prospects remain lackluster. After almost four years of stagnation, GDP growth is projected to rise to 1% in 2016, supported by a highly accommodative external environment, in particular sharply lower oil prices, a depreciated euro, and interest rates at historic lows. The initial rebound has been driven by household consumption and exports are set to pick up as well, however, investment has not yet responded and unemployment remains stubbornly high above 10%.

The budget deficit is projected to be below 3% in 2016 and has been on a declining path in the past few years but the protracted recession has contributed to a steady rise in the debt-to-GDP ratio. This has limited the room for fiscal policy to cushion the effects of the downturn.

The 5-Minute Economist projects Italy's EPI score to improve only gradually in the medium term from almost 86.1%, or a C level, currently to 90.3%, or a B-level, by 2021, driven by some GDP growth acceleration and a lower unemployment rate, despite a gradual pick-up in inflation.

▼ EPI COMPONENTS (2015)

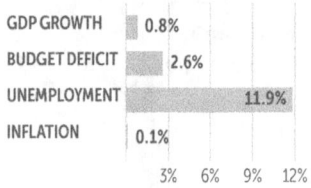

GDP GROWTH	0.8%
BUDGET DEFICIT	2.6%
UNEMPLOYMENT	11.9%
INFLATION	0.1%

3% 6% 9% 12%

▼ ECONOMIC PERFORMANCE INDEX (2000–2020) ——— ITALY ——— UNITED STATES

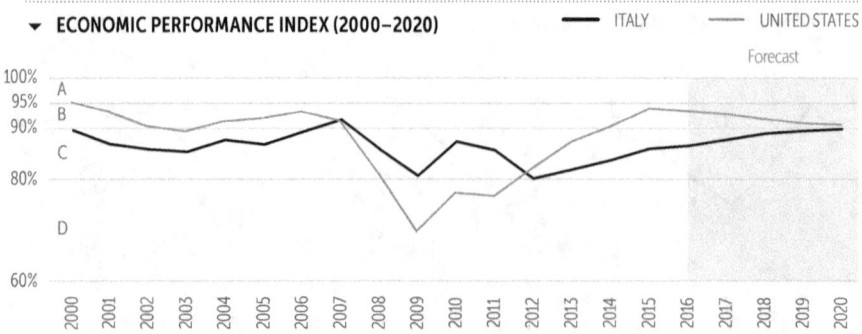

Forecast

JAPAN

End Secular Stagnation

JAPAN'S MODEST RECOVERY IS UNDERWAY, WITH THE EPI SCORE HAVING IMPROVED FROM 84.9% IN 2011 TO A PROJECTED 92.2%, OR A B LEVEL, IN 2016. EXPORTS HAVE STARTED TO RECOVER AND CONSUMPTION IS REGAINING ITS FOOTING, WITH THE LABOR MARKET SLOWLY IMPROVING, LEADING TO A MODERATE BUT HISTORICALLY IMPORTANT ACCELERATION IN WAGE GROWTH.

The equity market has been boosted by higher corporate profits, portfolio rebalancing and stock buybacks while the financial system's soundness has broadly improved. GDP growth is projected to accelerate to 0.5% in 2016, but long-term prospects still remain limited with growth unlikely to be above 1% per annum.

Lack of inflation combined with low GDP growth has always been an issue in Japan, as it was creating a circular stagnation in the economy – the economy could not grow either in real or in nominal terms. Still, inflation is expected to increase gradually, following the lagged effect of the recent episode of the yen weakening, combined with the Bank of Japan's (BoJ's) accommodative monetary policy. As a result, inflation is projected to rise gradually at about 1.2% per year by 2021.

The 5-Minute Economist projects Japan's EPI score to improve only gradually in the medium term from its current B level to 92.8%, still a B level, by 2021, mainly driven by a decrease in its budget deficit, while GDP growth and the unemployment rate are unlikely to change much, despite a gradual pick-up in inflation.

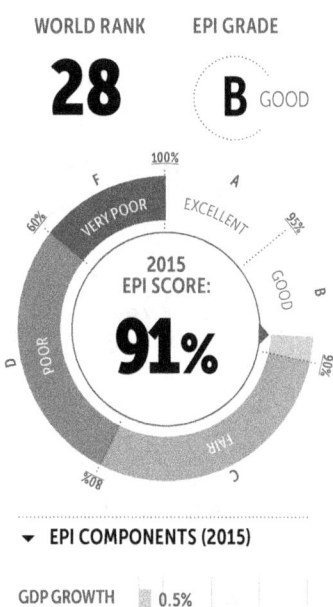

WORLD RANK 28

EPI GRADE B GOOD

2015 EPI SCORE: **91%**

▼ EPI COMPONENTS (2015)

GDP GROWTH	0.5%
BUDGET DEFICIT	5.2%
UNEMPLOYMENT	3.4%
INFLATION	0.8%

1%   3%   5%   7%

▼ ECONOMIC PERFORMANCE INDEX (2000–2020) — JAPAN — UNITED STATES

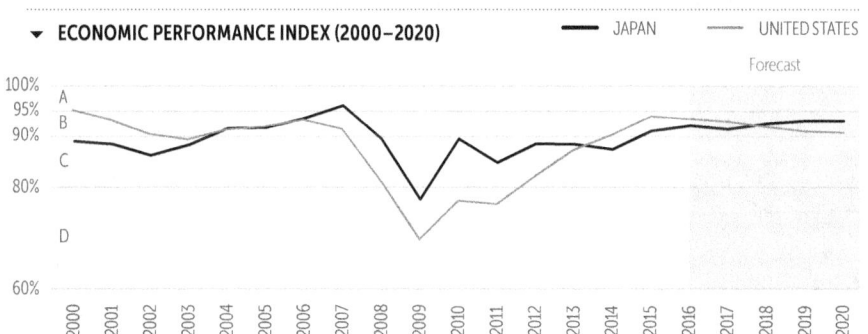

SOUTH KOREA

Seems Good But Only On Paper

THE KOREAN ECONOMY HAS BEEN ON A ROBUST GROWTH PATH, WITH THE EPI SHOWING AN A+/A ECONOMIC PERFORMANCE IN THE PAST FEW YEARS AND IS PROJECTED TO BE 98.2%, OR AN A LEVEL, IN 2016.

WORLD RANK

6

EPI GRADE

A XLNT

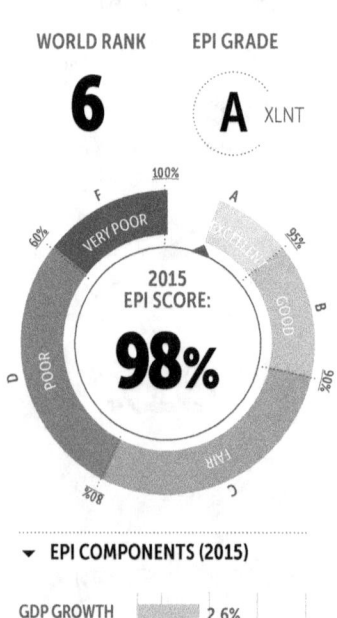

2015 EPI SCORE:

98%

GDP growth is projected to be 2.7% in 2016 with the unemployment rate staying below 4%. In order to boost economic growth, the government has adopted an expansionary fiscal stance and the budget is projected to turn into a small deficit in 2015-2016, after more than a decade of government surpluses.

As the government fails to engineer a structural shift away from the export-led growth model, the fate of the economy will become more tied to that of China's slowdown. It is more clear that President Park Geun-Hye is unlikely to be able to fulfil many of her campaign goals related to an increase in welfare-related spending and shifting the economy to a new model, driven by innovation and creativity rather than export-oriented manufacturing. Moreover, curbing the influence of the country's large family-run conglomerates, known as chaebol, and encouraging more competition in the economy has not been happening. Furthermore, the Sewol ferry disaster in April 2014 and then the outbreak of the Middle East respiratory syndrome (MERS) in June 2015 created additional challenges and complicated the government's agenda.

The 5-Minute Economist projects Korea's EPI score to stay around 99.6%, or an A level, until 2021, supported by relatively high GDP growth and budget surpluses.

▼ EPI COMPONENTS (2015)

GDP GROWTH	2.6%
BUDGET DEFICIT	0.2%
UNEMPLOYMENT	3.6%
INFLATION	0.7%

1%   3%   5%   7%

▼ ECONOMIC PERFORMANCE INDEX (2000–2020)

──── SOUTH KOREA   ──── UNITED STATES

Forecast

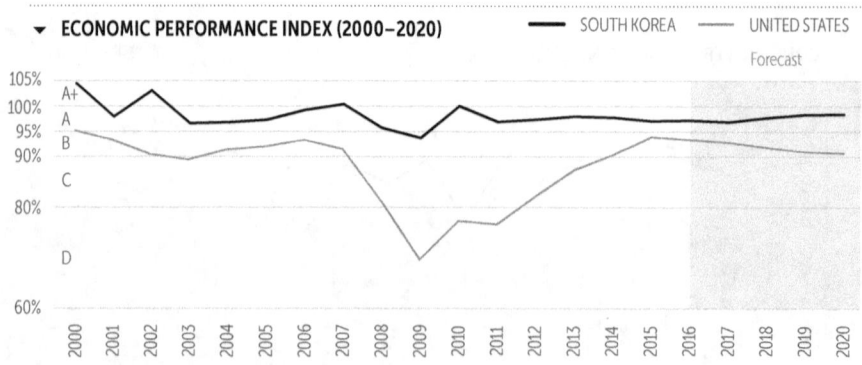

LUXEMBOURG

Small Economy, Big Ambitions

LUXEMBOURG'S ECONOMIC PERFORMANCE HAS BEEN RELATIVELY STRONG, WITH THE EPI SCORE PROJECTED TO BE 97.5% IN 2016, OR AN A LEVEL.

GDP growth is projected to be 3.5%, supported by consumer and firm sentiment. An improving labor market, low inflation and rising housing prices are also signals of improvement. The external outlook has weakened, as major trading markets adjust to the ongoing slowdown across emerging markets, but export of financial services will remain a key driver of growth.

The near-term outlook remains broadly positive, and *The 5-Minute Economist* projects Luxembourg's EPI score to stay around 95%, or an A- level, until 2021.

WORLD RANK

EPI GRADE

5

A XLNT

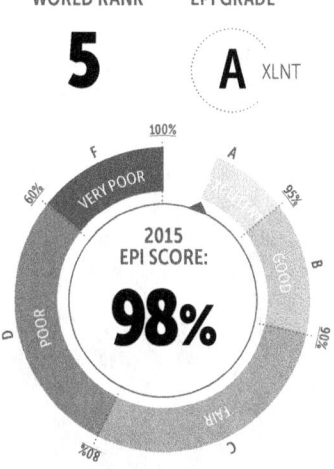

2015
EPI SCORE:

98%

▾ **EPI COMPONENTS (2015)**

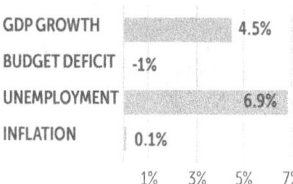

GDP GROWTH	4.5%
BUDGET DEFICIT	-1%
UNEMPLOYMENT	6.9%
INFLATION	0.1%

1% 3% 5% 7%

▾ **ECONOMIC PERFORMANCE INDEX (2000–2020)** — LUXEMBOURG — UNITED STATES

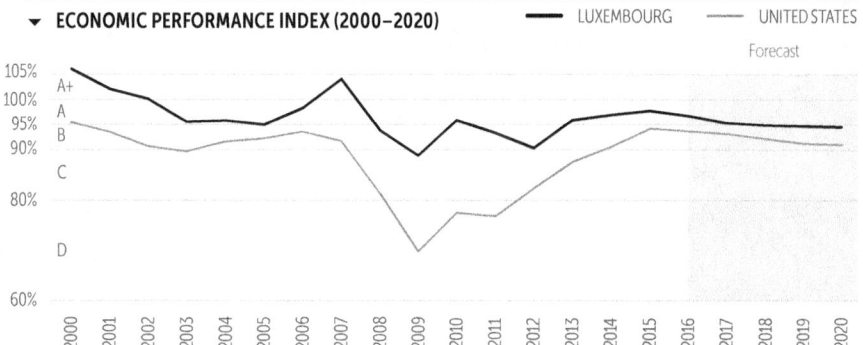

MALTA

Small, Open, And Exposed To Shocks

MALTA'S ECONOMIC PERFORMANCE HAS BEEN EXCELLENT, WITH THE EPI SCORE 97.4%, OR AN A LEVEL, IN 2015.

WORLD RANK

9

EPI GRADE

A XLNT

The Maltese economy is characterized by a high degree of openness to trade and financial flows and has enjoyed one of the fastest rates of GDP growth within the Eurozone. Growth is mainly based on internal factors and Malta's external sector performance has been largely unimpressive, reflecting the Eurozone weakness and a steady erosion of the country's export competitiveness.

The 5-Minute Economist projects Malta's EPI score to stay slightly below 95%, or a B+ level, until 2021.

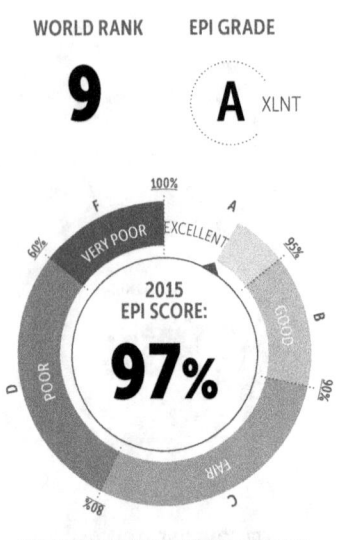

2015 EPI SCORE:

97%

▼ **EPI COMPONENTS (2015)**

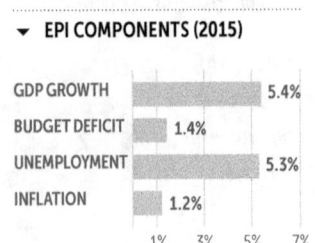

GDP GROWTH	5.4%
BUDGET DEFICIT	1.4%
UNEMPLOYMENT	5.3%
INFLATION	1.2%

▼ **ECONOMIC PERFORMANCE INDEX (2000–2020)**   —— MALTA   —— UNITED STATES

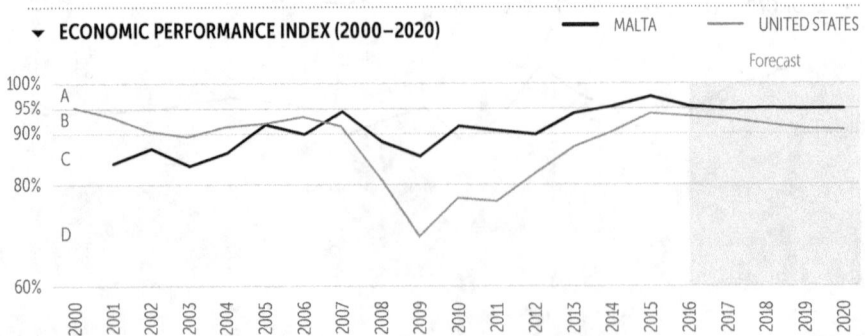

MEXICO

Headwind From Oil vs. Tailwinds From The US

MEXICO'S ECONOMIC PERFORMANCE HAS BEEN GOOD WITH THE EPI SCORE PROJECTED TO BE 92.0%, OR A B LEVEL, IN 2016. AFTER THE DROP IN OIL PRICES, MEXICO'S PRIMARY EXPORT, THE GOVERNMENT FACES THE SHORT-TERM CHALLENGE OF BOOSTING ECONOMIC GROWTH.

GDP growth has remained only slightly above 2% in 2015 and is projected to be 2.4% in 2016. At the same time, the recent improvements in the US growth perspectives are positive for Mexico, as this would boost Mexico's exports to its top trading partner. *The 5-Minute Economist* projects Mexico's EPI score to improve gradually to about 93.9%, or a B level, by 2021.

The government's fiscal outlook will be complicated by low oil prices, as around 10% of total government revenue comes from crude oil exports alone. The latest drop in oil prices has been taking a toll on the economy, as the peso lost a substantial share of its value and the budget deficit is likely to increase. The government will adjust fiscal policy in the light of weaker oil prices, but overall spending will remain high, causing the budget deficit to stay close to 3.5% in 2016.

Mexico's exports have been growing and it participates in most of the world's largest free-trade agreements. Still, the US accounts for over three-quarters of all Mexican exports and half of its imports. The upcoming trade expansion could be made through the Trans-Pacific Partnership and the Alianza del Pacífico.

Key reforms have been delayed, and the latest crisis of confidence related to corruption scandals and the investigation into the September 2014 Ayotzinapa student kidnappings has not only affected the government, but the political establishment as a whole, as all the main parties have been criticized for doing little to address rampant corruption and impunity.

WORLD RANK | EPI GRADE

26 | **B** GOOD

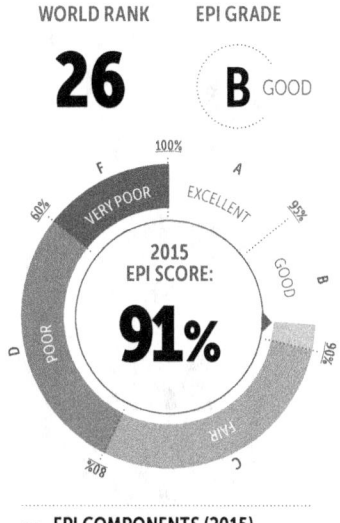

2015
EPI SCORE:

91%

▼ **EPI COMPONENTS (2015)**

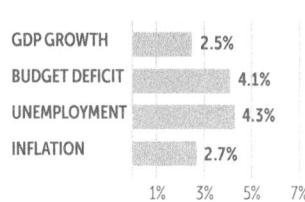

GDP GROWTH — 2.5%
BUDGET DEFICIT — 4.1%
UNEMPLOYMENT — 4.3%
INFLATION — 2.7%

1%   3%   5%   7%

▼ **ECONOMIC PERFORMANCE INDEX (2000–2020)**   ■— MEXICO   —— UNITED STATES

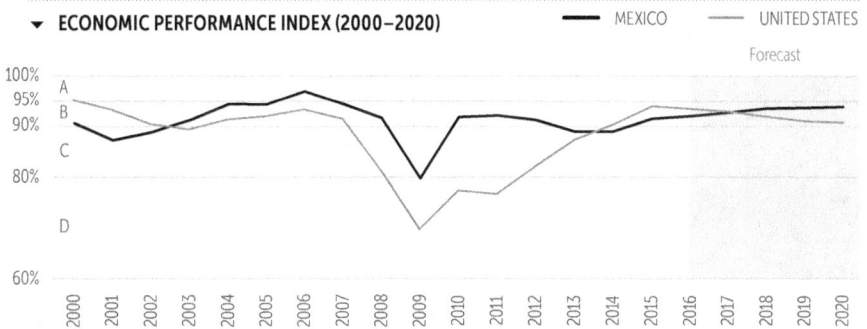

NETHERLANDS

In The Heart Of The Eurozone

THE NETHERLANDS' ECONOMIC PERFORMANCE HAS BEEN GOOD, WITH THE EPI SCORE PROJECTED TO BE CLOSE TO 93.4%, OR A B LEVEL, IN 2016. ECONOMIC CONDITIONS HAVE IMPROVED STEADILY OVER THE PAST TWO YEARS, WITH DOMESTIC DEMAND STRENGTHENING AND EXPORTS IMPROVING.

WORLD RANK

20

EPI GRADE

B GOOD

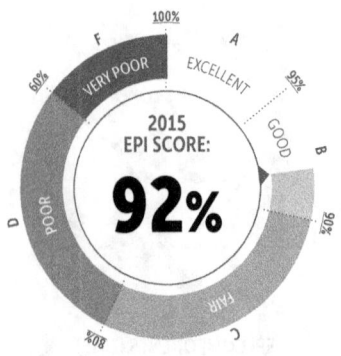

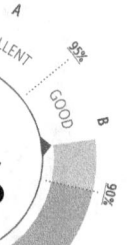

2015 EPI SCORE:

92%

Cheaper oil and a weaker euro have contributed to the improvement as well. Unemployment levels remain elevated, which is typical for European economies. *The 5-Minute Economist* projects the Netherlands' EPI score to improve only gradually to about 94.9% by 2021, but still stay at a B level.

On June 23, 2016, the British public decided to vote to "leave" the European Union. Renegotiation of trade and immigration agreements with the EU will determine the effects of separation. The negative effects of Brexit are likely to start materializing soon.

The general government deficit was 1.9% of GDP in 2015 and is projected to be 1.7% in 2016. The government's fiscal consolidation plans are aimed at keeping the deficit within 3% of GDP, in line with the EU's demands. Inflation is projected to be 0.3% in 2016, in line with a low inflationary environment in the Eurozone overall.

▾ **EPI COMPONENTS (2015)**

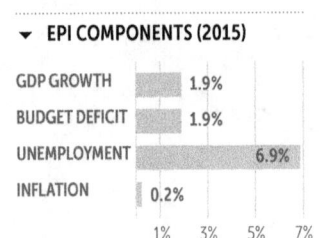

GDP GROWTH	1.9%
BUDGET DEFICIT	1.9%
UNEMPLOYMENT	6.9%
INFLATION	0.2%

1% 3% 5% 7%

▾ **ECONOMIC PERFORMANCE INDEX (2000–2020)**   NETHERLANDS   UNITED STATES

Forecast

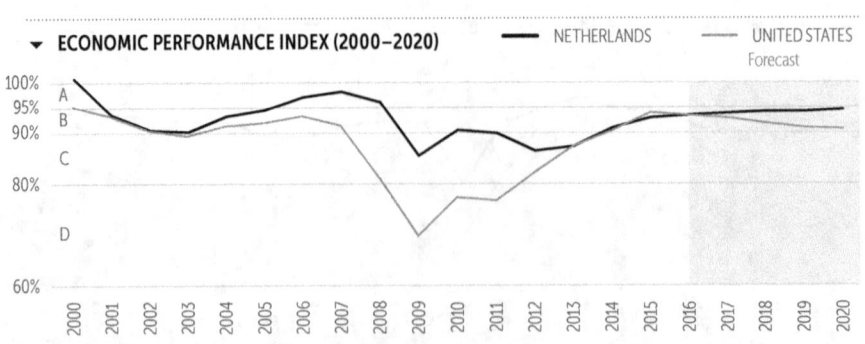

NEW ZEALAND
Too Far Or Too Close?

NEW ZEALAND'S ECONOMIC PERFORMANCE HAS BEEN GOOD, WITH THE EPI SCORE PROJECTED TO BE CLOSE TO 94.4%, OR A B+ LEVEL, IN 2016. ECONOMIC GROWTH HAS CHANGED ONLY SLIGHTLY FROM 3.0% IN 2014 TO 3.4% IN 2015 AND IS PROJECTED TO BE 2.0% IN 2016, MAINLY BECAUSE OF LOWER RESIDENTIAL INVESTMENTS.

The current unemployment level of 5.8% is relatively low and inflation is close to 0.3%, driven by low commodity prices. New Zealand has signed a series of trade agreements with Asian countries in the past decade as well as the Trans-Pacific Partnership (TPP) in 2015. Its major trade links with Australia and China make the economy dependent on Chinese economic growth and leaves it exposed to drops in commodity prices via Australia, which is a large iron ore exporter.

The 5-Minute Economist projects New Zealand's economic performance to improve to A- level in the next few years, driven by better deficits and GDP growth.

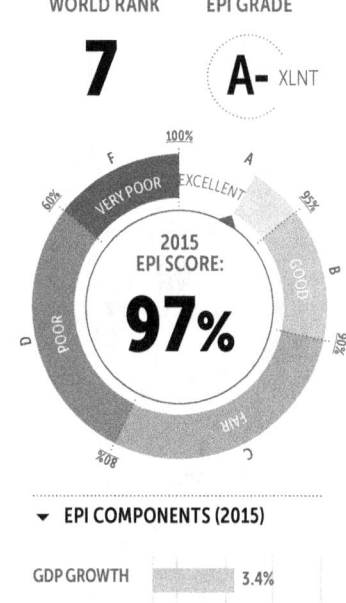

WORLD RANK

7

EPI GRADE

A- XLNT

2015 EPI SCORE:

97%

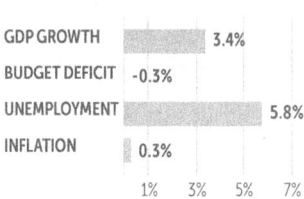

▼ EPI COMPONENTS (2015)

GDP GROWTH — 3.4%
BUDGET DEFICIT — -0.3%
UNEMPLOYMENT — 5.8%
INFLATION — 0.3%

1%   3%   5%   7%

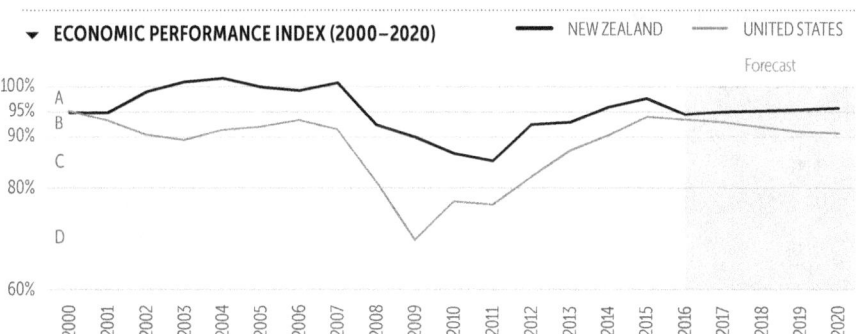

▼ ECONOMIC PERFORMANCE INDEX (2000–2020)   —— NEW ZEALAND   —— UNITED STATES

Forecast

NORWAY

Wealth From Oil Is Depleting

NORWAY'S ECONOMIC PERFORMANCE HAS BEEN OUTSTANDING, WITH THE EPI SCORE PROJECTED TO BE 99% IN 2016, A DROP FROM 105.1% TWO YEARS BEFORE, MAINLY BECAUSE OF LOWER OIL PRICES.

WORLD RANK

2

EPI GRADE

A+ SUPERIOR

2015 EPI SCORE:

100%

Norway is one of the richest nations in the world with a GDP per capita of more than $60K (by PPP). Still, most of the country's wealth is coming from exports of natural resources, as the oil and gas sector constitutes around 22% of Norwegian GDP and 67% of Norwegian exports. For many years Norway's government has been running large fiscal surpluses and has built up one of the largest national wealth funds in the world, with more than $800bn in assets.

The drop in oil prices hit the economy hard, with the Norwegian krone's value falling from about 6 krones per dollar in 2014 to above 8.5 krones per dollar in 2016. Economic activity remains weak, with GDP growth around 1.6% in 2015 and a projected 1% in 2016. Because of large government revenues coming from oil and gas exports, the government has been running double-digit fiscal surpluses. Lower oil prices have reduced government revenues and the government decided to continue a fiscal stimulus program. This combination reduced government budget surplus from about 13.5% of GDP in 2012 to about 5.4% in 2015 and 2016, the lowest level in the past decade.

The 5-Minute Economist projects Norway's economic performance to remain outstanding, with the EPI score remaining above 99-100% in the next few years, mainly driven by large fiscal surpluses of about 6% of GDP. Norway's inflation is likely to stay above 2%, still above most of its European peers, elevated mainly because of the currency devaluation that increased the prices of imported goods. Unemployment has increased slightly but is still relatively small, below 5%.

▼ **EPI COMPONENTS (2015)**

GDP GROWTH	1.6%
BUDGET DEFICIT	-5.4%
UNEMPLOYMENT	4.4%
INFLATION	2.2%

1%   3%   5%   7%

▼ **ECONOMIC PERFORMANCE INDEX (2000–2020)**   ▬▬ NORWAY   ── UNITED STATES

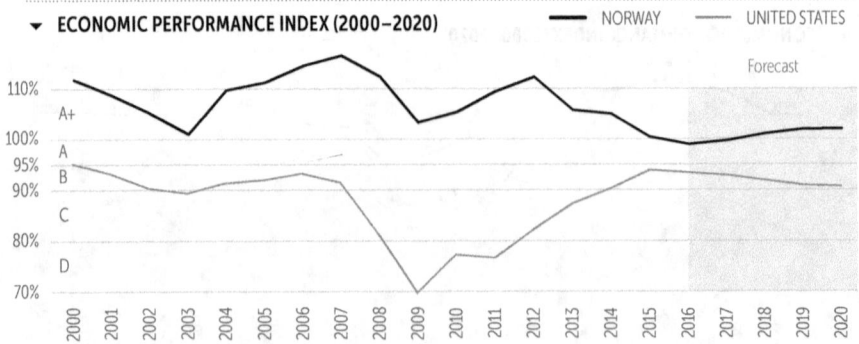

Forecast

110%
A+
100%
A
95%
B
90%
C
80%
D
70%

2000 2001 2002 2003 2004 2005 2006 2007 2008 2009 2010 2011 2012 2013 2014 2015 2016 2017 2018 2019 2020

POLAND

Strong Growth In Europe

POLAND'S ECONOMIC PERFORMANCE HAS BEEN GOOD, WITH THE EPI SCORE PROJECTED TO BE 93.6%, OR A B LEVEL, IN 2016. ECONOMIC GROWTH OF ABOUT 3.6%, DRIVEN BY INTERNAL CONSUMPTION AND HIGHER EXPORTS, SHOWS SIGNS OF IMPROVEMENT IN THE POLISH ECONOMY RELATIVE TO ITS EUROPEAN UNION PEERS.

Lower oil prices materially decreased food and energy prices, as Poland is an energy importer, pushing inflation into negative territory and supporting economic growth overall. The unemployment level of 6.9% in 2016 remains high but is on a declining path.

The 5-Minute Economist projects Poland's economic performance to remain good, with the EPI score remaining above 90% in the next few years, supported by strong GDP growth of about 3.5%. Inflation is likely to start picking up, once the deflationary effects of lower energy prices fade out. The budget deficit is projected to stay below 3.1%, in line with European Union standards.

WORLD RANK	EPI GRADE
24	**B** GOOD

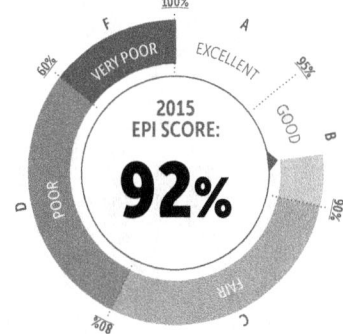

2015 EPI SCORE:

92%

▼ EPI COMPONENTS (2015)

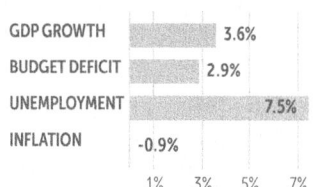

GDP GROWTH	3.6%
BUDGET DEFICIT	2.9%
UNEMPLOYMENT	7.5%
INFLATION	-0.9%

1%   3%   5%   7%

▼ ECONOMIC PERFORMANCE INDEX (2000–2020)   POLAND   UNITED STATES

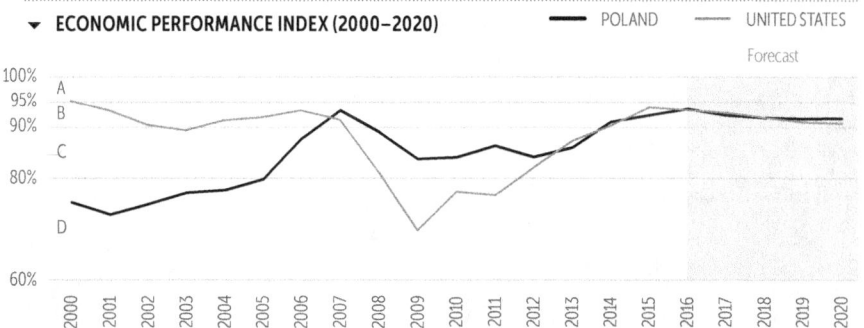

PORTUGAL

Successful Recovery From The Crisis

PORTUGAL'S ECONOMIC PERFORMANCE HAS BEEN IMPROVING IN THE PAST FEW YEARS, WITH THE EPI SCORE PROJECTED TO BE AROUND 84.1%, OR A C LEVEL, IN 2015, A LARGE IMPROVEMENT FROM THE CRISIS LEVEL OF 70% JUST A FEW YEARS AGO.

WORLD RANK

37

EPI GRADE

C FAIR

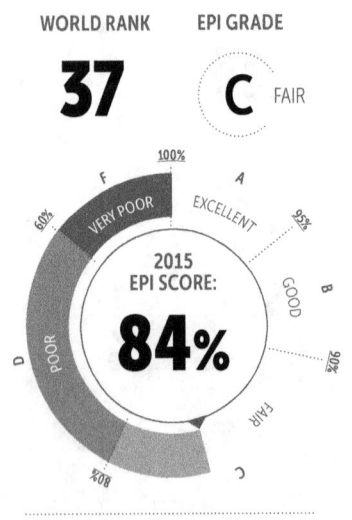

2015 EPI SCORE: **84%**

GDP growth turned positive in 2014 after a few years of recession and is projected to accelerate to 1.4% in 2016. Portugal successfully graduated from the European Union/International Monetary Fund bail-out program in mid-2014 and has been repaying funds to its international creditors ahead of schedule. Sovereign debt reached its peak level of 130% of GDP in 2014 and is projected to start falling in 2016, once the government repays its creditors.

The 5-Minute Economist projects Portugal's economic performance to continue improving gradually but to still remain poor, with the EPI score reaching 87.3% by 2021, supported by a falling unemployment rate and a modest GDP growth of about 1.2%. Portugal only partially benefited from lower oil prices in 2015, with food prices not falling as much as in other EU countries. Inflation is likely to start picking up, once the deflationary effects of lower energy prices fade out. The budget deficit is projected to stay below 3%, in line with European Union norms.

▼ EPI COMPONENTS (2015)

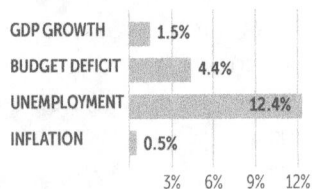

GDP GROWTH	1.5%
BUDGET DEFICIT	4.4%
UNEMPLOYMENT	12.4%
INFLATION	0.5%

3% 6% 9% 12%

▼ ECONOMIC PERFORMANCE INDEX (2000–2020)

—— PORTUGAL —— UNITED STATES

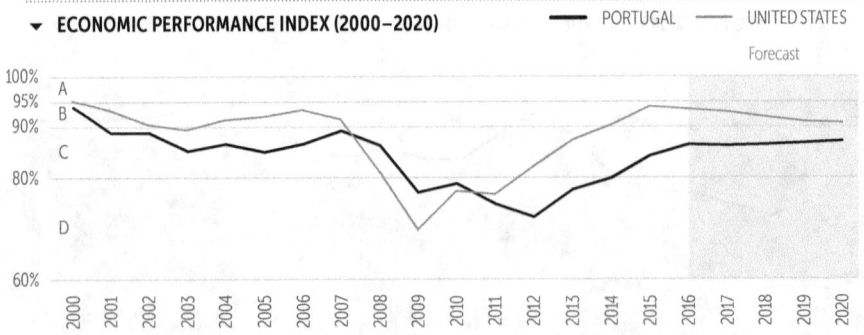

RUSSIA
Surviving The Crisis

RUSSIA'S ECONOMIC PERFORMANCE HAS BEEN VERY POOR AFTER THE DROP IN OIL PRICES IN 2015 THAT LED TO A DEEP RECESSION. THE EPI SCORE WAS CLOSE TO 71%, OR A D LEVEL, IN 2015, THE LOWEST LEVEL SINCE THE 2009 CRISIS, BUT IS PROJECTED TO IMPROVE TO 78.9%, OR A D+ LEVEL, MAINLY BECAUSE OF LOWER INFLATION.

For an economy with two thirds of exports and half of the government budget revenues coming from oil and gas, the latest downturn in the global oil market means Russia's recession may stretch into next year for the longest slump in two decades. The western sanctions on Russia related to the crisis in Ukraine have also played a role in amplifying the negative effects of lower oil prices on the Russian economy by limiting the ability of Russian companies to borrow money on the western financial markets.

GDP fell by about 3.7% in 2015, driven by a large drop in exports in dollar terms and a deep recession in the industrial sector, but is projected to fall by 1.8% in 2016. The ruble lost almost half of its value after the Central Bank of Russia stopped selling its reserves on the market to protect the currency. A large ruble devaluation increased the prices of imported goods, pushing inflation to almost 16% in 2015, up from about 8% in 2014. The government has already cut budget outlays and dipped into one of its sovereign wealth funds, the Reserve Fund, to help cover the shortfall. The unemployment level increased only slightly to 6.5% in 2016, up from 5.6% in 2015, driven by the recession in the economy.

With oil prices at below $50 dollars per barrel, the Russian economy is likely to go through a painful adjustment in the next few years. *The 5-Minute Economist* projects Russia's EPI score to improve in the medium term from a D level currently to a B by 2021, mainly driven GDP recovery after the recession and slowdown in inflation, if the ruble and oil prices stabilize.

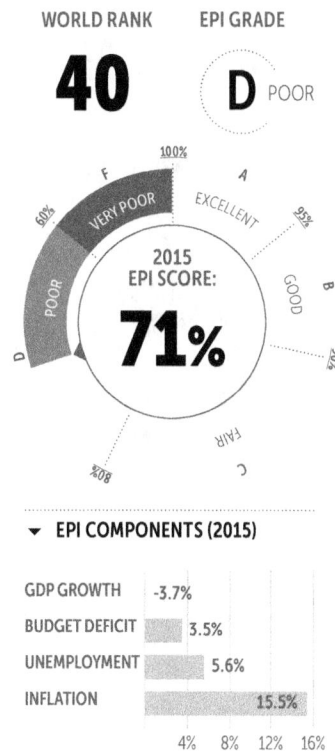

WORLD RANK — EPI GRADE

40   **D** POOR

2015
EPI SCORE:

71%

▼ **EPI COMPONENTS (2015)**

GDP GROWTH	-3.7%
BUDGET DEFICIT	3.5%
UNEMPLOYMENT	5.6%
INFLATION	15.5%

4%   8%   12%   16%

▼ **ECONOMIC PERFORMANCE INDEX (2000–2020)**   —— RUSSIA   —— UNITED STATES

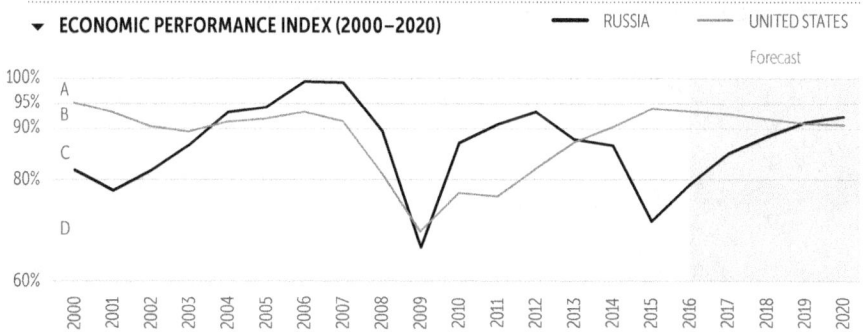

SINGAPORE

Outstanding Performance

SINGAPORE'S ECONOMIC PERFORMANCE HAS BEEN OUTSTANDING,
WITH THE EPI SCORE PROJECTED TO BE 101.5% IN 2016.

WORLD RANK

1

EPI GRADE

A+ SUPERIOR

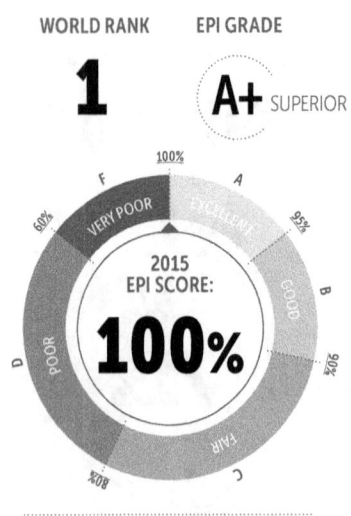

2015
EPI SCORE:
100%

Singapore has an extremely low unemployment rate of only about 2% and the city-state has been persistently running large government surpluses. Inflation is projected to be close to 0.2% in 2016, mainly reflecting lower oil prices. GDP growth is likely to be 1.8% in 2016, despite the fact that Singapore's economy is heavily dependent on trade flows, and that weaker growth prospects in China, Singapore's main trading partner, will have negative implications for trade. Still, economic growth is likely to be supported by government spending, which will remain strong, as the city-state continues to invest in its infrastructure.

Singapore has been running extremely large current account surpluses of about 25% of GDP, with projected exports of about $375bn and imports of $285bn in 2015. Lower global oil prices have acted as a double-edged sword in 2015, as Singapore's energy imports fell dramatically but exports decreased as well, as the city-state is one of the world's largest petroleum refining centers.

The 5-Minute Economist projects Singapore's EPI score to remain at an A+ level in the next few years.

▾ **EPI COMPONENTS (2015)**

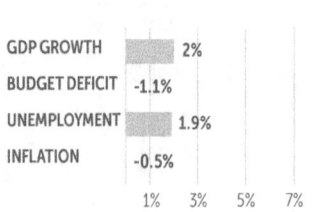

GDP GROWTH — 2%
BUDGET DEFICIT — -1.1%
UNEMPLOYMENT — 1.9%
INFLATION — -0.5%

1%   3%   5%   7%

▾ **ECONOMIC PERFORMANCE INDEX (2000–2020)**   —— SINGAPORE   —— UNITED STATES

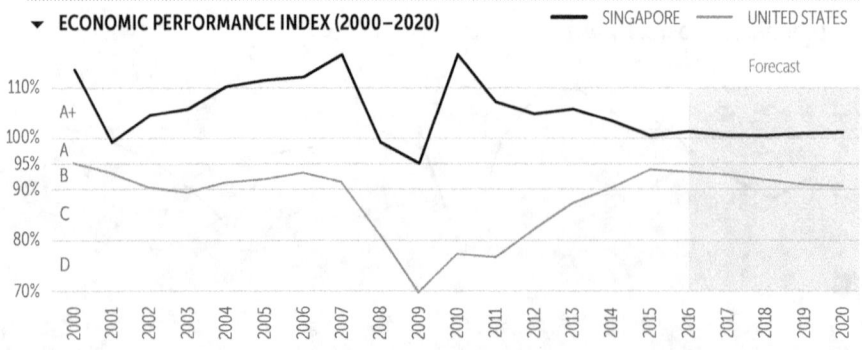

Forecast

SLOVAK REPUBLIC

Growth Model Change

THE SLOVAK REPUBLIC'S ECONOMIC PERFORMANCE HAS BEEN HELD BACK BY SLUGGISH DEMAND IN THE EUROZONE AND THE EFFECTS OF THE EU-RUSSIA SANCTIONS. IN 2016, THE EPI PROJECTS THE SLOVAK REPUBLIC TO HAVE A SCORE OF 90.6%, OR A SOLID B- GRADE.

Since the 2009 crisis, when EPI was at a D level, the economic model of the country has shifted from export-oriented (primarily to Germany) to more domestic demand-driven. In 2016, Slovakia's projected GDP growth of 3.3% is a sign of solid economic recovery. This is due, in part, to a particularly strong domestic demand and an increase in government spending.

The budget ballooned to 7.9% of GDP in the 2009 recession but is projected to narrow to 3.3% in 2016. The government follows EU budget rules and will keep the deficit below the 3% limit.

The main economic drag on the Slovak Republic's EPI score is unemployment. It is expected to fall slightly to 10.4% in 2016 and down to 9.0% by 2021. Still, this unemployment level is below the country's historic averages of about 15%.

Inflation is small and in line with other Eurozone economies. This reflects the effects of lower commodity prices and a slow recovery in the rest of the Eurozone.

By 2021, *The 5-Minute Economist* projects the Slovak Republic's EPI score to remain slightly above the current levels, around 90.6%, or a B- level. Economic growth will continue to be positive but is unlikely to accelerate further. Inflation will likely start picking up once lower commodity price effects fade out. This negative effect would be offset by slightly lower unemployment levels and lower budget deficits.

WORLD RANK **32**

EPI GRADE **C+** FAIR

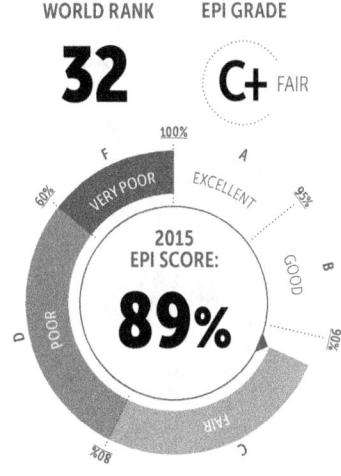

2015 EPI SCORE: **89%**

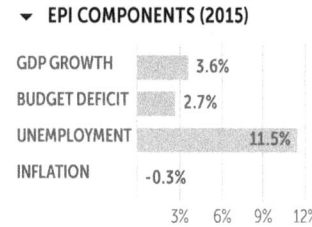

▼ **EPI COMPONENTS (2015)**

GDP GROWTH 3.6%
BUDGET DEFICIT 2.7%
UNEMPLOYMENT 11.5%
INFLATION -0.3%

3%   6%   9%   12%

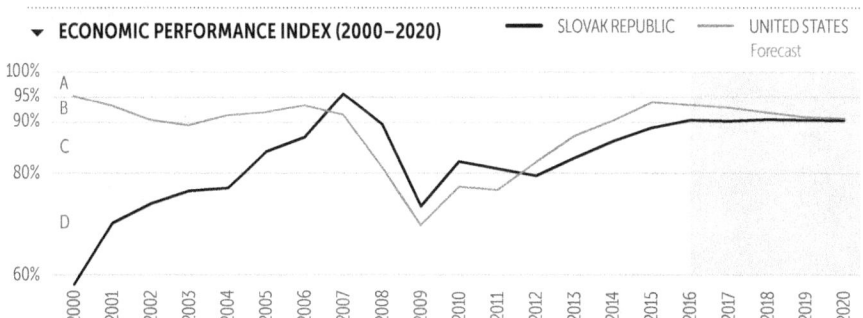

▼ **ECONOMIC PERFORMANCE INDEX (2000–2020)** — SLOVAK REPUBLIC — UNITED STATES Forecast

SLOVENIA

Reform Momentum

SLOVENIA'S ECONOMY HAS BEEN EMERGING SLOWLY FROM A RECESSION AND A BANKING CRISIS, WHILE THE ECB'S QUANTITATIVE EASING AND RECENT REFORMS PUSHED THE ECONOMY INTO A REBOUND. THE EPI GRADES SLOVENIA'S CURRENT ECONOMIC PERFORMANCE AT A C+ LEVEL, WITH THE EPI SCORE PROJECTED TO BE CLOSE TO 91.2% IN 2016.

WORLD RANK

29

EPI GRADE

C+ FAIR

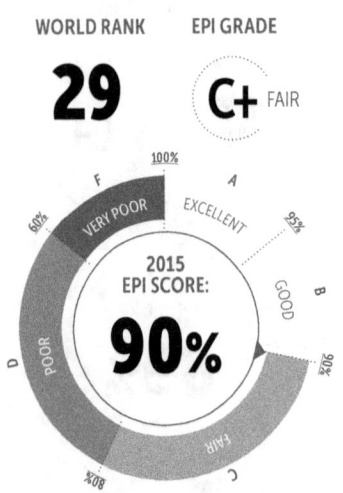

2015 EPI SCORE: **90%**

Slovenia has been recovering after a banking crisis in 2013, when the government had to recapitalize large government banks, which pushed the government's budget deficit to almost 14% of GDP. Being a member of the Eurozone and having a population of only two million people, Slovenia has been benefiting from improved export performance to the other Eurozone countries.

On the back of higher exports and a stabilizing financial system that is helping the internal demand to recover, GDP growth has been recovering and reached 2.9% in 2015 and is projected to be 1.9% in 2016.

The 5-Minute Economist projects Slovenia's EPI score to stay around 90%, or a B-/C level, until 2021, as unemployment is likely to stay relatively high, along with budget deficits.

▼ **EPI COMPONENTS (2015)**

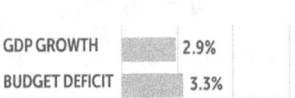

GDP GROWTH — 2.9%
BUDGET DEFICIT — 3.3%
UNEMPLOYMENT — 9.1%
INFLATION — -0.5%

3%   6%   9%

▼ **ECONOMIC PERFORMANCE INDEX (2000–2020)**　　— SLOVENIA　— UNITED STATES

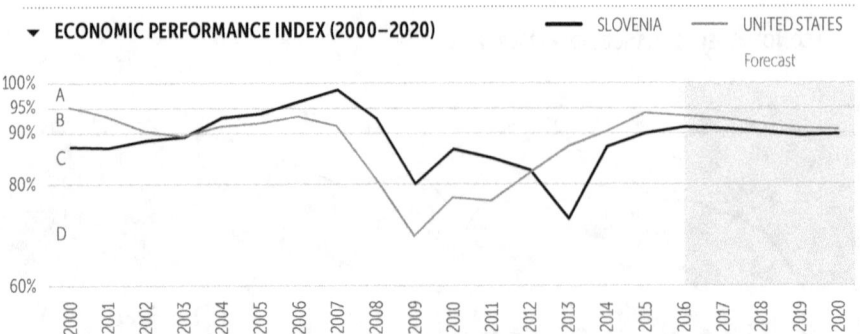

Forecast

SPAIN

Fighting Unemployment

SPAIN'S ECONOMY HAS BEEN EMERGING SLOWLY FROM A RECESSION, WHILE THE ECB'S QUANTITATIVE EASING AND RECENT REFORM EFFORTS IMPROVED MARKET CONFIDENCE. THE EPI GRADES SPAIN'S CURRENT ECONOMIC PERFORMANCE AT A D+ LEVEL, WITH THE EPI SCORE PROJECTED TO BE 79.2% IN 2016.

Spain's recovery has gathered speed, but an unemployment rate of more than 20% remains the key issue, as it remains stubborn and has only been declining very gradually in the past few years. Job creation has picked up, but more than 5 million people remain unemployed and new jobs still rely heavily on temporary and part-time contracts. Growth has picked up and is expected to be at 2.6% in 2016, well above the euro area average. Strong policy implementation has supported the return of confidence, and the private sector has started borrowing again after long-lasting deleveraging.

However, deep structural problems limit Spain's growth going forward, including the high structural unemployment and the lack of economies of scale. Public and private debt levels are still high and are likely to keep weighing on consumption and investment.

The 5-Minute Economist projects Spain's EPI score to gradually recover to only 83.2%, or a C level, by 2021, as unemployment is likely to remain very high.

WORLD RANK

39

EPI GRADE

D+ POOR

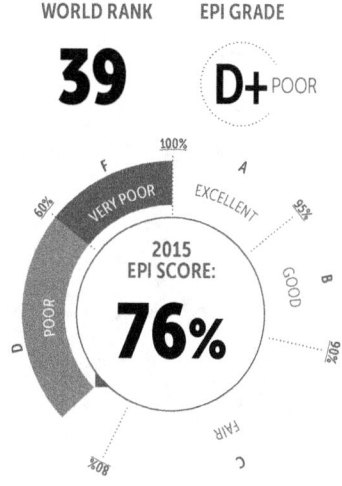

2015 EPI SCORE:

76%

▼ **EPI COMPONENTS (2015)**

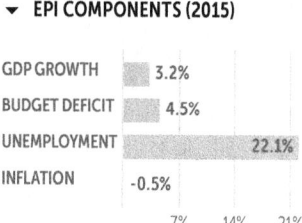

GDP GROWTH	3.2%
BUDGET DEFICIT	4.5%
UNEMPLOYMENT	22.1%
INFLATION	-0.5%

7%   14%   21%

▼ **ECONOMIC PERFORMANCE INDEX (2000–2020)** ——— SPAIN ——— UNITED STATES

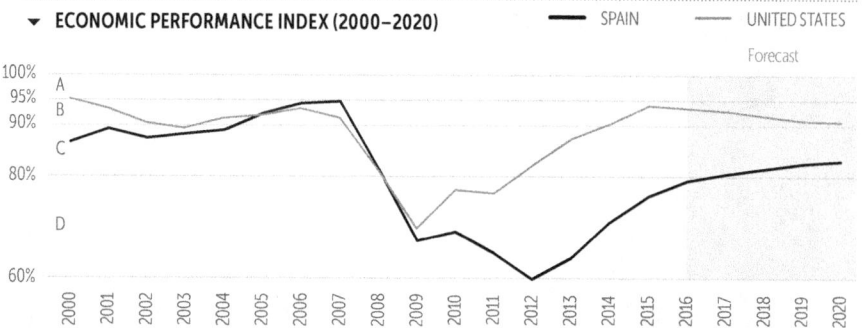

Forecast

SWEDEN

Nordic Recovery

THE EPI GRADES SWEDEN'S CURRENT ECONOMIC PERFORMANCE AT A B LEVEL, WITH THE EPI SCORE PROJECTED TO BE 94.9% IN 2016. STRUCTURAL PROBLEMS IN THE LABOR AND HOUSING MARKETS REMAIN THE MAJOR OBSTACLES TO FASTER ECONOMIC DEVELOPMENT.

WORLD RANK

14

EPI GRADE

A- XLNT

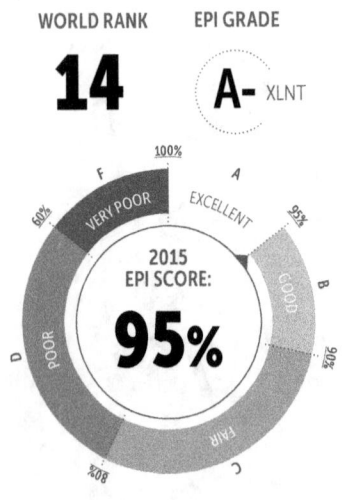

2015
EPI SCORE:

95%

Benefitting from supportive policies bolstering domestic demand, GDP growth of about 3.7% is expected to continue into 2016. Exports are also expected to pick up, but risks of an export decrease are related to trading partner demand, including the euro area, emerging markets, and Nordic neighbors. Inflation has picked up but remains below the 2% target. Fiscal policy is expected to be neutral over 2015-16, with the government budget deficit projected to be below 1%.

Structural problems in labor and housing markets are major road blocks to growth, while the low-skilled and foreign-born are a rising portion of the unemployed and the lack of affordable housing in the major cities also undermines labor mobility. Housing prices are rising fast from elevated levels, resulting in households taking on higher debt burdens and making the economy more vulnerable to shocks.

The 5-Minute Economist projects Sweden's EPI score to gradually recover to 93.1%, or a B level by 2021.

▼ **EPI COMPONENTS (2015)**

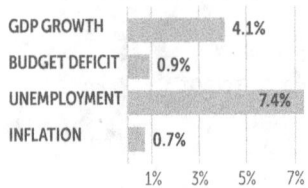

GDP GROWTH	4.1%
BUDGET DEFICIT	0.9%
UNEMPLOYMENT	7.4%
INFLATION	0.7%

▼ **ECONOMIC PERFORMANCE INDEX (2000–2020)**　　　━━ SWEDEN　　━━ UNITED STATES

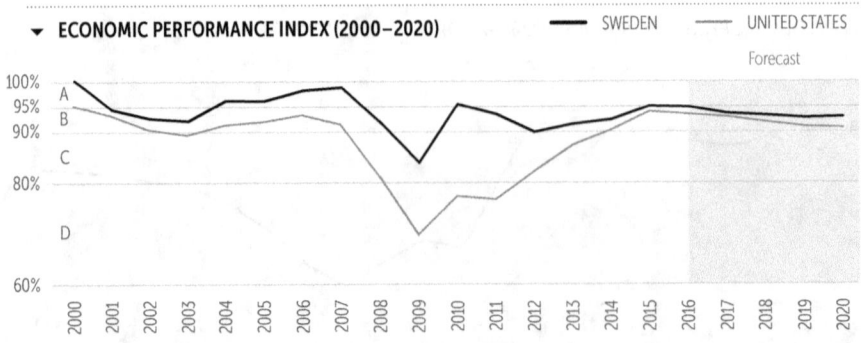

SWITZERLAND
Is Too Good Eventually Bad?

THE SWISS ECONOMY AND THE SWISS FRANC HAVE BEEN A SAFE HAVEN IN THE EUROZONE SINCE THE BEGINNING OF THE FINANCIAL CRISIS IN 2009. THE EPI GRADES SWITZERLAND'S ECONOMIC PERFORMANCE AT AN A LEVEL SINCE 2010, WITH THE EPI SCORE PROJECTED TO BE 96.9%, OR AN A LEVEL, IN 2016.

The inflation rate has been close to zero in the past few years, GDP growth has been small but positive, unemployment levels were around 3%, and the government has been running budget surpluses. Because of these strong economic fundamentals, the economy experienced large capital inflows and the Swiss National Bank (SNB) decided to fix the rate of the Swiss franc to the euro at 1.2 in 2011.

The Swiss franc appreciation has been the main shock to the economy. The SNB exited from the currency floor on January 15, 2015 and the frank appreciated almost 20% within one day. In late 2014 the SNB started intervening heavily to defend the floor in response to increased capital inflows arising from a combination of events, including the anticipation of the European Central Bank's quantitative easing program and geopolitical turmoil in Europe. To maintain the fixed rate of the Swiss franc, the SNB was buying euros and selling francs on the market in large quantities. When the SNB's balance sheet was approaching 90% of GDP, the SNB decided to exit the currency peg to avoid speculative risks of over-appreciation and further speculative pressures.

Following the appreciation, growth indicators have weakened, as Swiss goods became less competitive and inflation has fallen deeper into negative territory. The appreciated franc will weigh on growth in 2016, but the economy is expected to recover over the next few years. *The 5-Minute Economist* projects Switzerland's EPI score to stay at a similar level of about 98%, or an A level, in the next few years.

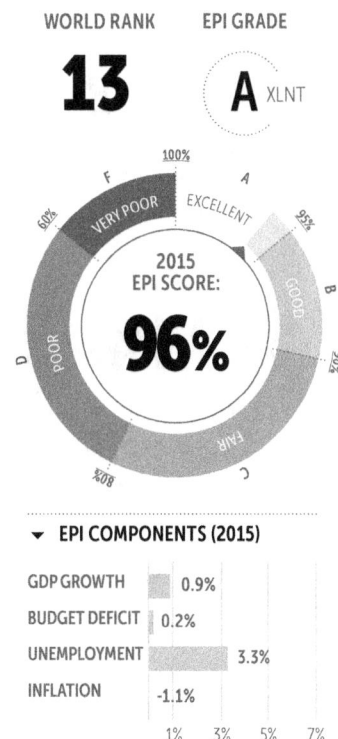

WORLD RANK **13**

EPI GRADE **A** XLNT

2015 EPI SCORE: **96%**

▼ EPI COMPONENTS (2015)

GDP GROWTH	0.9%
BUDGET DEFICIT	0.2%
UNEMPLOYMENT	3.3%
INFLATION	-1.1%

1%   3%   5%   7%

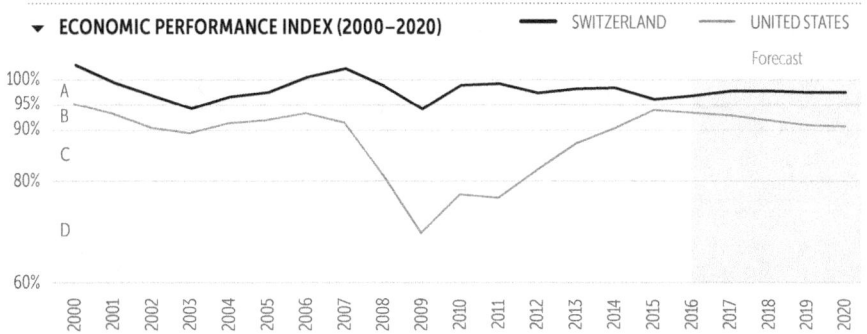

▼ ECONOMIC PERFORMANCE INDEX (2000–2020) —— SWITZERLAND —— UNITED STATES

Forecast

TAIWAN

Negative Spillovers From China

THE PERFORMANCE OF TAIWAN'S ECONOMY HAS BEEN EXCELLENT, WITH THE EPI SCORE PROJECTED TO BE 94.6%, OR A B+ LEVEL, IN 2016. AN ECONOMIC SLOWDOWN IN CHINA, TAIWAN'S MAIN TRADE PARTNER, HAS CREATED HEADWINDS TO THE TAIWANESE ECONOMY.

WORLD RANK

16

EPI GRADE

B GOOD

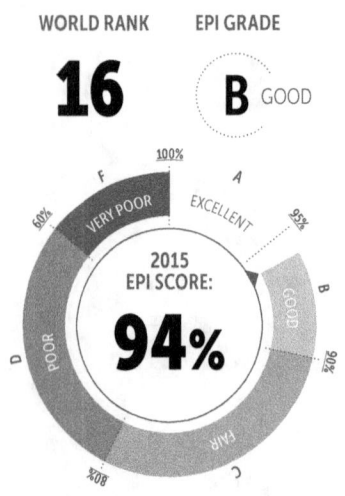

2015 EPI SCORE: **94%**

GDP growth slowed down slightly in 2015 and is unlikely to recover in 2016-2017, unless the Chinese economy turns to faster growth rates. Domestic demand is still likely to be the main driver that would support growth in 2016. Government spending is likely to start picking up later in 2016, after a slowdown created by the political conflict in 2015. Investment growth is likely to be subdued on poor sentiment and will not push GDP growth in 2016. Still, inflation is projected to be close to zero in 2016, driven by low oil prices.

The 5-Minute Economist projects Taiwan's EPI score to stay at an A- level in the next few years, with gradually increasing inflation compensated by improved GDP growth.

▼ EPI COMPONENTS (2015)

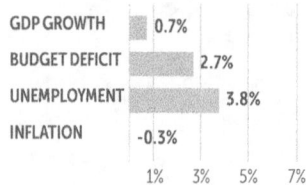

GDP GROWTH	0.7%
BUDGET DEFICIT	2.7%
UNEMPLOYMENT	3.8%
INFLATION	-0.3%

▼ ECONOMIC PERFORMANCE INDEX (2000–2020) — TAIWAN — UNITED STATES

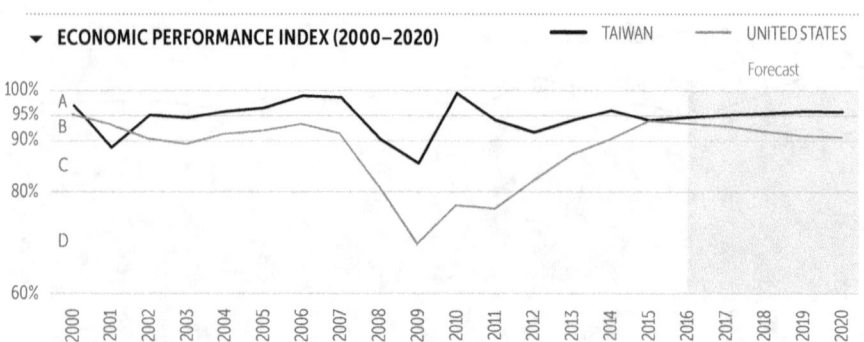

TURKEY

Fragile Economy

TURKEY'S ECONOMIC PERFORMANCE HAS BEEN POOR, WITH HIGH INFLATION
AND UNEMPLOYMENT RATES AND SMALL GDP GROWTH. THE EPI SCORE
IS PROJECTED TO BE 81.3%, OR A C- LEVEL, IN 2016.

After four elections in the past two years, the attemted military coup created new risks to political stability. GDP growth is projected to be close to 3.8% in 2016, driven by improved domestic demand and decreased imports, but is likely to be downgraded due to political uncertainty. Turkey is benefitting from lower oil prices but is exposed to overall emerging market turmoil. With persistent current account deficits of more than 4% of GDP, Turkey remains vulnerable to capital outflows and external sentiment shocks.

An increase in wages and a weaker lira have contributed to increased inflation, despite lower oil prices. Inflation is likely to be close to 9.8% in 2016 and would decelerate if the lira stabilizes. The victory of the ruling party in last year's elections came at a toll of a higher budget deficit for the current government. Promises to increase wages are likely to increase budget deficit above the current projection of 1.9% in 2016. The unemployment rate has been in the double digits and is likely to increase to 10.8% in 2016 from 10.2% in 2015.

The 5-Minute Economist projects Turkey's EPI score to stay at a C level in the next few years.

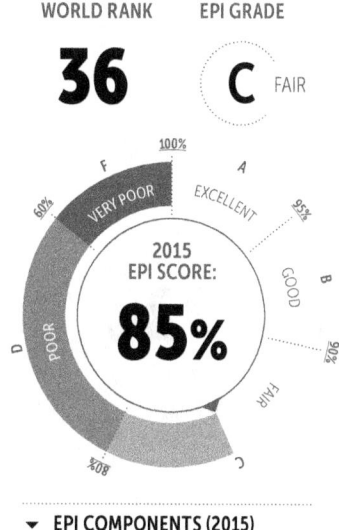

WORLD RANK **36**

EPI GRADE **C** FAIR

2015 EPI SCORE: **85%**

▼ EPI COMPONENTS (2015)

GDP GROWTH	3.8%
BUDGET DEFICIT	1%
UNEMPLOYMENT	10.2%
INFLATION	7.7%

3%   6%   9%   12%

▼ ECONOMIC PERFORMANCE INDEX (2000–2020)

—— TURKEY   —— UNITED STATES

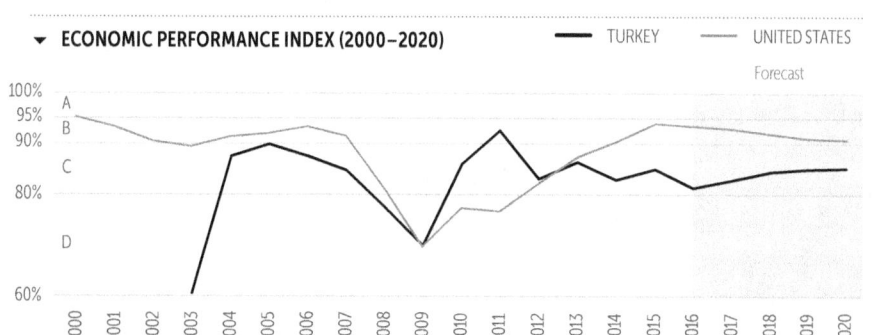

Forecast

UNITED KINGDOM
Life After Brexit

THE UNITED KINGDOM'S ECONOMY IS UNDER THE RISK OF RECESSION AFTER
THE BREXIT VOTE. STILL, THE EPI IS PROJECTED TO BE AT 92.4%, OR A B LEVEL,
IN 2016 WITH RISKS ON THE DOWNSIDE.

WORLD RANK

23

EPI GRADE

B GOOD

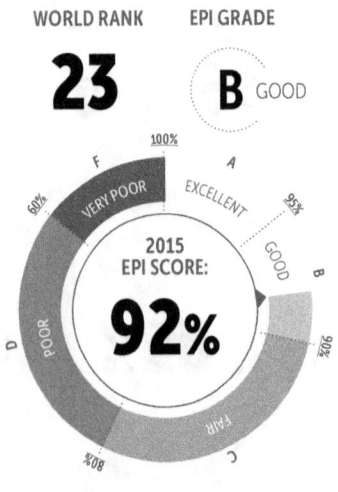

2015
EPI SCORE:
92%

On June 23, 2016, the British public decided to vote to "leave" the European Union. Renegotiation of trade and immigration agreements with the EU will determine the effects of separation. Many economists expect deterioration in growth and a recession beginning in 2016-2017. The British Pound fell by more than 10% after the vote to leave, signaling negative market expectations. The Bank of England will provide support to the economy, but negative consequences are inevitable.

The United Kingdom is one of the few European countries that managed to recover from the financial crisis. The policy of monetary easing and fiscal stimulus provided strong support to the economy in 2009-2010. A reversal towards more fiscal discipline in the past few years and potential rate hikes in 2016 have been signs of economic stability.

GDP growth is projected to slow down in 2016, driven by fiscal austerity and uncertainty of the separation from the EU. Inflation remains low due to low oil prices but could start increasing in 2016, due to the base effects of the past year. Unemployment has decreased to 5.6% in 2015 from 8.1% in 2011 and is on a declining path. The government has decided to unwind the fiscal stimulus package and the budget deficit has been gradually declining from 10.7% in 2009 to 3.2% in 2016.

▾ EPI COMPONENTS (2015)

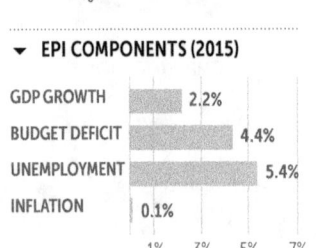

GDP GROWTH	2.2%
BUDGET DEFICIT	4.4%
UNEMPLOYMENT	5.4%
INFLATION	0.1%

1%   3%   5%   7%

▾ ECONOMIC PERFORMANCE INDEX (2000–2020) —— UNITED KINGDOM —— UNITED STATES

Forecast

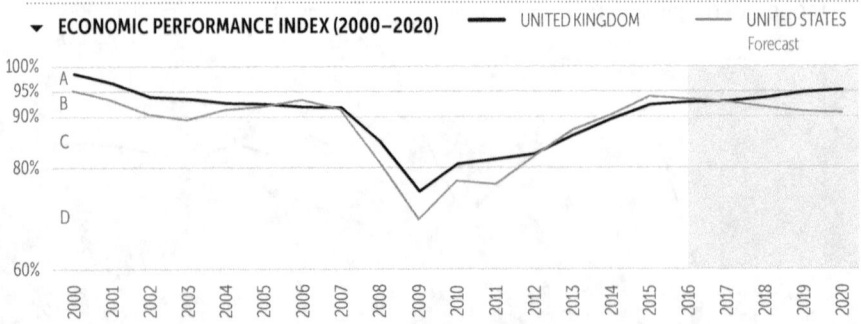

UNITED STATES The End Of The Great Recession

THE US ECONOMIC PERFORMANCE HAS BEEN GOOD, WITH ECONOMIC ACTIVITY EXPANDING AT A MODERATE PACE AND A PROJECTED EPI SCORE OF 92.9%, OR A B LEVEL, IN 2016, ALMOST THE SAME LEVEL AS IN 2015. A SOLID LABOR MARKET, ACCOMMODATIVE FINANCIAL CONDITIONS, AND CHEAPER OIL SHOULD SUPPORT A MORE DYNAMIC GROWTH PATH THIS YEAR.

The US economic performance has been good, with the economic activity expanding at a moderate pace and the EPI score is projected to be 93.2%, or a B level, in 2016, almost the same level as in 2015. A solid labor market, accommodative financial conditions, and cheaper oil should support a more dynamic path this year.

The Fed's policy of low interest rates and the government's fiscal support provided major economic stimulus to the economy since the 2008 crisis. The economy has been showing signs of robust growth and low unemployment levels in the past few years. The Fed began hiking rates last year, after strong signs that the economy is on the path to recovery. The housing sector is continuing to recover as well, as housing prices have recovered to pre-crisis levels.

The 5-Minute Economist projects the United States' EPI score to stay around the current levels of about 93%, or a B level, in the next few years. Inflation pressures remain muted, mainly due to the dollar appreciation and cheaper energy costs. Driven by robust economic growth and a strong hiring by the private sector, the unemployment level is likely to stay below 5% in the next few years. The government has been winding down its fiscal stimulus program and the budget deficit is projected to decrease to about 3.5% in the next few years. GDP growth will gradually increase but will stay below 3%, as interval drivers of the economy and high levels of private and government debt would limit the speed of economic growth.

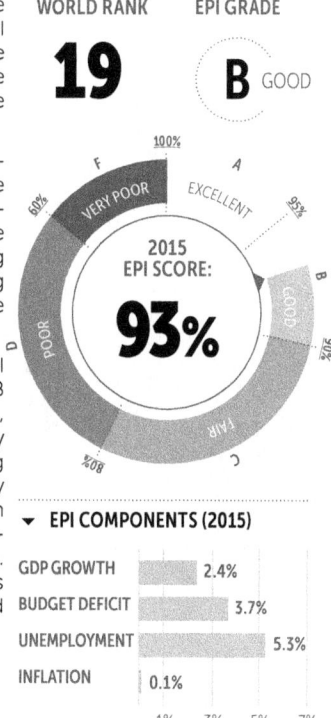

WORLD RANK 19

EPI GRADE B GOOD

2015 EPI SCORE: 93%

▼ EPI COMPONENTS (2015)

GDP GROWTH	2.4%
BUDGET DEFICIT	3.7%
UNEMPLOYMENT	5.3%
INFLATION	0.1%

1% 3% 5% 7%

▼ ECONOMIC PERFORMANCE INDEX (2000–2020) — UNITED STATES

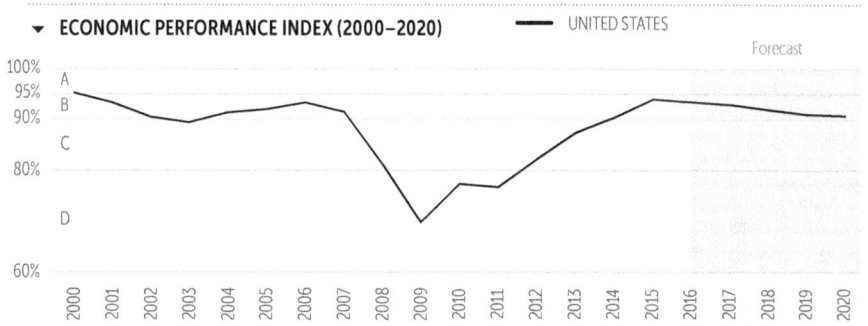

THE EPI AND US ECONOMIC HISTORY

In this section, we examine US economic history using the EPI as a tool to help explain overall economic performance. Economists and historians generally agree that the US has experienced a number of historical periods that included both favorable and unfavorable economic conditions. Each period is also characterized by a variety of sociological changes, domestic political upheaval, technological innovation, and exogenous shocks such as wars.

Since 1790, we have identified 14 general economic periods[1], commented on a number of important events in each period, provided a brief EPI analysis and then ranked each period's performance using the Index.

These periods include (see Chart 1 and 2):

1. The Founding Years: 1790-1811
2. The War of 1812: 1812-1815
3. Industrial Revolution: 1816-1860
4. The Civil War: 1861-1865
5. The Gilded Age: 1866-1889
6. The Progressive Era (excluding WWI): 1890-1913
7. World War I and its aftermath: 1914-1920
8. The Roaring 20s: 1921-1929
9. The Great Depression: 1930-1940
10. World War II (including the lifting of wartime controls): 1941-1947
11. The Post-War Prosperity: 1948-1967
12. Stagflation and Malaise:1968-1981
13. The Reagan Revolution and the New Economy: 1982-1999
14. The Post-Millennium Period: 2000-the present

---

[1] Historians generally agree on them with minor deviations.

With the exception of unemployment data, statistics from 1790 are generally available. Most historical statistical data for inflation, unemployment, budget deficits, and change in GDP was taken from *Historical Statistics of the United States: Millennial Edition* (2006)[2]. A complete discussion of data sources can be found in Appendix IV.

THE FOUNDING YEARS: 1790-1811

In 1787, the United States adopted the US Constitution which established a unified nation with a common market having no internal tariffs or taxes on interstate commerce. The national culture was dominated by three primary trends including the development of government institutions, western expansion and early industrialization marked by growth of small cities.[3] In the early years of the republic, a debate arose between those who wanted a strong federal government led by the First Secretary of the Treasury, Alexander Hamilton, and those that preferred a weak central government, led by Thomas Jefferson and James Madison, the third and fourth US Presidents. Hamilton, however held immense power and influence in Washington and envisioned a national economy built on diversified shipping, manufacturing and banking. He succeeded in building the nation's credit based on a national debt held by the wealthy and political classes and funded by tariffs on imported goods along with a tax on whiskey. In addition, he spearheaded the creation of the First Bank of the United States (1791-1811).[4]

---

[2] "Historical Statistics of the United States: Millennial Edition" (2006). Edited by Richard Sutch, Susan B. Carter, etc. Cambridge University Press.

[3] Jonathan Hughes and Lousi P. Cain (2007). American Economic History (7th edition, p.87).

[4] Curtis P. Nettels (1962). The Emergence of a National Economy, 1775-1815.

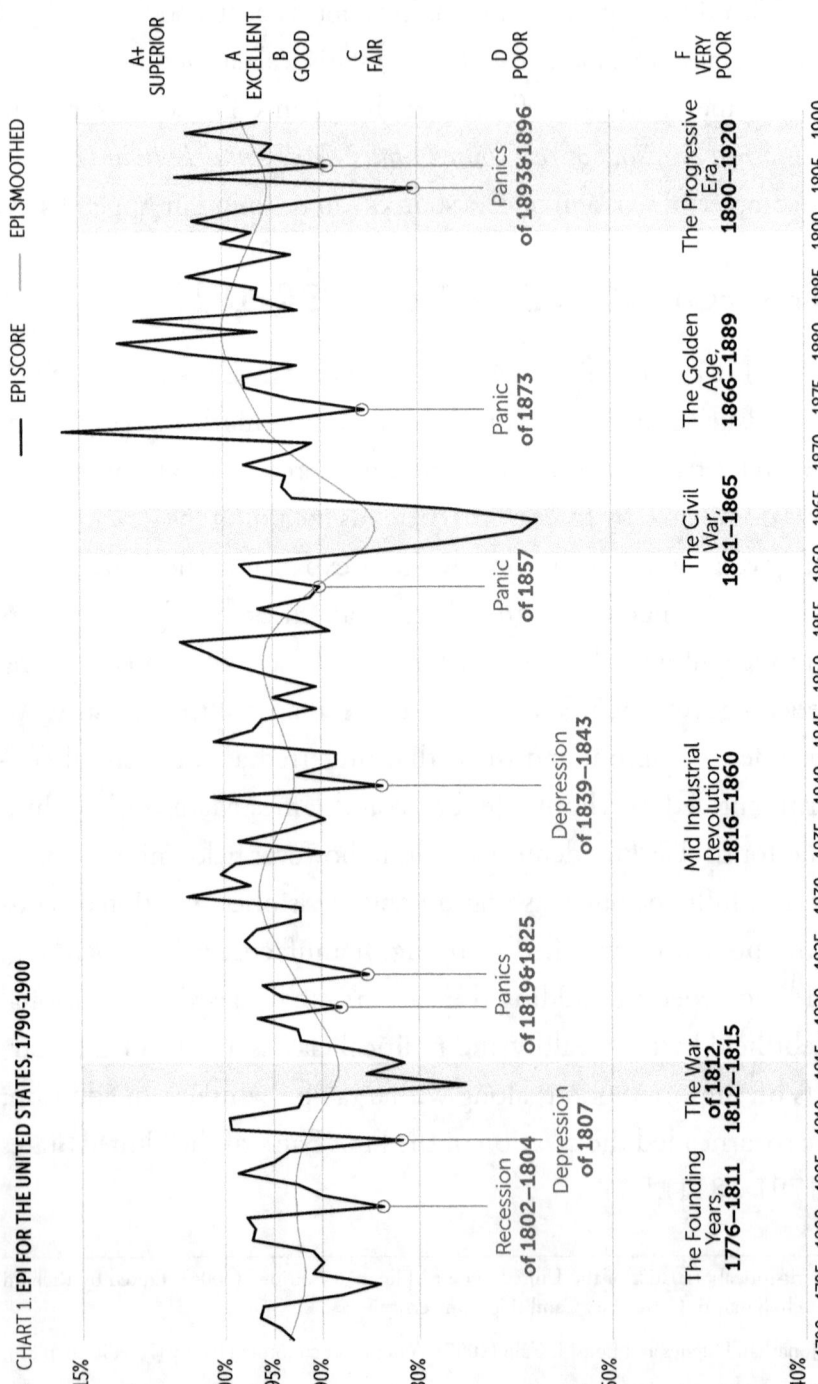

► CHART 1. EPI FOR THE UNITED STATES, 1790-1900

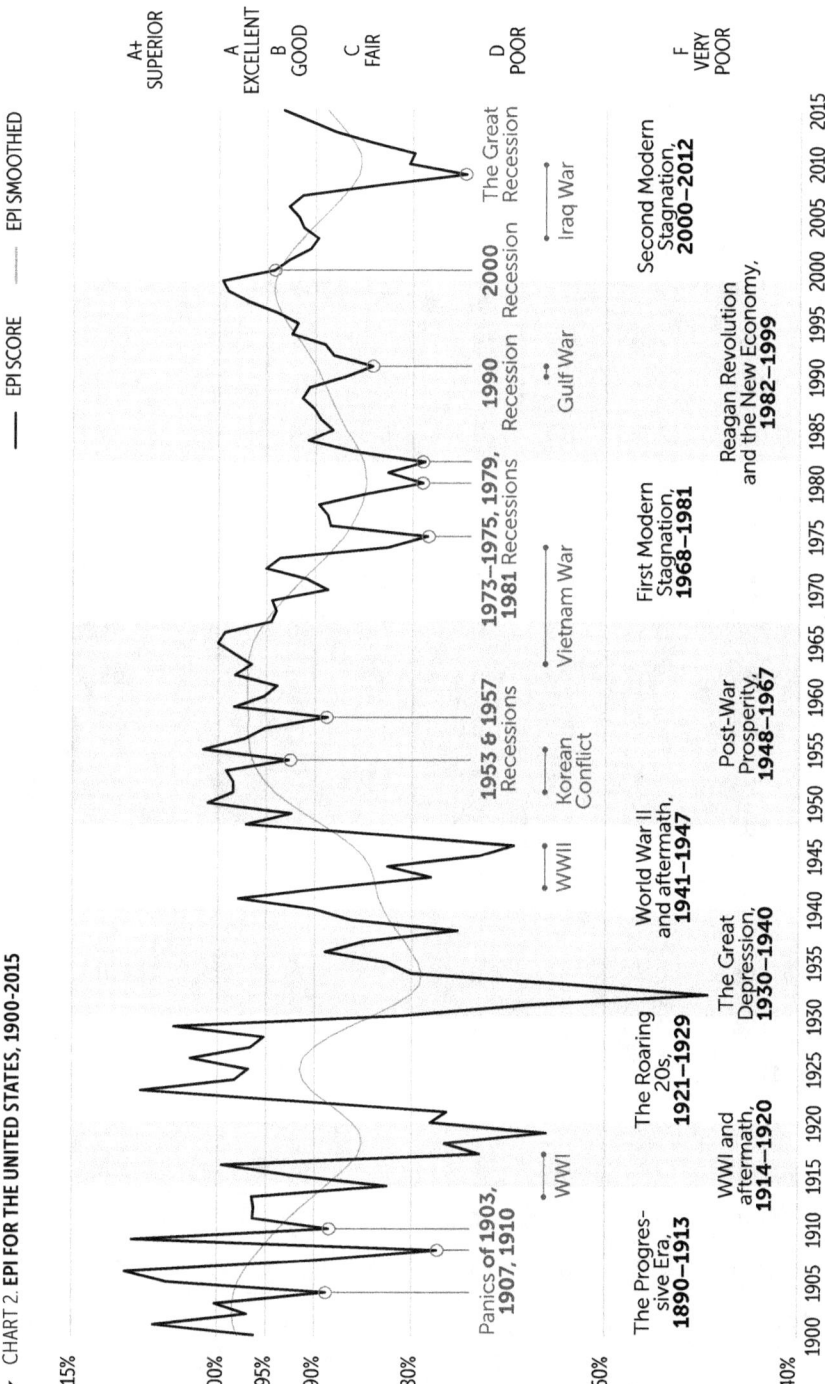

▸ CHART 2. **EPI FOR THE UNITED STATES, 1900-2015**

—— EPI SCORE   - - - EPI SMOOTHED

▼ **TABLE 1. THE FOUNDING YEARS, 1790–1811**

Year	Inflation Rate (%)	Unemployment (%)	Budget Deficit (% of GDP)	GDP growth (%)	EPI (%)	EPI Grade	Weighted EPI (%)	Weighted EPI Grade
1790	3.8	6.7	0.0	3.4	93.0	B	92.8	B
1791	2.7	6.7	0.0	3.6	94.2	B+	94.0	B
1792	1.8	6.7	0.4	5.1	96.3	A	95.9	A-
1793	3.5	6.7	0.0	6.2	96.0	A	95.5	A-
1794	10.9	6.7	0.4	5.9	87.9	C	87.1	C
1795	14.4	6.7	0.3	5.4	84.0	C	83.2	C
1796	5.3	6.7	-0.6	2.4	90.9	B-	90.8	B-
1797	-3.8	6.7	-0.5	-0.3	89.8	C+	89.9	C+
1798	-3.3	6.7	0.0	0.8	90.9	B-	91.0	B
1799	0.0	6.7	0.4	4.2	97.1	A	97.0	A
1800	2.0	6.7	0.0	5.5	96.8	A	96.4	A
1801	1.3	6.7	-0.6	5.0	97.6	A	97.3	A
1802	-15.7	6.7	-1.2	4.8	83.6	C	82.7	C-
1803	5.4	6.7	-0.5	1.4	89.8	C+	89.7	C+
1804	4.4	6.7	-0.5	3.0	92.4	B	92.2	B
1805	-0.7	6.7	-0.5	5.4	98.5	A	98.1	A
1806	4.3	6.7	-0.8	5.1	94.9	B+	94.5	B+
1807	-5.4	6.7	-1.1	4.3	93.3	B	92.9	B
1808	8.6	6.7	-1.0	-4.1	81.6	C-	82.0	C-
1809	-2.0	6.7	0.3	8.2	99.2	A+	98.5	A
1810	0.0	6.7	-0.1	5.9	99.4	A+	99.0	A+
1811	6.8	6.7	-0.8	5.0	92.4	B	91.9	B
Average	2.0	6.7	-0.3	3.9	92.7	B	92.4	B

In 1801, Thomas Jefferson was elected president. He promoted a more decentralized, agrarian democracy based on his philosophy that government policy should protect the common man from political and economic tyranny. He repealed a number of taxes imposed by his predecessors and despite misgivings, signed the Louisiana Purchase, which doubled the size of the United States in 1803, setting the stage for continental expansion ("Continentalism").[5] President James Madison continued Jefferson's decentralized policies letting the National Bank charter expire in 1811. However, Madison reversed his stance in reaction to the War of 1812 and supported the Second Bank of the United States (1816-1836).[6]

In the South, cotton became the primary cash crop following the invention of the cotton gin in 1793 and large plantations based on slave labor expanded in the Carolinas westward to Texas.[7] Great Britain became the United States' largest trading partner, receiving 80% of all US cotton and 50% of all other US exports.[8] Despite growing commerce, the British public and press became increasingly resentful of the growing mercantile and commercial competition.[9] Furthermore, Great Britain was at war with France and instituted a number of trade restrictions, which began to impede America's ability to trade. The United States' view was that Britain was in violation of a neutral nation's right to trade with any nation it

---

[5] Continental and Continentalism, www.sociologyindex.com.

[6] Bray Hammond (2001). Banks and Politics in America from the Revolution to the Civil War.

[7] Lewis Cecil Gray (1933). History of agriculture in the southern United States to 1860.

[8] Kate Caffrey (1977). The Twilight's Last Gleaming: Britain vs. America 1812-1815 (pp.50-51).

[9] Toll, Ian W. (2006). Six Frigates: The Epic History of the Founding of the US Navy (p.281).

saw fit and contested these restrictions as illegal under international law.[10]

Generally speaking, the economy performed at a B (Good) level prior to the War of 1812 (Table 1). Despite high inflation rates in 1794-1795 and considerable deflation in 1802, prices rose only 2% on average. Deficits were virtually non-existent as the budget was in balance or ran a surplus in 16 out of 21 years between 1790 and 1811. GDP growth averaged 3.9% during this period.

THE WAR OF 1812: 1812-1815

▼ TABLE 2. THE WAR OF 1812, 1812–1815

Year	Inflation Rate (%)	Unemployment (%)	Budget Deficit (% of GDP)	GDP growth (%)	EPI (%)	EPI Grade	Weighted EPI (%)	Weighted EPI Grade
1812	1.3	6.7	1.3	1.1	91.8	B	92.0	B
1813	20.0	6.7	2.1	3.9	75.1	D+	74.3	D
1814	9.9	6.7	2.8	4.7	85.3	C	84.8	C
1815	-12.3	6.7	2.0	2.4	81.4	C-	81.0	C-
Average	4.7	6.7	2.1	3.0	83.4	C	83.0	C

Within the larger context of the Napoleonic Wars, Britain was engaged in war with France and did not want America to trade with France, irrespective of any theoretical neutral right to do so. As a result, the British established a blockade of American ports resulting in American exports falling from $130 million in 1807

---

[10] Kate Caffrey (1977). The Twilight's Last Gleaming: Britain vs. America 1812-1815 (pp. 56-58).

to $7 million in 1814.[11] The blockade of American ports later tightened to the extent that most American merchant ships and naval vessels were confined to their port.

In 1812, the British Royal Navy was the world's largest and had 85 vessels in American waters.[12] In contrast, the United States Navy was only twenty years old and had only 22 commissioned vessels. That same year, the United States declared war on Great Britain in reaction to trade restrictions as well as America's opposition to the forced recruitment of US citizens into the Royal Navy and British military to support American Indians who were resisting the US expansion.[13] The war began poorly when an attempt to invade Canada was repelled by British troops, local militias and Indian tribes, which led to the British capture of Detroit. Hostilities flared in what are now Ontario, Québec, New Brunswick, Newfoundland, Nova Scotia, Prince Edward Island, Cape Breton Island, and Bermuda. Britain's strategy was to protect their merchant shipping to and from Canada and the West Indies and to enforce a blockade of major American ports to restrict trade with France. Due to naval inferiority, Americans were reduced to hit-and-run tactics and only engaged the Royal Navy under favorable circumstances.

The cost of the war is difficult to measure, however, the national debt rose from $45 million in 1812 to $127 million by 1815. Also costly was the depressive effect on exports. For example, flour exports fell from almost one million barrels in 1812 and 1813

---

[11] Robert Leckie (1998). The Wars of America (p.255).

[12] Ian W. Toll (2006). Six Frigates: The Epic History of the Founding of the US Navy (p.180). New York: W.W. Norton.

[13] Kate Caffrey (1977). The Twilight's Last Gleaming: Britain vs. America 1812-1815 (pp.101-104). New York: Stein and Day.

to 5,000 barrels in 1814. Maritime insurance rates skyrocketed, at times reaching 75%, leading to a virtual standstill in shipping. Overall, exports and imports fell and foreign trade declined from 948,000 tons in 1811 to just 60,000 tons by 1814.[14]

On August 24, 1814, British troops entered Washington D.C. Under orders not to occupy the city, General Robert Ross ordered the burning of government buildings. The Senate and House of Representatives were set ablaze along with the Library of Congress. The troops then marched toward the Presidential Mansion (the White House) moments after First Lady Dolly Madison fled with documents, art and other valuables. Upon arriving at the mansion, the British soldiers feasted in the dining hall, collected souvenirs and then set the building afire. The British also burned the Treasury Building and other government buildings while Americans burned much of the Washington Navy Yard including the frigate USS Columbia to prevent it from being captured. With the American Government in disarray, execution of the war became difficult over the following weeks.

Despite the success of the British blockade and the burning of the Capitol, there was little chance of any decisive military victory in North America. In short order, the war became a stalemate and by 1814 both sides began looking for a peaceful settlement. Prime Minister Lord Liverpool encountered increased opposition to continued war taxation and merchants increasingly wanted to restore trade with America. On December 24, 1814, diplomats from the two countries met in Ghent, in the Netherlands (now Belgium), and signed the Treaty of Ghent, which was ratified by on February 16, 1815.

---

[14] Donald R. Hickey (1990). War of 1812 (pp.172-4); Samuel E. Morison (1941). The Maritime History of Massachusetts, 1783-1860 (pp. 205-206).

The EPI clearly measures a fall in economic conditions during the war (Table 2). Inflation surged in 1813 and 1814, with prices rising almost 30%, followed by a fall in prices of just over 12% in 1815. While small by today's standards, budget deficits surged to 2.1% of GDP and the national debt tripled. Despite these problems, growth in GDP averaged a respectable 3% over the four-year period. The EPI, which had registered a rank of Superior only two years earlier, fell to B level during the first year of the war and then to Poor level in 1813. Overall, the average score was 83.4%, or a C level.

THE INDUSTRIAL REVOLUTION: 1816-1860

The Industrial Revolution, which began in north Europe in the late 18th century, had quickly spread to the United States by the early 19th century and gained speed following the War of 1812 (Table 3). The Whig Party, with the assistance of leading politicians including Henry Clay and John Quincy Adams, advanced a political philosophy of federalism where sovereignty was constitutionally divided between a central governing authority and constituent political units (i.e. states). Closely related was an economic philosophy championed by Henry Clay which he termed the "American System." This combination led to a number of policies designed to strengthen and unify the nation.

The most important tenets included:
• Support for a high tariff to protect American industries and generate revenue for the federal government
• Maintenance of high public land prices to generate federal revenue

▼ **TABLE 3. THE INDUSTRIAL REVOLUTION: 1816-1860**

Year	Inflation Rate (%)	Unemployment (%)	Budget Deficit (% of GDP)	GDP growth (%)	EPI (%)	EPI Grade	Weighted EPI (%)	Weighted EPI Grade
1816	-8.6	6.7	-2.0	-1.4	85.3	C	85.3	C
1817	-5.3	6.7	-1.3	2.9	92.1	B	91.9	B
1818	-4.4	6.7	-0.2	3.3	92.4	B	92.2	B
1819	0.0	6.7	-0.3	2.9	96.5	A	96.5	A
1820	-7.8	6.7	0.0	2.4	87.9	C	87.6	C
1821	-3.5	6.7	0.2	4.5	94.1	B+	93.8	B
1822	3.7	6.7	-0.6	5.8	96.0	A	95.5	A-
1823	-10.6	6.7	-0.7	1.8	85.1	C	84.8	C
1824	-7.9	6.7	0.1	5.7	90.9	B-	90.3	B-
1825	2.6	6.7	-0.6	5.3	96.6	A	96.2	A
1826	0.0	6.7	-0.8	3.7	97.8	A	97.7	A
1827	0.8	6.7	-0.7	3.5	96.6	A	96.5	A
1828	-5.0	6.7	-0.8	3.0	92.1	B	91.8	B
1829	-1.8	6.7	-0.9	-0.4	92.1	B	92.3	B
1830	-0.9	6.7	-0.9	10.5	103.8	A+	102.8	A+
1831	-6.3	6.7	-1.1	9.2	97.2	A	96.2	A
1832	-1.0	6.7	-1.1	6.8	100.2	A+	99.7	A+
1833	-1.9	6.7	-0.8	6.6	98.7	A	98.2	A
1834	2.0	6.7	-0.2	-2.0	89.6	C+	90.0	B-
1835	2.9	6.7	-1.2	6.8	98.4	A	97.8	A
1836	5.7	6.7	-1.3	4.4	93.3	B	92.8	B
1837	2.7	6.7	0.8	-0.4	89.5	C+	89.8	C+
1838	-2.6	6.7	0.5	1.9	92.1	B	92.1	B

Year	Inflation Rate (%)	Unemployment (%)	Budget Deficit (% of GDP)	GDP growth (%)	EPI (%)	EPI Grade	Weighted EPI (%)	Weighted EPI Grade
1839	0.0	6.7	-0.3	7.6	101.2	A+	100.7	A+
1840	-7.1	6.7	0.3	-2.3	83.6	C	83.9	C
1841	1.0	6.7	0.6	0.7	92.5	B	92.7	B
1842	-6.7	6.7	0.3	2.0	88.4	C+	88.2	C+
1843	-9.2	6.7	0.2	4.5	88.4	C+	87.8	C
1844	1.1	6.7	-0.4	8.3	100.9	A+	100.2	A+
1845	1.1	6.7	-0.4	4.5	97.0	A	96.8	A
1846	1.1	6.7	-0.1	3.7	96.0	A-	95.8	A-
1847	7.6	6.7	1.3	6.0	90.4	B-	89.8	C+
1848	-4.0	6.7	0.4	6.1	94.9	B+	94.4	B+
1849	-3.2	6.7	0.6	0.9	90.4	B-	90.5	B-
1850	2.2	6.7	-0.2	4.0	95.2	A-	95.0	A-
1851	-2.1	6.7	-0.2	7.8	99.2	A+	98.5	A
1852	1.1	6.7	-0.2	9.0	101.4	A+	100.7	A+
1853	0.0	6.7	-0.4	10.7	104.4	A+	103.5	A+
1854	8.6	6.7	-0.4	3.9	89.0	C+	88.6	C+
1855	3.0	6.7	-0.1	1.0	91.5	B	91.6	B
1856	-1.9	6.7	-0.1	4.9	96.4	A	96.1	A
1857	2.9	6.7	0.0	0.6	91.0	B-	91.1	B
1858	-5.7	6.7	0.7	3.1	90.0	B-	89.8	C+
1859	1.0	6.7	0.4	5.1	97.1	A	96.8	A
1860	0.0	6.7	0.2	5.1	98.2	A	98.0	A
Average	-1.3	6.7	-0.3	4.1	94.1	B+	93.8	B

• Preservation of the Bank of the United States to stabilize the currency and rein in risky state and local banks
• Development of a system of internal improvements (such as roads and canals) which would knit the nation together and be financed by the tariff and land sales revenues

Portions of the American System were enacted by the United States Congress. The charter of the Second Bank of the United States was renewed in 1816 for 20 years. High tariffs were maintained from the days of Alexander Hamilton until 1832. Millions of settlers moved to the more fertile farmland of the Midwest, partially encouraged by government-created national roads and waterways, such as the Cumberland Pike (1818) and the Erie Canal (1825).

Other Whig-sponsored improvements were frustrated by the Democratic Party and most[15] notably, President Andrew Jackson (1829–1837), who vetoed a bill in 1830 allowing the federal government to purchase stock in a road company which had been organized to construct a link between Lexington and the Ohio River in the state of Kentucky. Jackson also opposed the Second National Bank, which he believed favored the interests of his political opposition. After a political struggle, Jackson succeeded in closing the Bank by vetoing its re-charter passed by Congress and withdrawing US funds in 1833.

The bank's functions were absorbed by local and state banks which also became the beneficiaries of US funds. This led to an expansion of credit and speculation. At first land sales, canal construction, cotton production, and manufacturing boomed.[16] However inflation

---

[15] Digital History.

[16] Sparknotes.

resulted[17] because these banks issued paper banknotes that were not backed by gold or silver reserves. In 1836, Jackson issued the Specie Circular, which required buyers of government lands to pay in specie (gold or silver coins). The result was a great demand for specie. Unfortunately, many banks did not have sufficient gold and silver reserves to exchange for their notes, which led to their collapse, spawning the Panic of 1837 and a depression. Of the 850 banks in the United States, 343 closed, 62 partially failed and the State bank system never fully recovered. Interestingly, Jackson was the only president in history to have virtually retired the national debt during his term, having reduced it to $33,733.05, the lowest since the first fiscal year of 1791.[18] This accomplishment was short lived as falling economic activity caused by the Panic led to budget deficits.

The Panic of 1837 as well as other recessions did not curtail rapid US economic growth. Long-term demographic growth, expansion into new farmlands and the creation of new factories continued. New inventions and capital investment led to the creation of new industries and economic growth. As transportation improved, new markets continuously opened. The steamboat made river traffic faster and cheaper but the development of railroads had an even greater effect, opening up vast stretches of new territory for development. Like canals and roads, railroads received large amounts of government assistance in their early years in the form of land grants. Unlike other forms of transportation, however, railroads also attracted a good deal of domestic and European private investment. Railroads led to the creation of large-scale business operations which created

---

[17] The financial panic of 1837.

[18] Bray Hammond (2001). Banks and Politics in America from the Revolution to the Civil War; Taylor (1977). The Transportation Revolution 1815-1860.

a blueprint for large corporations to follow. They were the first to encounter managerial complexities, labor union issues and problems of competition. These innovations, considered radical at the time, combined with the discovery of gold which added to America's public and private wealth, enabled the nation to develop a large-scale transportation system creating a base for the country's industrialization.

By 1860, 16% of the population resided in cities of at least 2,500 and a third of the nation's income came from manufacturing. Urban industry was concentrated in the Northeast with cotton cloth production as a leading industry. The urbanization and industrialization was fed by immigrant labor that originated in Europe. An estimated 300,000 immigrants arrived annually between 1845 and 1855. Most were poor and remained in eastern cities, often at ports of arrival.[19]

THE CIVIL WAR: 1861-1865

▼ TABLE 4. THE CIVIL WAR: 1861–1865

Year	Inflation Rate (%)	Unemployment (%)	Budget Deficit (% of GDP)	GDP growth (%)	EPI (%)	EPI Grade	Weighted EPI (%)	Weighted EPI Grade
1861	6.0	6.7	0.5	0.1	86.9	C	87.0	C
1862	14.2	6.7	7.7	5.3	76.8	D+	76.2	D+
1863	24.8	6.7	8.2	8.8	69.1	D	67.8	D
1864	25.2	6.7	6.3	5.7	67.5	D	66.4	D-
1865	3.7	6.7	10.2	-2.9	76.4	D+	77.3	D+
Average	14.8	6.7	6.6	3.4	75.3	D+	74.9	D

---

[19] Walter Licht (1995). Industrializing America: The Nineteenth Century.

In contrast to the industrializing North, the South remained rural and dependent on the North for capital and manufactured goods. The economy of the South was also dependent upon slavery which could only be sustained through political power. This power was put in jeopardy when the Republican Party, organized in 1856, called for the end to the expansion of slavery, wishing instead to focus on industry, commerce and business. The Republican victory in the 1860 election resulted in seven Southern states declaring their secession from the Union even before the new President, Abraham Lincoln, took office on March 4, 1861. Eventually, eleven Southern slave states seceded and formed the Confederate States of America and fought against the US federal government, which was supported by all the free states and the five border slave states in the North.

As the war escalated, Washington required enormous funding. The Morrill Tariff, passed in 1860, was revised upward twice between 1861 and 1862. With the low-tariff Southerners gone, the Republican-controlled Congress doubled and tripled the rates on European goods, which reached 49 percent in 1868. Ironically, the US never put a tariff on goods from the Confederacy because the US never recognized the legal existence of the C.S.A. As the war progressed, the North blockaded the Southern states and very little legal trade occurred between either side because most goods were considered war contraband. Thus, the Confederacy collected only $3.5 million in tariff revenue during the war and had to resort to inflating their currency to pay for the war.

The American Civil War was the deadliest war in American history, causing 620,000 soldier deaths and an undetermined number of civilian casualties. The industrial advantages of the North secured a Northern victory and that victory sealed the destiny of the nation and its economic system. The war's legacy included the abolition of slavery in the United States, a plunge in the economic fortunes of the South, a rapid expansion of industry in the North, a restoration of the Union, and a strengthening of the federal government. The social, political, economic, and racial issues of the war decisively shaped the reconstruction era that lasted to 1877 and brought changes that made the United States a superpower.[20]

The EPI Index clearly records a dramatic fall in economic conditions during the war (Table 4). Inflation surged in 1862-1864 and by the war's end, the price level had almost doubled. Budget deficits also exploded with the deficit averaging 6.6% of GDP in each of the war years. One bright spot, if any, was the growth in GDP, which averaged a respectable 3.4%. However, this growth was concentrated in the North as the South was generally devastated. The EPI Index, which had achieved an Excellent rating in each of the two years prior to the war, dropped to Fair in 1861 and then remained Poor in each of the following 4 years. Overall, the EPI score averaged a 75.3%, or a D level, which represents the worst economic period in the country's history.

THE GILDED AGE: 1866-1889

The Gilded Age witnessed the creation of a modern industrial economy with a national transportation and communication network. In addition, the corporation became the dominant form of business organization and a managerial revolution transformed

---

[20] Ralph Andreano (1962) The Economic Impact of the American Civil War.

▾ TABLE 5. THE GILDED AGE: 1866–1889

Year	Inflation Rate (%)	Unemployment (%)	Budget Deficit (% of GDP)	GDP growth (%)	EPI (%)	EPI Grade	Weighted EPI (%)	Weighted EPI Grade
1866	-2.6	6.7	-0.4	1.7	92.8	B	92.9	B
1867	-6.8	6.7	-1.5	5.9	93.9	B	93.2	B
1868	-3.9	6.7	-0.3	3.8	93.5	B	93.3	B
1869	-4.1	4.0	-0.6	5.3	97.8	A	97.6	A
1870	-4.3	3.5	-1.2	-0.3	93.2	B	93.7	B
1871	-6.4	3.7	-1.1	-0.3	90.8	B-	91.2	B
1872	0.0	4.0	-1.0	19.7	116.8	A+	115.1	A+
1873	-2.0	4.0	-0.5	0.3	94.7	B+	95.2	A-
1874	-4.9	5.5	0.0	-4.3	85.4	C	86.1	C
1875	-3.6	5.8	-0.2	2.2	92.9	B	92.9	B
1876	-2.3	7.0	-0.3	6.6	97.7	A	97.1	A
1877	-2.3	7.8	-0.4	7.5	97.8	A	97.1	A
1878	-4.8	8.3	-0.2	5.1	92.3	B	91.7	B
1879	0.0	6.6	-0.1	10.0	103.5	A+	102.7	A+
1880	2.5	4.5	-0.6	17.3	110.9	A+	109.3	A+
1881	0.0	4.1	-0.8	-0.3	96.4	A	97.0	A
1882	0.0	3.3	-1.1	11.3	109.1	A+	108.4	A+
1883	-1.6	3.5	-1.1	-3.7	92.2	B	93.2	B
1884	-2.5	4.0	-0.9	2.2	96.6	A	96.8	A
1885	-1.7	4.6	-0.5	2.2	96.4	A	96.7	A
1886	-2.6	4.7	-0.7	10.2	103.6	A+	102.8	A+
1887	0.9	4.3	-0.7	3.1	98.6	A	98.8	A
1888	0.0	5.1	-0.8	-2.8	92.9	B	93.7	B
1889	-2.6	4.3	-0.6	6.3	100.0	A+	99.8	A+
Average	-2.3	5.1	-0.7	4.5	97.5	A	97.3	A

business operations. Industrial production and per capita income rose sharply and the United States grew in economic power second only to Great Britain. Heavy industry, railroads, steel, oil, sugar, meatpacking, agriculture, machinery and coal mining, financed by capital from the nation's financial market on Wall Street, dominated the economic landscape. New access to the American West and its natural resources supplied the raw materials for economic and corporate expansion while the completion of the rail system enabled the massive export of resources.[21]

Technology, mechanization and innovation drove increases in productivity, allowing corporations to produce more goods with fewer resources in less time. Changes in factory design increased the rate of production while undercutting the need for skilled labor as unskilled labor was able to perform simple and repetitive tasks under the direction of skilled foremen and engineers. In turn, skilled labor and engineers were drawn to machine shops which grew rapidly. Both the number of unskilled and skilled workers increased and their wage rates grew. Engineering colleges were established to supply the growing demand for expertise. Railroads, which tripled in mileage between 1860 and 1880, invented bureaucratic corporate structures using middle managers and set up specific career tracks for their employees. For example, young men were hired and promoted internally until they reached the position of locomotive engineer, conductor or station agent. The concept of career tracks spread from the railroads to other skilled blue collar jobs and for white collar managers which later expanded into finance, manufacturing and trade. Smaller businesses also thrived

---

[21] Jerome A. Greene and Douglas D. Scott (2006). *Finding Sand Creek: History, Archaeology, and the 1864 Massacre Site.* Norman: University of Oklahoma Press.

and together with the labor force employed by large business, a new middle class developed, especially in the Northern cities.

Americans had a strong sense of civic virtue and were often shocked by scandals in corrupt state governments and cities controlled by political machines where payoffs to secure government contracts were common. A widespread belief that government intervention in the economy inevitably led to favoritism, bribery, kickbacks, inefficiency, waste, and corruption led to pressure for a free market with low tariffs, low taxes, less spending, and a laissez-faire government. Many business and professional people supported these goals although there were often calls for high tariffs to insulate American workers from low wages in Europe. The period was also marked by long work hours and sometimes hazardous working conditions which led to the beginning of the Labor Movement despite strong opposition from industrialists and the courts. Labor activists and agrarians focused their attacks on monopolies and railroads, arguing they were unfair to the common man. Overall, Republican and Democratic political platforms remained remarkably constant during this period. However, Republicans often complained that high tariffs benefited industrialists more than their employees who, even at the time, were regarded by many as being exploited.

At times economic growth was interrupted by financial panics, most notably, the Panic of 1873 and the Panic of 1884. The Panic of 1873 was precipitated by the bankruptcy of the Philadelphia banking firm, Jay Cooke & Company, a major financier of railroad expansion, on September 18, 1873. It came right on the heels of a number of economic setbacks including the Black Friday panic of 1869, the Chicago fire of 1871, the outbreak of equine influenza in 1872, and demonetization of silver in 1873. The failure of the Jay Cooke bank set off a chain reaction of bank failures and temporarily closed the New York stock market. Factories began to lay off workers. Between 1873 and 1875, 89 railroads went bankrupt and a total of 18,000 businesses failed. Historians record that the panic led to the Long Depression which the National Bureau of Economic Research records as the longest-lasting contraction in US history. At 65 months, this period eclipses the Great Depression's 43 month contraction.[22] [23] In the case of the United States, the Long Depression is more myth than fact as the period was marked by deflation but not falling production and the GDP grew throughout the period except in 1874. The Panic of 1884, a relatively short downturn, occurred when a depletion of gold reserves in Europe led New York City national banks to reduce investments in the rest of the country and call outstanding loans. As a result, the Marine Bank of New York, the Penn Bank of Pittsburgh, the investment firm, Grant & Ward, and more than 10,000 small firms failed.

Despite the economic panics and recessions, the EPI Index records a period of excellent performance (Table 5). Inflation was non-existent as prices fell on average 2.3% per year. Budget deficits were also non-existent as the government ran surpluses averaging 0.7% of GDP. Most importantly, GDP growth averaged a very strong 4.5% per year with economic contractions over 1% occurring only in 1874, 1883 and 1888. The average EPI score was Excellent, at 97.5%, and the period ranks 1st out of 14 economic periods examined.

---

[22] *Business Cycle Expansions and Contractions.* National Bureau of Economic Research.

[23] Rendigs Fels (1949). *The Long-Wave Depression, 1873-79.* The Review of Economics and Statistics (Vol. 31, No. 1, pp. 69-73).

PROGRESSIVE ERA (EXCLUDING WWI): 1890–1913

Prior to the Progressive Era, politicians were generally reluctant to use the federal government to intervene in the private sector. Laissez-faire, a doctrine opposing government interference in the economy, was generally accepted by the public except in law and order issues and the railroad industry. By 1890, this attitude slowly began to change when a collection of labor movements, small businesses and farm interests slowly began lobbying the government to intercede on their behalf.[24] The middle class was beginning to reach critical mass and began to demonstrate a leeriness of both business elites as well as the radical farmer and labor movements who were coalescing around a fledgling Progressive movement, encouraged by journalists, known as Muckrakers, and authors such as Upton Sinclair.

Progressives, in contrast to earlier generations, favored government regulation of business to achieve, in their opinion, market competition and free enterprise. Their goal was to temper the power of trusts and monopolies that had created enormous wealth controlled by only a few individual industrialists whose names are legendary such as John D. Rockefeller (oil), Andrew Carnegie (railroads and steel), Jay Gould (finance and railroads), Leland Stanford (railroads), and Cornelius Vanderbilt (railroads).

Like the Gilded Age, the Progressive Era also had its share of recessions and panics. The most serious was the Panic of 1893. Like that of earlier crashes, it was caused by a series of bank failures this time caused by railroad overbuilding and shaky financ-

---

[24] Harold U. Faulkner (1951). *The Decline of Laissez Faire*, 1897-1917.

▼ **TABLE 6. PROGRESSIVE ERA: 1890–1913**

Year	Inflation Rate (%)	Unemployment (%)	Budget Deficit (% of GDP)	GDP growth (%)	EPI (%)	EPI Grade	Weighted EPI (%)	Weighted EPI Grade
1890	-1.8	4.0	-0.6	2.2	97.0	A	97.3	A
1891	0.0	4.5	-0.2	7.4	103.0	A+	102.8	A+
1892	0.0	4.3	-0.1	2.0	97.7	A	98.1	A
1893	-0.9	6.8	0.0	-3.3	89.0	C+	89.7	C+
1894	-4.6	9.3	0.4	-5.4	80.3	D+	80.7	D+
1895	-1.9	8.5	0.2	15.4	104.8	A+	103.1	A+
1896	0.0	9.3	0.1	-1.5	89.1	C+	89.3	C+
1897	-1.0	8.5	0.1	5.7	96.1	A	95.5	A-
1898	0.0	7.8	0.2	2.8	94.8	B+	94.7	B+
1899	0.0	5.9	0.5	9.9	103.6	A+	102.9	A+
1900	1.0	5.0	-0.2	2.1	96.3	A	96.5	A
1901	1.0	4.1	-0.3	11.5	106.7	A+	105.9	A+
1902	1.0	3.5	-0.3	1.1	97.0	A	97.5	A
1903	2.9	3.5	-0.2	6.5	100.3	A+	100.1	A+
1904	0.9	4.9	0.2	-5.0	88.9	C+	90.0	B-
1905	-0.9	3.9	0.1	10.2	105.3	A+	104.7	A+
1906	1.9	2.5	-0.1	13.8	109.6	A+	108.7	A+
1907	4.6	3.1	-0.3	-1.9	90.7	B-	91.5	B
1908	-1.8	7.5	0.2	-13.2	77.4	D+	79.1	D+
1909	-1.8	5.7	0.3	16.6	108.9	A+	107.4	A+
1910	4.6	5.9	0.1	-0.9	88.6	C+	88.9	C+
1911	0.0	7.0	0.0	3.4	96.4	A	96.3	A
1912	2.6	5.9	0.0	4.8	96.3	A	96.1	A
1913	1.7	5.7	0.0	4.0	96.5	A	96.4	A
Average	0.3	5.7	0.0	3.7	96.4	A	96.4	A

ing. Compounding market overbuilding and a railroad bubble was a run on the gold supply and a policy of using both gold and silver metals as a peg for the US dollar value. Only three years later, the US experienced another panic in 1896 and while it was sharp and resulted in the failure of the National Bank of Illinois in Chicago, it was less serious than other panics. It was caused by a drop in silver reserves and market concerns over the effects it would have on the gold standard. Deflation of commodities prices drove the stock market to new lows in a trend that began to reverse only after the 1896 election of William McKinley.

The most significant panic was the 1907 Banker's Panic. It occurred during an economic contraction, as measured by the National Bureau of Economic Research, which began in May 1907 and ended in June of 1908.[25] Robert Bruner and Sean Carr recite the economic damage in *The Panic of 1907: Lessons Learned from the Market's Perfect Storm*. During the contraction, industrial production dropped further than in any prior bank run. 1907 also saw the second-highest volume of bankruptcies to that date. Industrial production fell by 11%, imports by 26%, and unemployment rose from 3% to 8%. Immigration dropped to 750,000 in 1909, down from 1.2 million two years earlier.[26]

The history of the panic is insightful for underscoring the lack of institutional safeguards as well as the influence of specific groups and individuals on the markets. The panic began when an attempt to corner the market on United Copper Company stock failed.

---

[25] *US Business Cycle Expansions and Contractions*, National Bureau of Economic Research.

[26] Robert F Bruner and Sean D. Carr (2007). *The Panic of 1907: Lessons Learned from the Market's Perfect Storm*, Hoboken, New Jersey: John Wiley & Sons (pp. 103-107).

Banks that had lent money to the cornering scheme suffered runs that later spread to affiliated banks and trusts, leading a week later to the downfall of the Knickerbocker Trust Company, New York City's third-largest trust. The collapse generated fear throughout the city's trusts as regional banks withdrew reserves from New York City banks. The Panic spread nationwide as depositors in turn withdrew funds from their regional banks.

At the time, the United States did not have a central bank to inject liquidity into the banking system. Fortunately, J. P. Morgan, New York's most famous and well-connected financier, intervened and pledged support from his personal fortune while convincing other New York bankers to do the same. However, within hours of the banking crisis solution another potential panic emerged when one of Wall Street's largest brokerage firms, Moore & Schley, began to fail after borrowing heavily while using the stock of Tennessee Coal, Iron and Railroad Company (TC&I) as collateral. The value of this stock was under pressure and it was presumed that many banks would likely call the brokerage's loans forcing a sudden liquidation of the stock. If that occurred, it would have sent shares of TC&I plummeting, devastating Moore and Schley and causing a further panic in the market.[26] Again, Morgan stepped in, using his personal influence to arrange for US Steel Corporation to acquire TC&I, despite the fact that such an acquisition would violate the Sherman Antitrust Act. In what must have been perceived as a perfect storm, J.P. Morgan was immediately confronted with another situation following his banking interventions as concerns arose that the Trust Company of America and the Lincoln Trust might fail to open on Monday due to continuing runs. On a Saturday evening, Morgan hosted top bankers at his residence to discuss the crisis, with the clearing-house bank presidents in the East room, trust company executives in the West room, and those dealing with the Moore & Schley situation in his library office. There, Morgan told his counselors that he would agree to help shore up Moore & Schley only if the trust companies would work together to bail out their weakest members.[27] The discussion among the bankers continued late Saturday night but without any real progress. Then, around midnight, J.P. Morgan informed a leader of the trust company presidents of the Moore & Schley situation which was going to require $25 million and that he was not willing to proceed with any assistance unless the problems with the trust companies could also be solved. He also informed the trust companies that they would not receive further help and that they had to reach their own solution. As the discussions continued, Morgan locked them in his library and hid the key to force a solution while warning them that without a solution, the entire banking systems would fail.[28] Finally, at 4:45 in the morning, he persuaded the leaders of the trust companies to sign an agreement and allowed them to go home.[29] [30] The next day, Morgan and his representatives, along with US Steel's Gary and industrialist Henry Clay Frick, worked at the library to finalize the acquisition of TC&I by US Steel, yet one obstacle remained: the anti-trust crusading President Theodore Roosevelt who had made breaking up monopolies a focus of his presidency.[31]

---

[27] Ibid, p.122.

[28] Ibid, p.122.

[29] Ibid, p.124.

[30] Ibid, pp.124-127.

[31] Ibid, p.121.

Morgan sent Frick and Gary overnight by train to the White House to implore Roosevelt to approve the acquisition and set aside the principles of the Sherman Antitrust Act before the market opened. With less than an hour before the markets opened, Roosevelt and Secretary of State Elihu reviewed the proposed takeover and assessed the news of a potential crash if the merger was not approved.[32] [33] Roosevelt relented and when the news reached New York, confidence soared. The *Commercial & Financial Chronicle* reported that "the relief furnished by this transaction was instant and far-reaching."[34] The final crisis of the panic had been averted. But the frequency of previous crises and the severity of the 1907 panic added to widespread concern over the large role J.P. Morgan and other bankers played, which led to renewed calls for a national debate on reform.[35] The next year, Congress passed the Aldrich–Vreeland Act, which established the National Monetary Commission to investigate the panic and to propose legislation to regulate banking.[36] The result was that the Federal Reserve Act of 1913 took effect in November, 1914, when the 12 regional banks commenced operations.

Despite the increase in government intervention in the economy, the EPI indicator reports that economic conditions were generally excellent with very low rates of inflation, mild unem-

---

[32] Ibid, p.132.

[33] Ron Chernow (1990). *The House of Morgan: An American Banking Dynasty and the Rise of Modern Finance* (p.132), New York: Grove Press.

[34] Robert F Bruner and Sean D. Carr (2007). *The Panic of 1907: Lessons Learned from the Market's Perfect Storm*, Hoboken, New Jersey: John Wiley & Sons.

[35] Smith, B. Mark (2004). *A History of the Global Stock Market; From Ancient Rome to Silicon Valley* (pp.99-100), Chicago: University of Chicago Press.

[36] Jeffrey A. Miron (1986). *Financial Panics, the Seasonality of the Nominal Interest Rate, and the Founding of the Fed*, American Economic Review, 76 (1): pp.125-40.

ployment, budget surpluses or mild deficits, and a growth rate of 3.7% between 1890 and 1913 (Table 6). Exceptions to this favorable climate occurred in 1904, 1908 and 1910, which is consistent with recessionary business cycle activity. The economy enjoyed stable prices on average, mild budget deficits and surplus, low rates of unemployment and moderate growth in GDP.

WORLD WAR I AND IMMEDIATE AFTERMATH: 1914-1920

▼ TABLE 7. WORLD WAR I AND IMMEDIATE AFTERMATH: 1914–1920

Year	Inflation Rate (%)	Unemployment (%)	Budget Deficit (% of GDP)	GDP growth (%)	EPI (%)	EPI Grade	Weighted EPI (%)	Weighted EPI Grade
1914	1.0	8.5	0.0	-7.9	82.6	C-	83.6	C
1915	1.0	9.0	0.2	2.7	92.4	B	92.2	B
1916	7.9	6.5	-0.1	13.9	99.6	A+	98.1	A
1917	17.4	5.2	1.6	-2.7	73.0	D	73.2	D
1918	18.0	1.2	13.5	9.3	76.6	D+	76.2	D+
1919	14.6	2.3	17.5	0.4	66.1	D-	66.9	D-
1920	15.6	5.2	-0.3	-1.5	78.1	D+	78.1	D+
Average	10.8	5.4	4.6	2.0	81.2	C-	81.2	C-

Historians generally agree that the Progressive Era ended at the beginning of the 1920s. However, we have split the WWI economy from the Progressive Era due to the dramatic economic upheaval caused by the war.

The onset of WWI dramatically changed the economic landscape as spending on the war precipitated very large budget deficits in 1918 and 1919, a rapid increase in money creation and double digit inflation. By the final years of the Progressive era, economic conditions had deteriorated considerably with the EPI indicator registering Poor for the years 1917-1920 (Table 7).

THE ROARING 20S: 1921-1929

▼ TABLE 8. THE ROARING 20S: 1921-1929

Year	Inflation Rate (%)	Unemployment (%)	Budget Deficit (% of GDP)	GDP growth (%)	EPI (%)	EPI Grade	Weighted EPI (%)	Weighted EPI Grade
1921	-10.5	11.3	-0.7	-2.4	76.4	D+	76.1	D+
1922	-6.1	8.6	-1.0	6.0	92.3	B	91.4	B
1923	1.8	4.3	-0.8	13.3	108.0	A+	107.0	A+
1924	0.0	5.3	-1.1	2.5	98.3	A	98.4	A
1925	2.3	4.7	-0.8	3.1	96.9	A	97.0	A
1926	1.1	2.9	-0.9	6.1	102.9	A+	102.9	A+
1927	-1.7	3.9	-1.2	1.1	96.7	A	97.1	A
1928	-1.7	4.7	-1.0	0.8	95.3	A-	95.7	A-
1929	0.0	2.9	-0.7	6.8	104.6	A+	104.6	A+
Average	-1.6	5.4	-0.9	4.1	96.8	A	96.7	A

Following WWI, the political landscape changed significantly. In 1921, President Harding was elected promising "a return to normalcy." The inflation associated with the war fell dramatically, with prices actually falling in 1920 and 1921 in conjunction with a brief, yet sharp recession. Under the leadership of Treasury Secretary Andrew Mellon, tariffs were increased. However, high wartime taxes were reduced, including a reduction in the top rates from 73% to 24% leading to vigorous economic growth and government surpluses, which were used to retire about a third of the national debt between 1920 and 1930. In addition, Secretary of Commerce Herbert Hoover worked to introduce reforms by regulating many business practices. Also noteworthy was the rapid growth of the automobile industry, which stimulated other industries such as energy, glass, and road-building. These, in turn, strengthened tourism as consumers with vehicles enjoyed shopping further from their homes. Both small and large cities prospered as millions migrated from the country side, leading to sharp increases in construction for offices, factories and homes powered by the emerging electric power industry and connected by new telephones.

With the exception of agriculture, which never recovered from the wartime bubble in land prices, the 1920s enjoyed one of the best economies in US history. The EPI Index recorded seven consecutive years of an Excellent performance for the period of 1923-1929 (Table 8).

THE GREAT DEPRESSION: 1930-1940

In October 1929, eight months into newly elected President Herbert Hoover's term, the stock market crashed. Through a series of dramatic policy missteps, the Federal Reserve Board allowed the money supply to fall by almost one- third over the next three years and despite their mandate, the Fed made little attempt to assist banks. Today, it is widely believed by economists that this was one of the single most important contributors to the Depression.

▼ TABLE 9. THE GREAT DEPRESSION: 1930–1940

Year	Inflation Rate (%)	Unemployment (%)	Budget Deficit (% of GDP)	GDP growth (%)	EPI (%)	EPI Grade	Weighted EPI (%)	Weighted EPI Grade
1930	-2.3	8.9	-0.8	-8.6	81.0	D+	81.9	C-
1931	-9.0	15.9	0.6	-6.4	68.1	D	67.8	D
1932	-9.9	23.6	4.0	-13.0	49.5	F	49.2	F
1933	-5.1	24.9	4.5	-1.4	64.1	D-	62.5	D-
1934	3.1	21.7	5.9	10.8	80.1	D+	77.6	D+
1935	2.2	20.1	4.0	9.0	82.6	C-	80.5	D+
1936	1.5	17.0	5.5	12.9	89.0	C+	86.8	C
1937	3.6	14.3	2.5	5.3	84.9	C	83.7	C
1938	-2.1	19.0	0.1	-3.5	75.3	D+	74.6	D
1939	-1.4	17.2	3.2	8.1	86.3	C	84.6	C
1940	0.7	14.6	3.0	8.5	90.2	B-	88.8	C+
Average	-1.7	17.9	3.0	2.0	77.4	D+	76.2	D+

Help, if any, would have had to come from fiscal policy, but here too, policy missteps worsened the downturn. Hoover attempted to stop "the downward spiral" which contradicts many contemporary critics who accused Hoover of sharing Mellon's laissez-faire viewpoint.

In 1930, Congress approved and President Hoover signed the Smoot-Hawley Tariff Act which raised tariffs on thousands of imported items. The intent of the Act was to encourage the purchase of American-made products by increasing the cost of imported goods while raising revenue for the federal government and protecting farmers. However, other nations, also suffering the effects of the Depression, quickly increased tariffs on American-made goods in retaliation, leading to a reduction in international trade further worsening the Depression.[37] By 1932, the Great Depression had spread worldwide and in the US, unemployment had reached 24.9%. Combined with an agricultural drought, individuals, businesses and farmers defaulted on record numbers of loans leading to the collapse of over 5,000 banks. The sharp decline in incomes led to deficit in the federal budget, prompting Congress and the President to enact the Revenue Act of 1932 to pay for government programs. Under the Act, income taxes on the highest incomes rose from 25% to 63%, the estate tax was doubled, a 13.75% tax on corporations was passed, and a two-cent (over 30 cents in today's dollars) "check tax" was passed on all bank checks. As drastic as these measures seemed, they did not work.

Franklin Delano Roosevelt was elected President in 1932 without a specific program. Like Hoover, he felt the Depression was caused, in part, by people no longer spending or investing because they were afraid. He relied on a highly eclectic group of advisors who patched together many programs, known as "The New Deal." During Roosevelt's "First 100 Days," he sent Congress a record number of bills including the Emergency Banking Act, which declared a "bank holiday" and announced a plan to allow banks to reopen. The number of banks that reopened after the "holiday" was less than the number that had been open before.[38] In addition, he signed the Glass-Stegall Act that created the Federal Deposit Insurance Corporation.

---

[37] "Smoot-Hawley Tariff", US Department of State.

[38] Paul Anthony Samuelson (1964). *Readings in Economics.* McGraw-Hill. p.140.

The economy eventually recovered from the low point of the winter of 1932-33, with sustained improvement until 1937 when the Recession of 1937 brought back 1934 levels of unemployment. Government spending increased from 8.0% of GNP under Hoover in 1932 to 10.2% of GNP in 1936 under Roosevelt. While Roosevelt balanced the "regular" budget, the emergency budget was funded by debt, which increased from 33.6% of GNP in 1932 to 40.9% in 1936.[39] Deficit spending had been recommended by some economists, most notably John Maynard Keynes in Britain.

The EPI Index clearly shows the dramatic change in the economic environment between 1930 and 1933 when the indicator dropped from a Superior score of 104.6 at the end of 1929 to a Failing 49.5 at the end of 1933, the lowest annual score ever recorded by the EPI Index (Table 9). Interestingly enough, the EPI Index also records an improvement in the economy from 1934-1936, which is consistent with other indicators, and then a drop again in 1937 and 1938 when America experienced "a recession within a depression" in 1937. Again, the economy began improving in 1939 and 1940, but at no time during the Great Depression did the unemployment rate drop below 14% after the peak Depression year of 1933, despite unprecedented intervention by the federal government by the Roosevelt Administration.

WORLD WAR II (INCLUDING THE LIFTING OF WARTIME CONTROLS): 1941-1947

Economic comparisons between times of war and peace are difficult at best, and the economy during World War II operated under numerous new conditions including unprecedent-

---

[39] Historical Statistics (1976).

▼ TABLE 10. WORLD WAR II (INCLUDING THE LIFTING OF WARTIME CONTROLS): 1941–1947

Year	Inflation Rate (%)	Unemployment (%)	Budget Deficit (% of GDP)	GDP growth (%)	EPI (%)	EPI Grade	Weighted EPI (%)	Weighted EPI Grade
1941	5.0	9.9	4.3	17.1	97.9	A	95.9	A-
1942	10.9	4.7	14.2	18.4	88.6	C+	87.2	C
1943	6.1	1.9	30.3	16.4	78.1	D+	78.0	D+
1944	1.7	1.2	22.7	8.2	82.6	C-	83.4	C
1945	2.3	1.9	21.5	-1.2	73.1	D	74.8	D
1946	8.3	3.9	7.2	-11.1	69.5	D	71.3	D
1947	14.4	3.9	-1.7	-0.7	82.8	C-	82.8	C-
Average	7.0	3.9	14.1	6.7	81.8	C-	81.9	C-

ed government spending, price controls, bond campaigns, controls over raw materials, bans on new housing and automobiles, rationing, guaranteed cost-plus profits, subsidized wages plus the draft of 12 million soldiers. Nevertheless, the economy performed strongly in terms of GDP growth and much of the unemployment of the previous decade evaporated during the war effort but at a cost: massive government budget deficits and an unprecedented increase in the national debt.

The War Production Board was formed and charged with organizing the nation's productive capabilities so that military priorities would be met. This was achieved through the conversion of consumer-products plants for the purpose of filling military contracts. The best example was the Automakers who built tanks and aircraft. The government created the Office of Price Administration which tried to prevent inflation caused by scarce consumer products by rationing consumer items ranging from sugar to gasoline along with rents controls.[40] The labor force also began to shift as six million women took jobs in manufacturing and production (most were newly created temporary jobs in munitions or to replace men on military duty).

In the United States, the end of WWII was followed by uneasy and contentious conversion back to a peacetime economy. President Truman was faced with a sudden renewal of labor-management conflicts that had lain dormant during the war years, severe shortages in housing and consumer products, and widespread dissatisfaction with inflation.[41] Also challenging was a wave of strikes in major industries. In the spring of 1946, a national railway strike crippled all passenger and freight lines for over a month.

Most economic indicators report a tremendous resurgence in economic conditions during this period, which is correct if one only measures economic performance in terms of GDP growth. While GDP growth is very important, the EPI indicator contrasts this with other indicators as it also accounts for the tremendous increase in war-related deficit spending, which reduces the EPI Index (Table 10). While it is accurate to report that economic activity increased dramatically and unemployment fell during the war, what is often forgotten is that the United States also tripled its national debt between 1941 and 1946 which would take decades to reduce. For this reason, the EPI averaged Fair for the years 1941-1947.

---

[40] Harold G. Vatter (1985). *The US Economy in World War II.*

[41] David Grubin (1997). *The American Experience: Truman.*

THE POST WAR PROSPERITY: 1948-1967

The two decades following WWII and the wartime decommission are often referred to as the golden era of American Capitalism. During this period, inflation, unemployment and budget deficits remained at historical lows while economic growth averaged over 4% per year. The government, by historical standards, was increasingly involved in many aspects of economic planning, albeit at a level considerably below government involvement in Europe or the Marxist economies of the Soviet Union and the Warsaw Pact.

In 1953, Truman was succeeded by President Eisenhower who espoused a policy of dynamic conservatism.[42] In terms of domestic policy, he continued the New Deal programs that he had inherited and expanded Social Security, which he consolidated into a new cabinet-level agency: the Department of Health, Education and Welfare. The economy experienced a recession in 1953–1954, early in Eisenhower's first term. While he deployed traditional Republican rhetoric, Eisenhower supported an activist contra-cyclical economic approach that helped to establish Keynesianism (popularized during the Depression) as a bipartisan economic policy, including public works programs, easing credit and reducing taxes.

Towards the end of the Eisenhower Administration, the economy suffered two recessions in three years. Despite low inflation and interest rates, GDP had grown by an average of only 2.2% during the Eisenhower presidency and had declined by 1% during

---

[42] The Eleanor Roosevelt Papers. *Dwight Eisenhower. Teaching Eleanor Roosevelt*, ed. by Allida Black, June Hopkins, et. al. (Hyde Park, New York: Eleanor Roosevelt National Historic Site, 2003). http://www.nps.gov/archive/elro/glossary/eisenhower-dwight.htm [Accessed July 21, 2009].

▾ **TABLE 11. THE POST-WAR PROSPERITY: 1948–1967**

Year	Inflation Rate (%)	Unemployment (%)	Budget Deficit (% of GDP)	GDP growth (%)	EPI (%)	EPI Grade	Weighted EPI (%)	Weighted EPI Grade
1948	8.1	3.8	-4.6	4.3	97.1	A	96.7	A
1949	-1.2	5.9	-0.2	-0.5	92.5	B	92.9	B
1950	1.3	5.3	1.1	8.7	101.1	A+	100.5	A+
1951	7.9	3.3	-1.9	7.8	98.5	A	97.9	A
1952	1.9	3.0	0.4	3.8	98.5	A	98.7	A
1953	0.8	2.9	1.7	4.6	99.2	A+	99.5	A+
1954	0.7	5.5	0.3	-0.7	92.8	B	93.3	B
1955	-0.4	4.4	0.8	7.1	101.6	A+	101.4	A+
1956	1.5	4.1	-0.9	1.9	97.3	A	97.6	A
1957	3.3	4.3	-0.8	2.0	95.2	A-	95.4	A-
1958	2.8	6.8	0.6	-1.0	88.8	C+	89.1	C+
1959	0.7	5.5	2.6	7.1	98.4	A	98.1	A
1960	1.7	5.5	-0.1	2.5	95.3	A-	95.4	A-
1961	1.0	6.7	0.6	2.3	94.0	B	94.0	B+
1962	1.0	5.5	1.2	6.1	98.3	A	98.1	A
1963	1.3	5.7	0.8	4.4	96.6	A	96.5	A
1964	1.3	5.2	0.9	5.8	98.4	A	98.2	A
1965	1.6	4.5	0.2	6.4	100.1	A+	99.9	A+
1966	2.9	3.8	0.5	6.5	99.4	A+	99.2	A+
1967	3.1	3.8	1.0	2.5	94.6	B+	94.9	B+
Average	2.1	4.8	0.2	4.1	96.9	A	96.9	A

Eisenhower's last twelve months in office.[43] Still in recession when Kennedy took office, the economy accelerated early in his presidency. In response, Kennedy passed the largest tax cut in history in 1961, thus ending a period of tight fiscal policies while the Federal Reserve loosened monetary policy to keep interest rates low and encourage growth of the economy. The economy emerged from the recession and GDP expanded by an average of 5.5% from early 1961 to late 1963, while inflation remained steady at around 1% and unemployment began to ease.[44] [45] This rate of growth in GDP and industry continued until 1966.

Following the assassination of President Kennedy, Lyndon B. Johnson was sworn in to office. One of his first initiatives was the Revenue Act of 1964, which reduced individual income tax rates including a lowering of the top personal rate from 91% to 70% and a lowering of the top corporate rate from 52% to 48%. In addition, Johnson introduced "The Great Society" program and the "War on Poverty" which included aid to education, Medicare, urban renewal, beautification, conservation, development of depressed regions, a wide-scale fight against poverty, control and prevention of crime, and the removal of obstacles to the right to vote, all with government involvement and funding. Simultaneous with the dramatic increase in domestic spending, was Johnson's escalation of the increasingly unpopular Vietnam War. By 1968, federal spending had risen to more than 20% of GDP from about 17.2% years earlier, while the budget deficit, virtually non-existent in 1965, had risen to almost 3% of GDP.

---

[43] BEA: quarterly GDP figures by sector, 1953-1964.

[44] Bureau of Labor Statistics: Employment & Unemployment

[45] Statistical Abstract of the United States: Historical price indices

During the post-war years, the EPI indicator records nearly twenty years of low inflation, unemployment, modest deficits, and rapid growth with only one exception, the recession year 1958 (Table 11). On average, the economy performed at an Excellent level between 1948 and 1967.

STAGFLATION AND MALAISE: 1968-1981

▼ TABLE 12. STAGFLATION AND MALAISE: 1968–1981

Year	Inflation Rate (%)	Unemployment (%)	Budget Deficit (% of GDP)	GDP growth (%)	EPI (%)	EPI Grade	Weighted EPI (%)	Weighted EPI Grade
1968	4.2	3.6	2.9	4.8	94.1	B+	94.2	B+
1969	5.5	3.5	-0.4	3.1	94.5	B+	94.6	B+
1970	5.7	4.9	0.8	0.2	88.8	C+	89.1	C+
1971	4.4	5.9	2.0	3.4	91.0	B	91.0	B-
1972	3.2	5.6	1.4	5.3	95.1	A-	94.8	B+
1973	6.2	4.9	1.0	5.8	93.7	B	93.3	B
1974	11.0	5.6	0.3	-0.5	82.6	C-	82.7	C-
1975	9.1	8.5	3.7	-0.2	78.5	D+	78.4	D+
1976	5.8	7.7	3.3	5.3	88.5	C+	88.0	C+
1977	6.5	7.1	2.2	4.6	88.8	C+	88.4	C+
1978	7.6	6.1	2.1	5.6	89.7	C+	89.3	C+
1979	11.3	5.8	1.1	3.2	84.9	C	84.6	C
1980	13.5	7.2	2.7	-0.2	76.4	D+	76.2	D+
1981	10.4	7.6	2.6	2.6	82.0	C-	81.6	C-
Average	7.5	6.0	1.8	3.1	87.8	C	87.6	C

Many historians record that the period of post-war prosperity lasted until the recession of 1973; however the EPI Index records that the economy began deteriorating in the late 1960s as inflation and budget deficits grew while GDP growth decelerated (Table 12). After hitting a high of 100.1 in 1965, the Index dropped slightly the next year to 99.4, but then fell significantly to 94.6 in 1967, where it hovered for three years before falling to 88.8 in 1970. Overall, the EPI Index trend during this period was down as the overall trend in inflation, unemployment and budget deficits was up. While real changes in economic growth were considered good in a number of years, the overall average annual rate of growth slowed to 3.1% vs. 4.1% during the previous "Golden Age."

To make matters worse, the political leadership and economic policies of Presidents Nixon, Ford and Carter were particularly weak and misguided. Examples include the detachment of the dollar from gold resulting in the collapse of the "Bretton Woods" international monetary regime, wage and price controls, the rapid expansion of social insurance programs (which would later prove to be actuarially unsound), the unsuccessful WIN (Whip Inflation Now) initiative, a presidential PR effort to "talk" prices down, "windfall" profit taxes on energy, and increased taxes resulting from inflation-led "bracket creep." At the same time, there was a rise in costly environmental and consumer movements which included new regulations and regulatory agencies such as OSHA (the Occupational Safety and Health Administration), the Consumer Product Safety Commission, the Nuclear Regulatory Commission and others. These policies were accompanied by an excessive increase in credit by the Federal Reserve leading to further economic turbulence exacerbated by oil price shocks which were led by OPEC.

THE REAGAN REVOLUTION AND THE "NEW ECONOMY": 1982-2000

In 1981, President Ronald Reagan presided over a collection of fiscally expansive economic policies marked by a reduction in federal income tax rates by 25%. His combination of tax cuts and dramatic increases in defense spending, in conjunction with continued spending on social welfare and insurance programs supported by a Democratic Congress, led to large federal deficits, including a tripling of the national debt from $944 billion in 1981 to $2.6 trillion in 1988. While debt almost always increased under every president in the latter half of the 20th century, it declined as a percentage of GDP under all presidents after 1950 and prior to Reagan. At the same time, inflation dropped dramatically from 13.5% annually in 1980 to just 3.2% annually in 1983; this was associated with a sharp recession resulting from historically high interest rates caused by Federal Reserve Chairman Paul Volcker's tighter control of the money supply. Real GDP contracted in 1980 and 1982 and the unemployment rate peaked at 9.7% in late 1982. Following the recession, GDP growth rebounded and unemployment dropped sharply, falling to 5.3% at the end of Reagan's presidency in January 1989. In addition, the deregulation movement that had begun under Ford and Carter accelerated under Reagan and became a bipartisan operation removing many of the New Deal regulations from energy, communications, transportation, and banking.

President George H. W. Bush succeeded Reagan in 1988 and continued many of Reagan's policies at the start of his term.

▼ TABLE 13. THE REAGAN REVOLUTION AND THE "NEW ECONOMY": 1982–2000

Year	Inflation Rate (%)	Unemployment (%)	Budget Deficit (% of GDP)	GDP growth (%)	EPI (%)	EPI Grade	Weighted EPI (%)	Weighted EPI Grade
1982	6.2	9.7	4.0	-1.9	78.2	D+	78.3	D+
1983	3.2	9.6	6.0	4.6	85.9	C	85.4	C
1984	4.4	7.5	4.8	7.3	90.6	B-	90.0	C+
1985	3.5	7.2	5.1	4.2	88.4	C+	88.3	C+
1986	1.9	7.0	5.0	3.5	89.6	C+	89.6	C+
1987	3.6	6.2	3.2	3.5	90.5	B-	90.5	B-
1988	4.1	5.5	3.1	4.2	91.5	B	91.4	B
1989	4.8	5.3	2.8	3.7	90.8	B-	90.8	B-
1990	5.4	5.6	3.9	1.9	87.0	C	87.1	C
1991	4.2	6.9	4.5	-0.1	84.4	C	84.7	C
1992	3.0	7.5	4.7	3.6	88.3	C+	88.2	C+
1993	3.0	6.9	3.9	2.7	89.0	C+	89.0	C+
1994	2.6	6.1	2.9	4.0	92.4	B	92.4	B
1995	2.8	5.6	2.2	2.7	92.1	B	92.2	B
1996	2.9	5.4	1.4	3.8	94.1	B+	94.0	B+
1997	2.3	4.9	0.3	4.5	96.9	A	96.8	A
1998	1.5	4.5	0.8	4.5	97.6	A	97.6	A
1999	2.2	4.2	1.4	4.7	96.9	A	96.9	A
2000	3.4	4.0	2.5	4.1	94.3	B+	94.4	B+
Average	3.4	6.3	3.3	3.4	90.4	B-	90.4	B-

As a "compassionate conservative," Bush was viewed as more "moderate" than Reagan, but shared his views on a number of issues, including free trade. In 1988 Canada and the United States signed the Canada-United States Free Trade Agreement. America then entered into negotiations with the Mexican government for a similar treaty and Canada asked to join the negotiations in order to preserve its perceived gains under the 1988 deal. The result, the North American Free Trade Agreement (NAFTA) was signed in 1992 and created the largest trading block in the world. Bush partially reversed Reagan's policies on taxes while simultaneously entering into a war in the Persian Gulf. The economy dipped into a mild recession which contributed to the election of Bill Clinton in 1992. In contrast to many politicians, Clinton was viewed by many as being more "centrist," however, due to controversies early in his term, conservatives were swept into office in 1994, handing the Republican Party control of both houses of Congress for the first time in forty years. The election of conservatives all but assured a slowing of government involvement in the economy and a more disciplined approach to fiscal policy and deficits.

The EPI Index clearly shows an improvement in economic conditions from Poor to Good in the late 1980s followed by a worsening of conditions between 1990 and 1993 (Table 13). By the end of 1994, economic conditions improved strongly as inflation, unemployment and budget deficits fell and economic growth accelerated. Over the entire time frame, economic conditions trended up with an Excellent performance recorded in 1997 through 1999.

THE POST MILLENNIUM PERIOD: 2001-2015

▾ TABLE 14. THE POST-MILLENNIUM PERIOD: 2001-2015

Year	Inflation Rate (%)	Unemployment (%)	Budget Deficit (% of GDP)	GDP growth (%)	EPI (%)	EPI Grade	Weighted EPI (%)	Weighted EPI Grade
2001	2.8	4.7	0.6	1.0	92.8	B	93.2	B
2002	1.6	5.8	3.8	1.8	90.6	B-	90.9	B-
2003	2.3	6.0	4.7	2.8	89.8	C+	89.9	C+
2004	2.7	5.5	4.3	3.8	91.3	B	91.4	B
2005	3.4	5.1	3.1	3.3	91.8	B	91.9	B
2006	3.2	4.6	2.0	2.7	92.8	B	93.0	B
2007	2.9	4.6	2.9	1.8	91.4	B	91.8	B
2008	3.8	5.8	6.7	-0.3	83.4	C	84.0	C
2009	-0.3	9.3	13.2	-2.8	74.5	D	75.3	D+
2010	1.6	9.6	10.9	2.5	80.4	D+	80.4	D+
2011	3.1	8.9	9.6	1.6	79.9	D+	80.1	D+
2012	2.1	8.1	7.9	2.2	84.2	C	84.3	C
2013	1.5	7.4	4.4	1.5	88.2	C+	88.4	C+
2014	1.6	6.2	4.1	2.4	90.5	B-	90.7	B-
2015	0.1	5.3	3.7	2.4	93.3	B	93.6	B
Average	2.2	6.5	5.5	1.8	87.7	C	87.9	C

The economy entered into a mild recession in the final days of the Clinton Administration which was exacerbated by the terrorist attacks of September 11, 2001. Upon entering office, President George W. Bush faced opposition in Congress but ultimately succeeded in winning a $1.35 trillion dollar tax cut program, one of the largest in history. By 2004, the economy showed signs of improvement in terms of GDP growth. However, the EPI indicator declined mildly between 2001 and 2003 (Table 14). Despite the modest improvement, the EPI indicator remained mostly at a B or Good level between 2001 and 2007.

In December 2007, the United States entered the longest post-World War II recession, which included a housing market correction, a subprime mortgage crisis, soaring oil prices, and a declining dollar value. As the economy worsened, both President Bush and his successor, President Obama, engaged in a series of politically unpopular stimulus and bail-out plans designed to stabilize the economy. Nevertheless, the EPI Index registered a sharp decline in 2008 and 2009 marked by rising unemployment, negative GDP growth and large budget deficits not experienced since WWII. Despite heavy government intervention, the recession continued. Although the economy slightly recovered in 2010, it did not return to pre-recession performance in 2012.

For the fifteen-year period of 2001-2015, average was manageable (2.2%), the combined impact of high unemployment (6.5%), a less-than-optimal deficit-to-GDP-growth ratio (5.5%), and lackluster GDP growth (1.8%) led to the Economic Performance Index score of 87.7%—a C grade, on par with the 1970s.

ALL ECONOMIC PERIODS

In order to bring historical perspective to the EPI Index, we have segregated US economic performance into fourteen distinct periods (Table 15). Most of these periods are already recog-

▼ TABLE 15. ALL ECONOMIC PERIODS

Period	Years	Inflation (%)	Unemployment (%)	Budget Deficit (% of GDP)	GDP growth (%)	EPI average Score	Performance	Lowest Score	Highest Score
1 The Founding Years	1790-1811	2.0	6.7	-0.3	3.9	92.7	B	81.6	99.4
2 The War of 1812	1812-1815	4.7	6.7	2.1	3.0	83.4	C	75.1	91.8
3 The Mid Industrial Revolution	1816-1860	-1.3	6.7	-0.3	4.1	94.1	B+	83.6	104.4
4 The American Civil War	1861-1865	14.8	6.7	6.6	3.4	75.3	D+	67.5	86.9
5 The Gilded Age	1866-1889	-2.3	5.1	-0.7	4.5	97.5	A	85.4	116.8
6 The Progressive Era (excluding WWI)	1890-1913	0.3	5.7	0.0	3.7	96.4	A	77.4	109.6
7 World War I and its aftermath	1914-1920	10.8	5.4	4.6	2.0	81.2	C-	66.1	99.6
8 The Roaring 20's	1921-1929	-1.6	5.4	-0.9	4.1	96.8	A	76.4	108.0
9 The Great Depression	1930-1940	-1.7	17.9	3.0	2.0	77.4	D+	49.5	90.2
10 World War II and War Decommission	1941-1947	2.1	3.9	14.1	6.7	81.8	C-	69.5	97.9
11 Post War Prosperity	1948-1967	7.4	3.0	12.8	4.9	81.7	C-	69.5	97.1
12 1st Modern Stagnation	1968-1981	7.5	6.0	1.8	3.1	87.8	C	76.4	95.1
13 Reagan Revolution and the New Economy	1982-2000	3.4	6.3	3.3	3.4	90.4	B-	78.2	97.6
14 The Post Millennium Period: 2000-present	2001-present	2.2	6.5	5.5	1.8	87.7	C	74.5	93.3

nized by historians and economists but we have added a raw EPI score and descriptive rankings to provide a sense of relative economic performance between each period. For example, the Gilded Age (1866-1889) and the Post-WWII Prosperity (1947-1967) periods rank first and second while the Great Depression (1930-1940) and the Civil War (1861-1856) periods rank thirteen and fourteenth (last). Also included is a chart containing each historical period in chronological order with a description of economic conditions, major events and the minimum, maximum and average EPI scores.

APPENDIX III

RAW AND WEIGHTED EPI

T he Raw EPI (or just EPI) was used throughout the book and is a simple metric that assigns equal weights to each of its subcomponents. The Raw EPI score is calculated as: 100% minus the absolute value of the inflation rate, minus the unemployment rate, minus the budget deficit as a percentage of GDP, plus GDP growth.

To overcome problems of consistency during periods of high economic volatility and to make scores comparable across countries, we normalize the data by introducing weights to each sub-component. The weights are determined by calculating the inverse standard deviation of each economic variable multiplied by the average standard deviation of all variables such that the average of weights is equal to one. In this way, scores are smoothed so as to capture trends without being distorted by short-lived volatility. The Weighted EPI formula is:

$$\text{Weighted EPI} = 100\% - W_{\text{Inf}} \bullet |\text{Inf}(\%) - I^*| - W_{\text{Unem}} \bullet (\text{Unem}(\%) - U^*) - W_{\text{Def}}(\text{Def/GDP}(\%) - \text{Def/GDP}^*) + W_{\text{GDP}} \bullet (\Delta\text{GDP}(\%) - \Delta\text{GDP}^*),$$

where W_i is the weight of each component of the indicator, calculated by the formula:

$$W_i = \frac{1}{\text{StD}_i} * StDev_{Av}$$

where StD_i is a standard deviation of each variable (inflation, or unemployment, or deficit as a share of GDP, or GDP growth) and $StDev_{Av}$ is the average standard deviation, calculated as:

$$StDev_{Av} = \frac{1}{4}\sum_{i=1}^{4} StD_i$$

Note that the average of the weights is equal to one. This weighting scheme allows keeping the same unit of measurement—percent—across all four variables. The Weighted EPI assigns smaller weights to more volatile variables and bigger weights to less volatile variables. This approach is similar to the ones used for the Chicago Fed National Activity Index (CFNAI) and the Conference Board Coincident Economic Index® (CEI), both of which use variables normalized by their standard deviations and then assign weights to each of them, by applying affine transformations.

Next, we nominally define the desired values for each of the indicator's subcomponents as follows:
- The desired inflation rate (I*) is 0.0%;
- The desired unemployment rate (U*) is 4.75%;
- The desired value for government deficit as a share of GDP (Def/GDP*) is 0.0%, consistent with a balanced budget
- The desired change in GDP (ΔGDP*) is a healthy real growth rate of 4.75%.

In our research, we calculate both raw and normalized EPI scores. It is worth noting that for developed economies, there are only small differences between the scores. However, for emerging market economies, differences can be significant and normalized data is essential to presenting a true picture of economic performance.

We calculate both the Raw and Weighted EPI scores for the US from 1790 to 2015 (chart below). The Raw EPI gives equal weights to its components, while the Weighted EPI uses in-

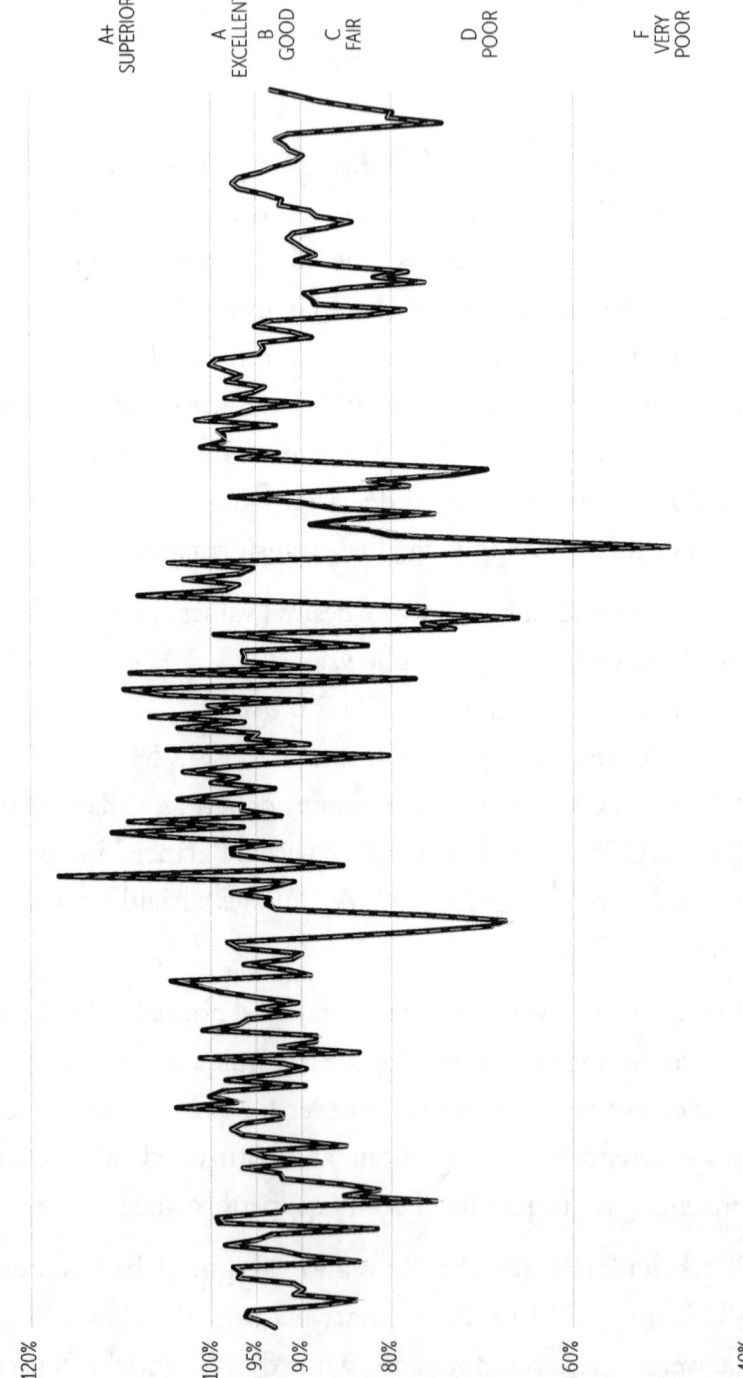

▶ 1. RAW EPI AND WEIGHTED EPI SCORES FOR THE US, 1790–2015

verse standard deviations. The standard deviations are calculated based on the whole data sample (not recursively) and are constant. The calculated weights for the US economy are close to unity for all EPI components, as volatilities of inflation, GDP growth, unemployment, and the budget deficit were relatively similar in the US over time. Note that, as the budget deficit and GDP growth have slightly bigger standard deviations, the weights that are used for calculation of the Weighted EPI are less than unity, while weights for inflation and unemployment are higher than unity.

The dynamics of both indexes are close to each other and the correlation between the Raw EPI and the Weighted EPI of 0.998, almost a perfect correlation. Comparing the Raw EPI and the Weighted EPI, we note that their main statistical moments are close to each other too. The same can be said about their autocorrelation coefficients, pointing to the fact that both indexes produce very similar dynamics.

As we mentioned earlier, a very similar dynamic for the Raw EPI and the Weighted EPI can be explained by the fact that the weights in the Weighted EPI formula are close to one, while the Raw EPI uses weights that are equal to one. We note that for other economies, weights might very be different. For example, many emerging market economies had periods of high and volatile inflation rates, pointing to the idea that inflation should have lower weight in the formula of the Weighted EPI.

APPENDIX IV

DATA SOURCES

COUNTRY DATA

Data on inflation, budget deficit, unemployment, and GDP growth were taken from the International Monetary Fund's April 2016 International Monetary Fund's World Economic Outlook database (http://www.imf.org).

US STATES DATA

Data was taken from the Bureau of Labor Statistics (http://www.bls.gov) and the Bureau of Economic Analysis (http://www.bea.gov).

US HISTORICAL DATA

For the US, we mainly used the International Monetary Fund's World Economic Outlook database for the latest data and historical data provided by *Historical Statistics of the United States: Millennial Edition* (2006). For some indicators and periods, the International Financial Statistics databases from International Monetary Fund was used.

REAL GDP GROWTH

1929-2015: the US Bureau of Economic Analysis (BEA) and the International Monetary Fund's World Economic Outlook database.

1869-1929: the estimates of real gross national product (GNP) were converted to 1996 prices. These figures were then converted to gross domestic product by subtracting net income earned abroad. The resulting time series was then shifted to make a smooth link at 1929.

1860-1869: as there are no direct estimates of national output for the years 1861-1868, the figure for 1869 was estimated. The figure for 1860 is taken from Weiss (1992, 1993).

1840-1860: for 1840, 1850, and 1860 Weiss's (1992, 1993) estimates of GDP in 1840 prices are used. For the intercensal years, interpolation is used.

1800-1840: estimates for 1800, 1810, 1820, and 1830 were established by the conjectural method (David, 1967) for farm output and nonfarm output.

1790-1800: estimates are based on the sum of farm output and nonfarm output, using backward extrapolation from 1800 for farm output and backward extrapolation using the David's index of industrial production for nonfarm output.

INFLATION

For 1774-1974, estimates by David and Solar (1977) are used, smoothed and merged with the US Bureau of Labor Statistics (BLS) consumer price index for all urban consumers for 1913-2003 (to splice at the year 1913 to a base of 1982-1984 = 100).

UNEMPLOYMENT

1948-2008: the US Bureau of Labor Statistics (BLS) data.

1890-1947: unemployment as a percentage of a civilian labor force used from Weir (1992).

1869-1899: vernon (1994) estimates.

1790-1868: we use the average unemployment rate of 6.7%.

DEFICIT AS A SHARE OF GDP

We separately discuss the data sources of deficit and nominal GDP data.

1959-2009: the IMF data for a Government balance and nominal GDP is used.

1789-1929: *Federal government finances-revenue, expenditure, and debt: 1789-1939* data from US Department of the Treasury.

1929-2008: Budget of the United States Government.

Nominal GDP is constructed as a product of real GDP and price deflator. For the construction of nominal GDP, the price deflator is used:

• 1869-1929: Balke and Gordon (1989) deflator of GNP, converted to 1996.

• 1860-1869: deflator is interpolated between the values for 1860 and 1869 using the David and Solar (1977) consumer price index.

• 1840-1860: deflator is interpolated between Weiss's estimates for 1840, 1850, and 1860 using a simple average of the David-Solar consumer price index, and the wholesale price index for all commodities, converted to a 1996 base by linking at 1860.

• 1800-1840: Weiss's estimates for 1800, 1810, 1820, 1830, and 1840, converted to a 1996 base by linking at 1860.

Since 1840, data on nominal GDP is available. Before 1840, nominal GDP was constructed from real GDP estimates and the data on the GDP deflator for 1800, 1810, 1820, 1830, and 1840. Using this data, the deficit as a share of nominal GDP is constructed directly.

APPENDIX V

REFERENCES

1. Bray Hammond (2001). Banks and Politics in America from the Revolution to the Civil War.

2. Charles W. Calomiris and Gary Gorton (1992). "The Origins of Banking Panics: Models, Facts and Bank regulation", in Hubbard, R. Glenn (ed.). Financial Markets and Financial Crises, Chicago: University of Chicago Press.

3. Curtis P. Nettels (1962). The Emergence of a National Economy, 1775-1815.

4. David Grubin (1997). The American Experience: Truman.

5. Donald R. Hickey (1990). War of 1812.

6. George Taylor (1977). The Transportation Revolution, 1815-1860.

7. Harold G. Vatter (1985). The US Economy in World War II.

8. Harold U. Faulkner (1951). The Decline of Laissez Faire, 1897-1917.

9. Historical Statistics of the United States: Millennial Edition (2006). Edited by Richard Sutch, Susan B. Carter, etc. Cambridge University Press.

10. Ian W. Toll (2006). Six Frigates: The Epic History of the Founding of the US Navy. New York: W.W. Norton.

11. Jeffrey A. Miron (1986). "Financial Panics, the Seasonality of the Nominal Interest Rate, and the Founding of the Fed," American Economic Review, 76 (1).

12. Jerome A. Greene and Douglas D. Scott (2006). Finding Sand Creek: History, Archaeology, and the 1864 Massacre Site.

13. Jonathan Hughes and Louis P. Cain (2007). American Economic History, seventh edition.

14. Kate Caffrey (1977). The Twilight's Last Gleaming: Britain vs. America 1812-1815. New York: Stein and Day.

15. Lewis Cecil Gray (1933). History of agriculture in the southern United States to 1860.

16. Paul Anthony Samuelson (1964). Readings in Economics. McGraw-Hill.

17. Paul David (1967). The Growth of Real Product in the United States Before 1840: New Evidence, Controlled Conjectures, The Journal of Economic History, Cambridge University Press, vol. 27(02).

18. Paul David and Peter Solar (1977). A Bicentenary Contribution to the History of the Cost of Living in America. Research in economic history.

19. Ralph Andreano (1962). The Economic Impact of the American Civil War.

20. Rendigs Fels (1949). "The Long-Wave Depression, 1873-79". The Review of Economics and Statistics. Vol. 31, No. 1.

21. Robert F Bruner and Sean D. Carr (2007). The Panic of 1907: Lessons Learned from the Market's Perfect Storm, Hoboken, New Jersey: John Wiley & Sons.

22. Robert F Bruner and Sean D. Carr (2007). The Panic of 1907: Lessons Learned from the Market's Perfect Storm, Hoboken, New Jersey: John Wiley & Sons.

23. Robert Barro and Charles Redlick (2009). Macroeconomic Effects from Government Purchases and Taxes.

24. Robert Leckie (1998). The Wars of America.

25. Ron Chernow (1990). The House of Morgan: An American Banking Dynasty and the Rise of Modern Finance, New York: Grove Press.

26. Samuel E. Morison (1941). The Maritime History of Massachusetts, 1783-1860.

27. Smith, B. Mark (2004). A History of the Global Stock Market; From Ancient Rome to Silicon Valley, Chicago: University of Chicago Press.

28. Walter Licht (1995). Industrializing America: The Nineteenth Century.

ABOUT
THE AUTHORS

VADIM KHRAMOV, PHD

Economist Vadim Khramov, PhD formerly served as advisor to the Executive Director of the International Monetary Fund in Washington, D.C., before becoming Vice President for Global Research and Director for EEMEA Strategy at Bank of America Merrill Lynch in London. Dr. Khramov co-founded the Center for Economic Performance and co-patented the Economic Performance Index to further the public's understanding of economic policies. He has been interviewed for CNN, CNBC, Bloomberg, *The Financial Times*, *The Wall Street Journal*, and *Foreign Policy*, among others. Vadim was voted leading macro strategist by *Institutional Investor* in 2016. Vadim holds a master's degree and a PhD in economics, both from the University of California, Los Angeles. Vadim currently works for an asset management company and lives with his wife in Boca Raton, FL.

JOHN RIDINGS LEE, JR.

The late John Ridings Lee, Jr. was a businessman and influential political activist. After a career in finance that included serving as CFO of North American National Life Insurance Company and CEO and co-founder of the Akuratus Corporation, John co-founded the Center for Economic Performance with Dr. Vadim Khramov and patented the Economic Performance Index, the first ever patent of its kind to be issued. He lobbied for better economic policies to congressmen and national figures at the GOP National Headquarters, Heritage Foundation, and CATO Institute, among other venues. He was an avid artist, exhibiting original paintings and producing movies in Hollywood. John held degrees in business, political science, and economics from Southern Methodist University and an advanced economics degree from Stanford University. Originally from Dallas, TX, he resided in Malibu, CA.

www.ingramcontent.com/pod-product-compliance
Lightning Source LLC
Chambersburg PA
CBHW070225190526
45169CB00001B/88